PROVOCATIVE
COLUMNS
Volume II

PROVOCATIVE COLUMNS

Volume II

✦

A Liberal Rabbi Reflects on Beliefs, Israel & American Politics

Bruce Warshal

iUniverse LLC
Bloomington

PROVOCATIVE COLUMNS Volume II
A Liberal Rabbi Reflects on Beliefs, Israel & American Politics

iUniverse books may be ordered through booksellers or by contacting:

iUniverse LLC
1663 Liberty Drive
Bloomington, IN 47403
www.iuniverse.com
1-800-Authors (1-800-288-4677)

ISBN: 978-1-4917-2556-6 (sc)
ISBN: 978-1-4917-2557-3 (e)

Printed in the United States of America

iUniverse rev. date: 02/20/2014

For Lynne, my wife of 53 years, my harshest critic and demanding editor, yet done with compassion and love. She has saved me from many embarrassments. Also, for my three grandchildren, Emily, Jack and Andrew. When they mature my hope is that they will read these columns and they will affect their views of Judaism and the world.

Acknowledgements

I want to thank my three children, Eric, Michael and Sue, who read my columns and encourage me to continue this task. Special thanks to the Tribune Company, the parent corporation of the *Jewish Journal* for its commitment to freedom of the press Throughout the years it has stood against censorship demands and have given me space to critique the world as I see it. Thanks to Andy Polin who introduced me to the craft of journalism. Also, special thanks to Alan Goch, editor of the *Journal*. We have been colleagues for 22 years, and it is always a pleasure to work with him. He is most accommodating when I modify a column while he is fighting a deadline.

Introduction

In 2003 I began writing weekly columns in the South Florida *Jewish Journal*. I had just retired from publishing the paper and assumed the title of publisher emeritus, a state of being that required little exertion. Writing a column seemed like a fun thing to do. Little did I know how time-consuming and difficult it could be. Five and a half years later in 2009 I assembled the first selection of columns for publication. Crass commercial plug: Volume One of Provocative Columns is still available at Amazon and Barnes & Noble. The vast majority of those columns have great current application.

It is now five years since the first volume and I have assembled a new collection. What sets these columns apart from the usual opinion pieces found in Jewish media is that they do not follow the official talking points from the Jewish establishment. I view my community with the eye of an outsider, all the while being an active participant on the inside. I attribute this ability to the fact that I grew up in a small Pennsylvania coal town where I was the only Jew in my class from first to 12th grade. These columns are not meant to be provocative; it's just that they merely reflect the world as I see it.

This book is not intended to be read linearly from page one onward. One can read columns at random or focus on particular topics. Looking at the Table of Contents you can see that the book is divided into three parts: Judaism, Israel and the United States. But I write from the viewpoint of a rabbi and my sense of Jewishness suffuses this entire book, not merely Part One. Also, these parts are not thematically hermetically sealed. There is much overlap. A few examples: the column on abominations in the bible could easily be part of a discussion on gay rights in the American political section; the column in the U.S. Part Three discussion of separation of church and state reviewing tax exemptions for West Bank settlements could be included in the Part Two Israel section.

I have included the publication date of each column because it often presents the context of the discussion. Since many of these columns were written years apart I have had to restate certain basic assumptions and facts in the later columns; thus there is a minimum amount of redundancy throughout the book. I have not attempted to rectify this since it would destroy the basic structure of an individual column.

Note that in the Part One Judaism section I have included seven columns on Islamophobia. With the exception of the Israeli peace process, I have given this more prominence than any other topic in the book. This reflects my belief that anti-Muslim animus in the Jewish community is a plague affecting 21st century American Jewry. I am ashamed and distressed and both intellectually and emotionally committed to its eradication. If nothing else in this book is read, I urge you to read those columns.

A newspaper column presents the writer with the challenge to present complex issues in every-day language. It forces one to use the vernacular rather than academic lingo. I believe this is a plus rather than a negative. This is especially true when discussing Jewish belief systems. I purposely use that phrase rather than Jewish philosophy or theology. We should be able to speak about sophisticated beliefs in simple language. I am frustrated with philosophers or theologians who leave you mystified after reading them. If an idea is worth something, it should be able to be communicated simply.

The title of this book is Provocative Columns and I realize that some of these columns may disturb the reader, but that is the result of my belief that the role of a columnist and a rabbi is to challenge conventional wisdom. In fact, that should be the role of religion, to challenge as well as to soothe us. In *Mishkan Tefilah*, the new Reform prayer book for the Sabbath, there is a prayer that epitomizes my understanding of the role of religion. It reads in part: "Disturb us, Adonai, ruffle us from our complacency. Make us dissatisfied with the peace of ignorance . . . Disturb us, O God, and vex us; let not your Shabbat be a day of torpor and slumber; let it be a time to be stirred and spurred to action." If in some small way these columns spur you to action, then I will consider my life successful.

I am accessible. My email address is brucewarshal@comcast.net and I am open to any comments of praise or condemnation. Happy reading.

Bruce Warshal
March, 2014

Table of Contents

THE JEWISH LOBBY

ISRAEL-U.S. RELATIONS

THE SOUL OF ISRAEL

HISTORY—PAST AND FUTURE

ISRAEL AND GAZA

ADDITIONAL TOPICS

PART THREE—UNITED STATES

POLITICAL PARTIES AND THE ELECTORAL PROCESS

SENATE FILIBUSTER

CHURCH AND STATE

THE SUPREME COURT

THE UNION MOVEMENT

ADDITIONAL TOPICS

PART ONE—JUDAISM BELIEF SYSTEMS

Where was God during the Holocaust?
12/18/13

I came to this column in a circuitous way. Menachem Rosensaft, general counsel of the World Jewish Congress, a child of Holocaust survivors and a teacher of the laws concerning genocide at the law schools of Columbia, Cornell and Syracuse Universities, delivered a sermon at New York's Park Avenue Synagogue on Shabbat Shuva, the Sabbath between Rosh Hashanah and Yom Kippur.

He also published it on the *Washington Post's* On Faith blog and sent a copy to Pope Francis. Being a mensch and a religious leader who reaches out to Jews, the Pope answered Rosensaft, and his answer was also published on the On Faith blog. Then the *Forward*, a national Jewish newspaper, picked up the story, highlighting the Pope's concurrence in Rosensaft's conclusion (more on the Pope's comment later). This sent me to the original *Washington Post* blog where I obtained a copy of the entire sermon.

Rosensaft begins by admitting that there are portions of the Torah that are very disturbing, where God promises to wreak destruction on the Jews for not following his commandments. He promises that "I will hide My countenance" from the Israelites in moments of their greatest distress (Deuteronomy 32:20). Based on these verses, some Jewish rabbinical leaders have concluded that God was indeed involved in the Holocaust; in fact, it was direct punishment from him.

Rabbi Joel Teitelbaum, the Satmar Hasidic Rebbe blames the Holocaust on Zionists who refused to wait for the Messiah before founding the State of Israel. The late Rabbi Eliezer Schach, spiritual leader of the ultra-Orthodox non-Hasidic Jews in Israel, declared that the Holocaust was God's divine punishment for all the perceived heresies committed by Jews under the influence of Zionists, socialism and the Enlightenment.

Rosensaft comments: "To his credit, Rabbi Menachem Mendel Schneerson, the Lubavitcher Rebbe, categorically rejected this approach . . . Nevertheless, the Lubavitcher Rebbe insisted that the Holocaust had to have been part of a divine plan, even if human beings could not comprehend God's reasons." Rosensaft does not comment on Schneerson's position. To me, it is incomprehensible in the puristic sense of that word. It defies logic. If God had a plan that included the Holocaust it is *ipso facto* punishment from him.

Rosensaft has more than a philosophical stake in figuring out where God was during the Holocaust. For him it is a gut issue. He writes: "My parents' entire immediate families were murdered in the Shoah. My mother's five-and-a half year old son, my brother, was one of more than one million Jewish children who were killed by the Germans . . ." Obviously, he needs an answer to preserve his Jewishness. He writes: "How can we pray to or have any relationship with God if we believe . . . that He abandoned us, and handed us over to the enemy?"

His answer: "What if God was very much there during the Holocaust, but not with the killers, with the forces that inflicted the Holocaust on humankind? What if he was in fact alongside and within the victims, those who perished and those who survived? Perhaps God was . . . within every Jewish parent who comforted a child on the way to a gas chamber . . ." He concluded his sermon, referring to his parents who survived the camps, writing: "Perhaps it was a divine spirit in them that enabled them to survive with their humanity intact. And perhaps it is to that God that we should be addressing our prayers during these Days of Awe and throughout the year."

Pope Francis replied, in part: "I felt within me that you had transcended all possible explanations and . . . that you were speaking to us the logic of First Kings 19:12 . . . Thank you from my heart. And please, do not forget to pray for me. May the Lord bless you." First Kings 19:12 explains that God is found in the "still small voice" within each of us.

Try as I might, I cannot accept this conclusion. If God could implant his essence in the hearts of the Jewish victims, why did he not do so to the Nazis, as well? Let us admit that God was just absent. Which presents us with the original problem, why wasn't he there?

Let me answer this briefly within the confines of a newspaper column by reviewing five possible definitions of God. First, God exists and looks down on humankind and answers prayers. Under this conception of God we must face the question as to where he was during the Holocaust. Second, a traditional God exists but he does not break into the natural order of the universe. The Torah was not dictated by God but was the product of mankind reaching toward God in search of life's meaning.

Third, God is another word for a supernatural force in the universe, but such force has no relationship to our traditional concept of God. Fourth, God is the word that we apply to pantheism, the concept that we are all part of nature. As the flower flourishes and eventually returns to the earth, so mankind is also part of the cycle of birth and death. God is the realization that we have the cosmos, not chaos. This was Rabbi Mordecai Kaplan's definition and the impetus for his founding the Reconstructionist Movement. Fifth and finally, God is purely a concept, a literary figure that mankind creates to define to our best ability the attributes that make us better human beings. When Torah says that we are made in the image of God, it beckons us to list the attributes that a God would possess, and thus we self-define what God is—and in the process make ourselves more God-like.

Personally, I vacillate from definitions number two to five. No matter which one you choose, if you exclude number one then you don't have to answer Rosensaft's question as to where God was during the Holocaust. The God of numbers two through five is not involved in the intricate workings of the world, and he is not expected to be at Auschwitz or any other place on earth. He is the basis of our religious devotion, the lynchpin of our search for meaning and the foundation of our obligation for performing Tikun Olam (repair of the world), but he/she/it has no direct tie to the Holocaust.

Religious conundrum solved. Now we can focus on mankind's responsibility for the Holocaust and not God's.

A Viable Philosophy for Reform Judaism
8/10/11

The Great Recession has impacted Reform Judaism. Congregations have experienced decreased membership as unemployment and general hard times plague the middle class, Jews included.

As a response Reform rabbis and lay leaders are questioning the status quo, including dues structures, liturgy, and even the philosophical basis of the movement.

It is this last category that interests me. I have been mulling over two opinion pieces that appeared in the *Forward* some months ago by Reform Rabbi Dana Evan Kaplan. Kaplan places the current malaise not on economics but on the lack of a clear Reform theology.

In a column entitled "The theological Roots of Reform Judaism's Woes" he bemoans the fact that Reform Judaism encompasses pluralistic theologies and focuses on individual autonomy. From my perspective these are its crucial strengths. If I wanted to be told what to believe I would join an Orthodox congregation.

I acknowledge that there are many Jewish beliefs about God and man and that in my quest for personal truth I can daven in schul and partake in community without having to wear a philosophical straight jacket. In a typical Reform congregation as we each read the Shma we may be experiencing several different personal religious experiences. Whether Rabbi Kaplan likes it or not, personal autonomy is part of Western Culture and religion must conform to this, not vice versa.

But Kaplan has a diametrically opposed view of Reform than I. He writes: "Judaism is the true religion . . . its doctrines are taken from the revelations of God in His works and words." He quotes Rabbi Maurice Eisendrath, the head of the Reform Movement in the mid 20th century: "We Reform Jews believe that God gave us the Torah . . . we are participating in the process of bringing God's revelation to human beings. That is Reform Judaism's mission, and it is a compelling one."

But Kaplan has a problem. He must distinguish himself from Orthodoxy, which also believes literally in the word of God. Kaplan explains that Reform believes in the academic study of Torah. He writes: "Orthodox Jews, by contrast, tend to read the Torah with pre-critical naiveté, by which I mean that they take it for granted that the five books of Moses are exactly what their pious teachers have told them it is—a word-for-word and letter-for-letter text given by God to Moses on Mount Sinai. While this belief enables the Orthodox to create religious communities of deep commitment, it is intellectually untenable."

This may surprise some readers, but I want to defend Orthodoxy. It is a very tenable assumption that I do not believe, but it is not intellectually naïve. It presents many philosophical problems that I won't discuss here for lack of space, but it is a totally coherent system once one accepts the basic premise of revelation from God, which I don't—but more on that later.

I believe that Kaplan's philosophy (and all of the Conservative Movement and a good portion of the Reform Movement, which share his approach) is intellectually untenable. He states that the Torah is God-given, yet we can alter its message through intellectual games. Sure, many parts are vague and open to interpretation, but other parts are not. My favorite nonsense passage is the statement in Deuteronomy (Chapter 22, verse 11, referred to as shatnez) that one should not wear garments that are a mixture of linen and wool. One cannot intellectualize around that law. How many Conservative and Reform Jews follow this?

But what right do we have to pick and choose what words of revelation we will follow if the books are truly the word of God. If God took time out of his busy day to instruct us on appropriate clothing, it is not up to us to ignore him. Strict Orthodox adherence to revelation makes more intellectual sense than watered-down revelation.

I don't have this problem. I believe that all of the books of Torah and the whole bible were written by men (literally by men, not women, because we have a sexist history) in our search to find meaning in life, in our attempt to define the image of God, which should reflect human ethical conduct. Yes, this leaves humankind without clear edicts from God to guide us. We have to work at our religion because each and every generation has the obligation to challenge the status quo in a continual process of tikkun olam, of repairing the world. Religion becomes a process rather than an all encompassing answer to our queries. It becomes an intellectual journey as well as an emotional roller coaster—but that is life. To deny that and to curl up in the cocoon of revelation is to run from life rather than embracing it.

I believe that the overriding vision of the Reform Movement is not some kind of ersatz revelation but a celebration of the Grand Quest for Meaning. We search together, we create community, we pray on Shabbat, and some of us pray for the ability to pray, we work toward tikkun olam *together*—that is the key word. Together we eschew anonymity and replace it with responsibility and community. I think that God would rather we do this than worrying over the blend of our clothing. (I wonder what God would think of the mixture of linen and the latest combination of micro-fibers.)

I do not mean to personally attack Rabbi Kaplan. If I am ever in Albany, Georgia I would love to meet him. It's just that he reflects a muddled philosophical position that is all too common in liberal Judaism.

I believe that the current problems of Reform will be fixed when this country gets its act together and pulls us out of this recession. Philosophically, we're OK.

Jewish fundamentalism and Reform Judaism
9/18/13

You may have noticed that I put my email contact at the end of each column. Most of my correspondents spew hatred, such as, "I wish you and all the other lefties would have died in the camps," or you are a "self-hating Jew," or "Shame on you and stop calling yourself Rabbi."

For the occasional civil respondent I try to answer in kind. A tourist from Lakewood, N.J. who happened to read one of my columns while on vacation in South Florida emailed me his basic religious assumption: "Our holy Torah that was given to us at Mt. Sinai by God is the essence of the world and mankind. It is a Torah that is pure goodness and kindness." Now I love Torah study because it was written by man in his quest to find ethics and God. But as a man-made product it is less than pure goodness and kindness—witness the portions that allow slavery or the killing of a child who is rebellious or a bride who is found not to be a virgin.

Another reader wrote: "Rational thought and modern science have nothing to do with Torah law. It is as if one is saying that they are smarter and wiser than HaShem (God)." It is precisely this assumption that leads Jewish fundamentalists to fear the outside world and to isolate themselves from it. This leads the ultra-Orthodox to either circumscribe or ban outright the use of the Internet. You may remember last year's mass rally at Citi Field (home of the New York Mets) where 40,000 men (women were excluded) filled the stadium, with an overflow of another 20,000 in Arthur Ashe Stadium (home to the U.S. Open tennis matches), to hear what the event's organizers called the dangers of the Internet.

The event was sponsored by the "Union of Communities for the Purity of the Camp" (translation from its Yiddish title). One of the most prominent rabbis backing the event and protecting the purity of fundamentalist Judaism was Matisyahu Salomon, spiritual leader of the largest yeshiva in Lakewood, N.J. As long ago as 2005 the Orthodox schools in Lakewood issued a proclamation forbidding children and high school students from using the Internet. In reference to the Citi Field rally, Rabbi Salomon commented that coming together they would be asking God's help in fighting evil inclinations.

This fear and isolation from the outside world leads to both internal repression and external violence. The fundamentalists at City Field and Lakewood, N.J. are *misnagdim*, rabbinic Jews sharing the same heritage as Modern Orthodox, as opposed to Hasidic Jews. But the Hasidim also either limit or outlaw the Internet and eschew the outside world. The internal repression by the Hasidic community of Brooklyn was highlighted in a front page article in the *New York Times*. It reported that, "shadowy, sometimes self-appointed modesty squads use social and economic leverage to enforce conformity."

These vigilantes, who could not operate without the blessings of rabbinical leaders, confiscate iPads and computer equipment deemed inappropriate for Orthodox children. Rabbi Allan Nadler, director of the Jewish studies program at Drew University in Madison, N.J. commented: "They walk into a store and say it would be a shame if your window was broken or you lost your clientele. They might tell the father of a girl who wears a skirt that's too short and he's, say, a store owner: 'If you ever want to sell a pair of shoes, speak to your daughter.'" Rabbi Nadler concludes, "They operate like the Mafia."

It is when Jewish fundamentalists act like the Mafia toward the outside world they become truly dangerous. Fundamentalism inexorably leads to violence against those who hold non-conforming beliefs. We see this in the gentile world where abortion clinic doctors are assassinated, and we see it in history where Jews were burned at the stake during the Inquisition. We see it today in Israel.

Yigal Amir, a former settler and student at an Orthodox university, was not alone in assassinating Yitzhak Rabin. He would not have acted without the blessings of his fundamentalist, radical, settler rabbis. And the danger abides today. West Bank ideological terrorists have threatened a Peace Now employee whose job it is to report on settler activity. They sprayed death threats on her Jerusalem home, writing: "Hagit Ofran, Rabin awaits you."

In July of this year Rabbi Shalom Cohen, a leader in the Sephardic religious party Shas, compared Jews active in *Habayit Hayehudi* (Jewish Home), another religious party in Israel, as Amalek. The bible calls for the annihilation of all Amalekites—men, women and children. One member of the Knesset lamented, "The road to violence on the ground has gotten shorter."

Earlier in this column I wrote that I respect Torah as man's quest to find ethics and God. Let me juxtapose this quest, which is for me the basis of Reform Judaism, with the fundamentalism described above. I want to quote another email that I received two years ago in response to one of my columns. Jeffrey Kaufman, a resident of Boston who works for a cancer research foundation, wrote:

"When divinity is placed within each human, it forces greater respect for each individual. And it permits each person to appraise the appropriateness of his/her own actions in the timeless and incorporeal realms of justice and loving-kindness. In my mind, Jews who insist on a literal interpretation of the Torah have turned the book into a graven image."

He continues: "A loving, fair and useful life is lived by acknowledging our own ignorance and wrestling to reconcile the messy ethical problems we face within ourselves every day. To me, the most beautiful and praiseworthy aspect of Reform Judaism is how goodness is not a victory march. Instead, Reform Jewish goodness is a tortured discussion of well-meaning souls trying to figure out the right thing to do in a complicated world with plenty of gray."

Thank you, Jeffrey, from the bottom of my heart. That is my personal quest. That is the real Judaism of the 21st century, not the fundamentalism that turns Torah into a graven image.

The Jewish Experience—Secular, Cultural or Religious?
3/20/13

Recently Rabbi Eric Yoffie, President Emeritus of the Union for Reform Judaism, wrote an opinion piece on the Huffington Post entitled, "The Self-Delusion of Secular Jews." Although he is the ex-leader of the Reform Movement he writes as if he were an Orthodox rabbi. He complains that absent a belief in a God that speaks to the Jewish people, "the Jewish people withers and dies."

Yoffie writes: "They (secular or ethnic Jews) refuse to accept the dictates of the divine or the absolutes of the Jewish religion . . . God has made a covenant with them, and this covenant provides the ground for all Jewish existence."

From this I assume that Yoffie believes that God actually dictated the Torah to Moses on Mount Sinai—Moshe, take a ballpoint and put the rules down. I find it difficult to believe this, as I suspect most cultural or secular Jews do, and if I did I would be an Orthodox rabbi, not Reform.

This is the crux of the religious divide between conservative and liberal Judaism. Here's my take on the Sinai experience: It is a magnificent myth, but I prefer not to use the term myth; rather I call it our Master Story—and I believe in the Master Story.

To me Sinai represents the Jewish quest to find meaning in life, including rules that protect us from chaos, striving for ethical conduct, boundaries that define a caring community and rituals that enrich our daily lives. It matters not to me whether God spoke to Moses, or whether there actually was an event on that mountain. The story, the questing, is what is important.

Let me further explain the concept of a Master Story by contrasting a subsequent reason for being Jewish. The philosopher Emil Fackenheim famously wrote that we should remain Jewish so that we do not give Hitler a posthumous victory. Rather than reaching back to ancient strivings, he focuses on a recent catastrophe. This creates a new Master Story based on a negative premise that produces the victim mentality that is so prevalent in our community. (Needless to say, we should always remember the Holocaust, but it cannot be the basis for our Jewish commitment.)

When I use the term Sinai experience I do not limit it to a point in time. Tanach (the Jewish bible) was written over an eight hundred year period. We can see the later books correcting earlier beliefs—one good example is the Book of Job challenging Deuteronomy on the problem of evil. The questing does not stop with the codification of the bible. We ethically evolve in the Talmud, essentially a commentary on the bible, and continue to grow through the medieval commentaries and on to current Jewish thinkers.

Yoffie presents a false dichotomy between a believing Jew and a secular or cultural Jew. One can believe in the Sinai odyssey without believing that God speaks to us or that God even exists, and a secular Jew is more "religious" than he/she realizes because he has internalized the quest for justice and meaning that is the Sinai experience.

Leonard Fein and Steven M. Cohen wrote a rebuttal to Yoffie defending secular Jews on the Huffington Post. Fein also discussed this issue in the *Jewish Journal* where he wrote: "For Yoffie, the roots—God—are essential ingredients in the struggle for social justice. And it is true that without roots, branches cannot long survive. But visualize in place of rootless branches mighty oaks that drop acorns that sprout, usually a good distance (20 to 30 meters) from the mother oak. The new trees to which they give birth do not look to the mother tree for guidance; they have their own work, the work of growing, to attend to. And yes, in the scheme of things—both ecological and mystical—that is sacred work."

A beautiful thought, but I believe that Fein is sucked into the dichotomy that Yoffie sets up. These secular Jewish social justice activists are related to the very roots of Judaism which is the continuing quest for justice and meaning that is encompassed in the Sinai Master Story. And we are not talking about just philosophy, but of the whole physical experience of our people—roaming the world, experiencing the Inquisition, finding acceptance in the Western World and, yes, destruction in the Holocaust. The bad and the good—from the ashes of destruction to the rebirth of the State of Israel and the miracle called America.

All of these mental and physical strivings are in people whom we call cultural or secular Jews. They have internalized the Master Story. They are both "religious" and "secular." They are not bifurcated. They are what they are and sometimes it is very difficult to label them. Let me give you one example. I have a close relative who is an ardent and vocal atheist. Yet he belongs to a Conservative synagogue, attends High Holy Day services, Passover Seders and occasionally a Shabbat or two. He gives extensively to Jewish charities as well as to secular groups and is a certified political liberal.

I have never asked him how he would characterize himself as a Jew, but I think that there is a fifty percent chance that he would answer either secular or cultural. I would call him religious.

But one thing of which I am sure—whether he knows it or not, he believes in the Master Story of Sinai because he is constantly questing for meaning in life and striving for Tikun Olam (the repair of this world). Yoffie is wrong. Our roots are in the quest, not in God talking to us. And the quest is what makes Judaism a liberal religion.

The Concept of Evolving Law—Secular and Jewish
9/23/09

I have said this before, but it merits repeating. I take great pride in the fact that when I was publisher of the *Jewish Journal* I initiated the concept that the paper would not take a weekly editorial stand on current events, but rather would publish opinion pieces reflecting both the right and the left in political and religious dialogue. Personally, I am not excited about bland centrist columns that are neither *milchik* nor *flaishik*.

That's the reason that the *Journal* has the most exciting opinion pages in Jewish publishing. Leonard Fein (weekly) and Zel Lurie and I (twice monthly) represent the left. On the right are many guest columnists including Rabbi Avi Shafran, who appears in the *Journal* quite frequently.

I enjoy reading Rabbi Shafran because he is such a good writer, but I rarely agree with anything that he writes. But he does move me to respond to him. Last month he wrote such a column. It was entitled "Justice Sotomayor and the Jews." Rabbi Shafran praised Justice Sotomayor for renouncing her famous "wise Latina woman" comment in which she said in a 2001 lecture that often a wise Latino could come to a better decision than a white male.

We will get back to Rabbi Shafran and the Jews, but let's discuss this renouncement by the Justice that it was merely a "rhetorical flourish that fell flat," and that "it was bad."

Was it bad and was it wrong? It was neither; in fact, it was true. I am not saying that Justice Sotomayor was wrong to play along with the charade before the Senate because that's how you play the game these days. One pays tribute to the inane concept that there is the law and a judge or justice merely follows that pre-set law. In testimony Justice Sotomayor made the analogy to sports. She proposed that a judge is like an umpire. He or she calls the shots according to established order, but does not change the rules, which would be "judicial activism,"

Nothing could be farther from the truth. Let's take the Equal Protection Clause of the 14th Amendment to the Constitution: A group of white males on the Supreme Court in 1896 declared that under this Amendment separate schools for the races treat everyone equally. It was their understanding of what was essentially fair. That's all that the Amendment requires—fair treatment for everyone. We know that in 1954 the Supreme Court decided that separate but equal is not fair.

The 8th Amendment to the Constitution prevents "cruel and unusual punishment." What is not cruel for one generation may be for another. The truth is that the Constitution is a short and very vague document that requires each generation to read into it what are acceptable standards. Concerning capital punishment, in years past states pronounced the death sentence upon juveniles and developmentally disabled people. In recent years the Supreme Court decided that this was cruel punishment. God only knows what the founding fathers considered cruel or not. The only thing we know for sure is that it is up to the living to decide what is or is not cruel, reflecting the norms of our current society.

Justice Sotomayor was correct in her wise Latina statement. What is fair or not fair is a reflection of one's background. A member of a minority, be he black, Latino, Jew or Catholic, brings to the bench a different perspective than a white Anglo Saxon male, the traditional occupants of the Courts that brought us the Dred Scott decision and the separate but equal conclusion. Diversity on the Court is healthy.

The fact is that an umpire in baseball can call a ball in or out of bounds because the difference is a clear line on the field. But the boundary of what is fair or not is not a fixed line that never changes. It is a fuzzy line in present time and it can change over time.

This brings us back to Rabbi Shafran. Why his interest in American law and Justice Sotomayor? He wrote, "The job of a judge, as Judge Sotomayor rightly concluded, is to apply laws, not feelings." He continues: "It is common these Jewish days to read of how this or that group or individual is promoting a new more 'sensitive,' 'contemporary' or 'caring' approach to *halacha*. And all too many Jews (are) falling into the conceptual trap from which Judge Sotomayor laudably extricated herself."

Here Rabbi Shafran, who is the director of public affairs for the ultra-Orthodox Agudath Israel movement, is attacking the Conservative movement's interpretation of *halacha* (Jewish law based on the Talmud).

What we have here is the Jewish counterpart of the southern Republicans who want "strict construction" of the Constitution, whatever that may legally mean. It is a call that means no change in society. In Rabbi Shafran's case it means no change in religion. In both cases it represents a futile cry against the nature of what it means to be a human being who must face society in his or her succeeding generations.

As a Reform rabbi I feel that I am not bound by *halacha*, even though I may look to it for guidance. But I applaud the Conservative movement for attempting to bring the Talmudic legalism into the 21st century, the same way that the Supreme Court must bring the Constitution into the contemporary milieu.

I look forward to Rabbi Shafran's next column. One of these years we may just agree on something.

Where is the "Holiest Place in Judaism"?
7/10/13

Recently we have been surfeited with news concerning the Western Wall in Jerusalem (The Kotel, in Hebrew) where feminist women have been physically attacked by the Orthodox for praying at the Wall while wearing *talit* (prayer shawls) and *tefillin* (phylacteries). In all of the media coverage the Wall has been referred to as the "holiest place of Judaism." This idea is so ubiquitous that recently my wife purchased a box of matzo meal imported from Jerusalem. The box was adorned with a picture of the Wall with the inscription, "The Kotel represents Judaism's holiest site." It seems a Jew cannot prepare matzo balls for chicken soup without being reminded of this "truth."

My column today is devoted to the history and to the supposed religious importance of the Wall.

First the history: The Wall is not the last remaining part of the ancient Temple. It is merely an embankment wall. On the eastern edge of the Temple Mount there is a natural cliff, but on the western side the mount tapered off so that earth had to be added to the effect that the mount would be gloriously high above the surrounding lowland. The Western Wall was erected to contain this artificial mountain. Atop this platform the Temple stood until destroyed by the Romans in 70 CE. The present Wall was erected by King Herod approximately 25 BCE.

It was not always the "holiest place of Judaism." I thank the Israeli blogger Uri Avnery for bringing my attention to the work of the historian Karen Armstrong. In her book "Jerusalem" she reports that the Sultan Suleiman the Magnificent, after building the existing walls surrounding the Old City of Jerusalem in 1516 CE, set aside a special place of worship for Jews who at that time were escaping from the Church's Inquisition (a nice reminder to contemporary Jewish hate-mongers of how well we have been treated by Islamic regimes). To make the Wall more towering Suleiman lowered the floor of the alley facing it. The existing piazza in front of the Wall was created after 1967 by tearing down an adjacent Muslim neighborhood. Before Suleiman's gesture the main praying place for Jews was the Mount of Olives.

Now to the spiritual significance of the Wall: The Wall and the Temple Mount itself are not really the focus of spirituality—it is the ancient Temple where God received animal sacrifices and which was the power base of the High Priest. Let's be honest here. Only the radical Orthodox fundamentalists really want the Temple rebuilt. With it would come animal sacrifices in lieu of prayer and priests instead of rabbis. The best thing that ever happened to Judaism was the destruction of the Temple.

Starting approximately 200 BCE the emerging rabbi class vied for dominance with the priesthood. One became a rabbinical leader through education while one was born a priest, no intelligence needed. By the time of the Maccabean uprising (for which we celebrate Hanukah) the priesthood was corrupt and dysfunctional. It was also detrimental to evolving Judaism. The priests felt nothing could be added to the strictures of the Torah because that was where their authenticity was based. The rabbis felt that religion must evolve and they developed the Talmud which is the basis of modern Orthodox Judaism. The competition between the rabbis and the priests was resolved by the Romans when they destroyed the Temple and put the priests out of business. For which we thank God.

There is also the religious question as to where God resides. To the modern mind there is an obvious answer—everywhere, including in our hearts and our very being. But to the ancient Jews this was not obvious. Torah presented us with a God that was tied to the Jewish people and specifically to the land of Israel. The Temple was his literal abode in that is where he communicated with the people. And only the High Priest could enter its innermost sanctuary.

After the destruction of the First Temple in 586 BCE when many Jews were exiled to Babylonia, the prophet Jeremiah (in Chapter 29 of the Book of Jeremiah), remaining in Jerusalem, wrote to the exiled Jews that they should worship God there. This, too, seems obvious to the modern mind, but it was not then. God was assumed to be the God of Israel, not of the whole universe, and after the defeat by the Babylonians it was perfectly reasonable to assume that their God was more powerful than ours. The philosophical basis of Jeremiah's letter was that our God was truly the God of all humanity and that the Babylonians were triumphant because our God allowed them to be. It was a major step into the concept of a full-blown monotheism.

What is important to us is that it was a statement concerning how to relate to God. There was no Jewish Temple in Babylonia and no ability to offer animal sacrifices. Thus a new mode of communication with God had to evolve. Prayer from the heart and the institution of the synagogue eventually filled the void.

Which leads me to my final conclusion: concerning physical location, the "holiest place in Judaism" is not the Wall or any other tomb, be it Rachel's or Joseph's or some revered ancient rabbi. The holiest place is your local synagogue where Jews assemble to either thank God, attempt to seek God, even to deny God, but find introspection and community. Also, one can argue that the "holiest place in Judaism" is within our hearts and actions, assuming that we as individuals strive to validate the premise that we are made in the image of God, as Torah tells us we are.

A Plea for Social Action Judaism
2/8/12

The columnist and seminal Jewish thinker Leonard Fein wrote one of the most elegant and insightful paragraphs recently in a column that appeared in the *Jewish Journal* in early January. Let me share it with you:

"Our tradition knows no radical distinction between politics and culture. Ours is a profoundly political religion, not a pietistic faith. We are enjoined to reject the world-as-it-is, to love it for what it may yet be, and to help transform it from the one into the other. To be interested in a serious Jewish culture means, necessarily, to be interested in politics—in whether the hungry are fed and the naked clothed, in whether justice is pursued and mercy loved. Judaism does not tell us which tax reform plan to favor; it does tell us that no tax plan that slights the downtrodden is acceptable."

This interest in politics is a natural outgrowth of Judaism's emphasis on communal responsibility. In previous columns I have pointed out that tzedakah is mistranslated as charity, which is a freewill offering. Judaism tells us that we have to support the needy whether we like it or not. The core of the Hebrew word tzedakah means justice. It is not within our free will to deny justice. Communal responsibility trumps individual preference (think of the required mandate to support health care for all). On Yom Kippur we Jews do not pray for atonement for "the sins which I have committed." No, the liturgy says "for the sins which *we* have committed." We pray on behalf of the entire congregation. That is the epitome of communal responsibility.

So how do we translate this into practical politics without making us into an organized political party? The tale of two rabbis may explicate this. The first rabbi serves a congregation in my home town in Pennsylvania. He is a committed political conservative who writes about politics in his bulletin and preaches it from his pulpit. He believes in everything that I do not. But he is not an uncaring person. He honestly believes that less government is the correct way to tikun olam, to repairing the world. In fact he is a mensch and a fine rabbi. I would defend his right to preach his brand of politics as the correct reflection of the aims of Judaism.

Rabbi number two I do not know personally, but I hear from the rabbinic grapevine that he just lost his job after attacking Islam in a sermon. If I were on his board I would vote post haste to get rid of him, as I am told was the case. Now what's the difference between these two rabbis? Why should one be revered and the other fired? Are they not both preaching politics in the name of Judaism?

The answer is no. The second rabbi is preaching hate in the service of politics while the first rabbi is preaching politics in service of tikun olam, even though I believe his politics is wrong. It is his motivation that counts. But there is no room for hate in Judaism. The second rabbi's attacking Islam (which is very fashionable in right wing circles) is no different from the Reverend John Hagee's outburst against the Catholic Church, labeling it as "The Great Whore." (Incidentally, this is the same Hagee that receives great applause at AIPAC conferences because of his "pro-Israel" stance—so much for contemporary Jewish ethics!) Attacking Islam, instead of attacking those who distort that religion through terrorism, has an equivalent hate factor equal to those who use the N-word and preach that African-Americans are genetically inferior.

I admit that I make fine distinctions here. But I also believe that the firing of the second rabbi was warranted. Hate is an insidious emotion that must be carefully used and mostly circumscribed, especially when it is coupled with religious fervor. It was hate that moved the Church from a theological argument with Judaism into burning us at the stake and expelling us from half of Europe during the Inquisition. Hate quickly deteriorates into dehumanization and that allows putting people in ovens and lesser atrocities as mass ethnic cleansing.

This whole topic is very important because in real life most conservative rabbis do not have a problem with this. Very few of them have to answer for conservative statements from the pulpit, especially as it relates to Israel. But liberal rabbis face another reality. I can tell you, from that rabbinic grapevine and from personal acquaintances, that most liberal rabbis live in fear of expressing Judaism through social action. What was once a great tradition, especially in the Reform Movement, has withered on the vine. It has been replaced by an emphasis on spiritual communion with God. Emotion has trumped righteousness. The travails of the downtrodden and the pursuit of peace (both in this country and Israel) are issues that can cost a liberal rabbi his or her job.

Congregants and boards of trustees have forgotten the truth so beautifully expressed in the Leonard Fein quote. Judaism is a political religion. It is our strength, and it's about time that we get back to Social Action Judaism.

JEWISH COMMUNITY

Challenges Facing Reform Synagogues in America
12/10/10

Last month I was privileged to present the featured address at Shabbat services celebrating the 30th anniversary of Temple Judea in Palm Beach Gardens, a Reform congregation that is the fastest growing synagogue in Palm Beach County. I share this with you because I believe that what follows is pertinent not only to Reform Judaism but to synagogues and Judaism in general. I discussed the role of the synagogue as the institution of American Jewish survival and its future challenges. Here are some excerpts:

I was a Federation executive director for 13 years and it was very fashionable in the 1980's for Federations to use the slogan that they were the "central address of the Jewish community." As a Federation director I strenuously objected to this. Here's why: If all the peripheral Jewish institutions were eliminated—the day schools, the JCC's, the family services, the Hadassahs, the ORT's, etc.—but with synagogues remaining, we would be an impoverished Jewish community, but we would survive and ultimately even flourish. But if the reverse were true—all of the existing Jewish institutions were to remain, but the synagogues would be eliminated—then I believe that the future of Judaism would indeed be imperiled. There is no central address to a vibrant Jewish community, but in the plural, the central addresses are our synagogues.

As to the challenges: First, we must continue to outreach to the intermarried and welcome the stranger into our synagogues. We must not look upon intermarriage as a problem, but as an opportunity to bring good people into our community, whether they formally convert or not. We must respect the partner who wants to share the Jewish experience with his or her spouse, even without conversion. Ultimately one who feels a part of our community is in fact Jewish whether that person converted or not.

The bottom line is identity, not legalities. Remember that the bedrock of ethical Judaism is not in ritual, as important as that is, but in understanding the "other" and treating him or her as a home-born, as directed in our Torah. The Reform Movement has been a leader in outreach, but we have not gone far enough. Much work needs to be done.

Second challenge: We must become more creative in passing along Jewish identity. Everyone knows of the Birthright Israel experience where we send college age Jews to Israel free of charge to cement their Jewish identity. As good as this program is, I believe that it is about 15 years too late in the life of a Jewish child. We should be instilling Jewish identity in grade school, not college.

How to do that? I propose that we spend greater resources on Jewish camping. I know that the Reform Movement runs wonderful summer camps. I have been on the faculty at many of these camps and my children attended Camp Coleman. But they are limited, especially because they are expensive. The Jewish community should send every child without charge to a summer camp at an early age, rather than waiting to spend the money on a trip to Israel. Someday a synagogue like Temple Judea will figure a way to send every one of its kids *each and every summer* to a Reform camp free, with the proviso that a family can contribute what it feels it can afford. No applications for subsidy, just a free-will offering. (Obviously this applies as well to the Conservative and Orthodox movements that run excellent summer camps.)

Number three: As important as our love of Israel is, we must find a way to inculcate Jewish ethics and identification into our children without relying on the glories of the Israeli experience. We live our lives in America and our Judaism must reflect the American Jewish experience. We must be authentic American Jews rather than ersatz Israelis. As Israel matures and its politics become more complex it becomes a more real country rather than an ideal, mystic experience in the American Jewish psyche. It can play a role in our Judaism, but it cannot be the dominant force in our community that it played in the second half of the 20th century. American Jewry has to become more sophisticated in its love of Israel if we expect to retain the commitment of our youth who do not share our generation's historical experiences of prejudice and the miraculous rise of an independent Jewish state.

Finally, challenge number four: We must keep alive prophetic Judaism. Now that we are part of mainstream America we must never forget the needy amongst us, nor should we stand idle when other minorities are scapegoated the way we once were. We should stand with the Islamic community of America and proclaim a stop to Islamiphobia. The guilt of a few should never be foisted upon a whole community. We must remember the Father

Coughlins, the Henry Fords and the numerous other anti-Semites who maintained that Jews could never be good Americans.

The next time someone attacks Muslims, remember that there but for the sake of God go we. We have done well in this regard, but I am saddened that some of the most rabid anti-Muslims are Jews who mistakenly think that they are doing Israel a favor by delegitimizing 1.3 billion Muslims. They are ignorantly and unethically turning a struggle over land into a religious struggle that we 14 million Jews could never win.

Our ethics also require us to care for the poor and needy. Societal needs must be met even if our income taxes rise by a few percentage points. Inevitably political considerations become religious considerations. Reform Judaism always understood this. Liberality is our religion. That's what the prophets taught us. As we get richer and more comfortable the challenge will be to continue our commitment to social action and prophetic Judaism.

Would that all synagogues, from Orthodox to Humanistic and everything in between, were to meet these challenges.

Challenges to the Conservative Movement
4/21/10

Recently I was privileged to present the keynote address at the 25th anniversary celebration of a local Conservative synagogue. Along with the expected accolades, I included a few challenges concerning the Conservative Movement. I share them with you today.

A previous speaker made reference to an American Management Association planning seminar that he attended. When asked, "What's the fundamental objective of an enterprise?" everyone responded that it was to make a profit. The lecturer responded, "No, the fundamental objective is to serve a market need better than the competition." Profits then follow.

The question that we have to ask today: Is the Conservative Movement meeting the needs of the majority of American Jews, and if not, why? Let's start with statistics. In the 1950's over half of the American Jews identified themselves as Conservative. It was the dominant form of American Judaism. According to the American Jewish Committee's 2008 Annual Survey of American Jewish Opinion only 28 percent of American Jews considered themselves Conservative. In the 2009 poll that number slipped down to 24 percent. I am fearful that we will continue to see further erosion.

Since the mid-1950's Reform grew from the low twenties to 30 percent in 2008. What is alarming is that in 2009 fully 36 percent of American Jews considered themselves "Just Jewish." I'm happy that they consider themselves Just Jewish but I fear such an identity will erode the crucial part that congregational affiliation plays in Jewish survival.

Obviously, no stream of Judaism is doing a great job of defining the market needs of American Jews, including the Orthodox, whose figures hover between only eight to nine percent in 2008 and 2009. But Reform is growing and Orthodoxy is remaining constant while Conservative Judaism is shrinking. It behooves us to think in terms of market needs.

I believe that we have to review the early history of the Conservative Movement to appreciate the vital role that it played in this country. When my grandparents came to these shores from Eastern Europe they knew that they did not want to be Orthodox and they certainly knew that they did not identify with those Reform Jews from Germany who actually prayed (rather than davened) with bare heads.

And so my grandparents, along with millions of other immigrants, swarmed to the Conservative Movement and it brilliantly met their emotional and intellectual needs. It provided a delicate balance between modernity and tradition. The need was for community and succor in a not always inviting Christian dominated society. The market need was met and profit ensued— profit not in the form of money but of membership and vitality.

But market needs change from generation to generation as the greater society and its relationship to its Jewish minority changes. Jews today interact differently with non-Jews than our fathers and grandfathers, and our children and grandchildren interact differently than we do.

For an institution to survive it has to recognize this new landscape and to adapt. Otherwise it shrinks from over 50 percent of the market to under a quarter. This is a disaster not only for the Conservative Movement but for all of the Jewish community, because we desperately need a vital Conservative Judaism for the future well being of American Jewry.

I understand that I speak as a Reform rabbi, but one with deep roots in the Conservative Movement, and one who cares passionately about its future success.

The bedrock of Conservatism is the balancing of Halacha with modernity. Halacha is important, but the movement has to finally make up its mind as to whether it is a reform movement (that's with a small R) or a watered down Orthodoxy. Halacha plays an important role in analyzing Jewish history and beliefs. But the Movement has to decide whether the ultimate decisions are made by people striving toward God or by God speaking through Halacha. This determines its flexibility and how quickly the Movement can change to meet the needs of 21st century Jews.

The prescription for success for the Conservative Movement was presented by Mordecai Kaplan, that great Conservative rabbi who taught at the Jewish

Theological Seminary, when he proclaimed his now famous statement that, "The past has a vote, but not a veto."

In simple language, the Conservative Movement found a way to Halachicly accept mixed seating, driving on the Shabbat, aliyas for women, the ordination of women (and by the way, the current president of the Rabbinical Assembly is a woman rabbi) and finally the acceptance of gays and lesbians into JTS. Albeit, most of these advances were done too slowly, which is reflected in the loss of market share. It is now time to find a way to Halchicly face new challenges.

Lest you think that I place market share above theology or Halacha, let me explain that I believe that Judaism and in fact all religions exist to meet the needs of people—our need to find meaning in life, to strive for ethical conduct, to find warm embracing community and so forth. I do not believe that we exist merely to serve God.

I do not believe that God really needs our praise in prayer or adulation through a specific ritual. If God is God, the Almighty does not need to be flattered. So if people are not identifying with us and are not joining our congregations, be they Orthodox, Conservative, Reform, Reconstructionist or Humanistic, then we are not meeting their needs and we are not really serving God.

So here's the specific challenge of the Conservative Movement—move faster. Utilize Halacha (even the Reform Movement does that these days) but face up to modern day challenges before everyone walks out the back door. Three specific areas must be faced:

First: How to respond to intermarriage. I propose the "radical" idea that we can't automatically turn away mixed couples when they ask our rabbis to marry them. Whether we like it or not, an immediate negative response drives many of them from Judaism. We should be able to perform certain intermarriages where children will be reared Jewishly and where other religions will not be part of the family environment. Yet today if a Conservative Rabbi were to perform such a ceremony he or she would be thrown out of the Movement.

Second, the Conservative Movement must do a much better job in welcoming mixed couples into its congregations. If a family comes as a unit it is told that only the Jewish partner is eligible for membership. What does this say to the partner who wants to share the Jewish experience with his or her spouse? And I must say that ultimately one who practices Judaism and feels a part of our community is in fact Jewish whether that person officially converts or not. Even Orthodox commentators have said that those non-Jews who followed their spouses into the extermination camps died as Jews without formal conversion. The bottom line is identity, not legalities.

Finally, the Conservative Movement must recognize patrilineal as well as matrilineal descent. In an age of 50 percent intermarriage, not to do so is communal suicide. How can we say that a child of a Jewish father and a non-Jewish mother who attends a Jewish day school, a Jewish summer camp, and is a bar or bat mitzvah is not Jewish? And how can Orthodoxy say that a child of a Jewish mother and non-Jewish father who attends a Christian School, is baptized, and believes that Jesus died for his or her sins is Jewish?

This is placing Halacha above common sense and the needs of modernity. And may I remind you that patrilineal descent was the norm of Torah. The most prominent example is that Joseph's two sons, Ephraim and Menassah, the children of a non-Jewish mother (indeed, the daughter of an Egyptian priest) inherited Joseph's portion when the land was divided among the Israelite tribes.

I go back to an earlier statement that I made: The Conservative Movement has to decide whether it is a reform (with a small R) movement or is a watered-down Orthodoxy.

The Travails of the Orthodox World
8/24/11

In my last column, two weeks ago, I critiqued Reform rabbis who attempted to base their relationships with God on revelation. I argued that they do not have the right to cherry-pick what part of Torah they want to believe is the word of God and what other part they arbitrarily decide is not God's word but man's distortion of God's intent.

In that column I defended Orthodoxy's reliance on Torah as the word of God as intellectually coherent. I don't believe it, but I respect it as an intelligent assumption. (As discussed in the last column I believe that the Torah is the product of humankind reaching toward God. It is the reflection of Judaism trying to create an ethical society.)

Having said that, there is still room in any orthodoxy to moderate the rough edges of documents written (or dictated by God) thousands of years ago; room to read into the texts modern concepts that our God-given intelligence can apply, concepts that derive from science, literature and philosophy, that are available to us and were not available to our ancestors. From this methodology we derive Modern Orthodoxy.

Admittedly there is danger in the Reform Movement's liberal non-revelationary approach to Judaism. People have the intellectual option of opting out of Judaism, and some do (although other questing souls opt in). Although Orthodoxy proclaims itself as the guardian of Jewish identity, it presents a different problem to the Jewish community—the danger of turning itself into a rigid medieval system that guarantees that it will lose the vast majority of modern Diaspora Jews. It is this danger that I discuss in this column.

It is no secret in Judaism (no secret within Orthodoxy itself) that the phrase Modern Orthodoxy is becoming an oxymoron. As Orthodoxy moves further and further to the right it widens the distance between it and the liberal wings of Judaism—widens it to the point where there is hardly anything in common.

Let me share with you some examples of medieval Judaism in the guise of Orthodoxy. Rabbi Avi Shafran, the official spokesperson for Agudath Israel of America, wrote in a column in this newspaper in the wake of the Haitian earthquake that natural disasters were God's punishment for humankind's misdeeds.

He is not alone among fundamentalists in this strain of thought. The Reverend Pat Robertson (or was it Jerry Falwell?) proclaimed that Hurricane Katrina destroyed New Orleans as punishment because the lesbian comedian Ellen DeGeneres hailed from that city.

Just this past month we read about the tragedy of 8-year-old Leiby Kletzky's abduction and murder in Brooklyn. Rabbi Yehuda Levin, an official spokesperson for the Igud HaRabbonim (Rabbinic Alliance of America), an ultra-Orthodox body, declared that little Leiby was cut into pieces and stored in a refrigerator by a deranged Hasidic Jew because it was God's punishment since Jews did not protest same sex marriage and abortion.

We have here a God of Punishment directly out of Torah without the filter of 21st century intelligence. But there is the fundamentalist flip side to this God. Our good deeds can save us from disaster. Shafran wrote in a more recent column in the *Journal* concerning a real event that occurred in Lyon, France in 1943. An anti-Semite entered the rear of the Great Synagogue with three hand grenades on a Friday evening during services with the intent of lobbing them into the congregation. At that very moment the congregation turned to face the main doors of the synagogue. Of course, it was the last stanza of L'cha Dodi when Jews turn to welcome the Shabbat bride. Looking into the faces of the entire congregation, the assailant fled and the Jews were spared. True story.

Shafran comments: "No mortal can identify the special merit of the Lyon worshippers. Maybe it was the fact that the city's Jewish community had provided sanctuary for Jewish refugees from other parts of France. Maybe it was the very fact of the synagogue stubbornly continuing to hold services during such trying times. Or something else, unknown. Or many things. But merits there were . . . What we can know though, is that we have a Guardian."

Really? Where was God the Guardian when the rest of European Jews went to the gas chambers? Did they not have merit? Shafran's theology leads us to the conclusion that they deserved to die in the Holocaust. He's not a far distance from the Reverend John Hagee (a darling of the Jewish right because he supports Netanyahu) when he declared that God caused the Holocaust because my grandparents migrated to America instead of the Holy Land as commanded by God. There is not much space separating Christian and Jewish fundamentalists.

The lurch to the right in Orthodoxy may have reached its pinnacle as reflected in the recent news concerning the Skver Hasidim in New Square, Rockland County, New York. By order of the Grand Rabbi David Twersky New Square residents must walk streets strictly divided by gender, with women on one side and men on the other. Women are not allowed to drive— shades of Islam in Saudi Arabia; and we criticize them. Maybe we should look closer to home.

This community found itself in the news because one of its residents sought to pray outside the village's main synagogue at a nursing home where a friend was suffering from cancer. His children were harassed in school. On a Sabbath morning more than 300 people gathered outside his home chanting for him to leave the community. Finally an 18-year-old assistant to the Grand Rabbi attempted to torch his home and in the process severely burned himself and his target. The police are investigating whether it was at the direction of Rabbi Twersky.

These are the wages of sin. Sorry, wrong sermon. These are the wages of fundamentalism. It may be too late, but for the sake of Judaism as a whole a serious effort within Orthodoxy must be waged to resurrect a sane and modern version of Judaism, the kind of Orthodoxy that my grandparents practiced, the kind of Judaism that for generations was the bedrock of American Jewry, not just a peculiar sideshow.

Can American Jewry Exist Without Israel?
10/3/12
Rabbi Bruce Warshal

Daniel Gordis is an American Conservative rabbi who made *aliyah* (emigrated to Israel—translation for our non-Jewish readers, and there are many). There he moved to the right, both religiously and politically, and is now a Senior Vice President at the Shalem Center, an Israeli think tank.

Tablet, the on-line Jewish magazine, published an excerpt from his recently published book. The title of the article was; "No Jewish People Without Israel."

Needless to say, I support the survival of Israel and would be devastated if it were extinguished; but to proclaim that the continuance of American Judaism depends on the existence of Israel is, to me, an unfounded assertion. It is important to review his thesis, not just for academic reasons but for an understanding of what exactly is the essence of our Judaism in America.

Before getting to his main assertion, Gordis argues that the centrality of Judaism has always been Israel or the longing for the existence of the state. He cites the annual conclusion of the Passover Seder, "Next year in Jerusalem." He could have cited the many references to Jerusalem and Israel in our liturgy. This reflects the reality that Jews have always related to Jerusalem in particular and all of the land of Israel to a lesser extent. It is certainly a part of our culture, but is it the "core of (our) national sensibilities and dreams," as Gordis would have it?

I believe that history answers this question. During the early and mid 1800's German Jews flocked to the United States, not to Israel (then Palestine). It could be argued that they were assimilated and estranged from their Judaism and did not relate to this core of which Gordis writes.

But how can he explain the fact that millions of eastern European Jews (including my beloved grandparents) flocked to the United States while only a trickle went to Palestine? They were the products of an intense Orthodox milieu, yet they did not choose the supposed core as their destination. They repudiated Gordis's thesis in the most dramatic fashion—they spoke with their feet. Gordis mistakes liturgy for reality. Zion was always a component of Judaism, but only one of many components of a multifaceted religious experience.

This is a good segue to the question of exactly what is the Jewish people. Are we a nation or are we a religion? Citing the writings of Emory University professor Jacob Wright, Gordis maintains that the aftermath of the fall of Judea (586 BCE) and the Babylonian Exile produced a new concept in history—a nation that was severed from its land, but still maintained its existence as a nation. Gordis looks upon world Jewry as part of this unique international nation that is tied to Israel by some kind of emotional umbilical cord. He writes that without Israel "Jews would become stateless like the Chechnyans, the Tibetans, or the Basques." This is great fodder for anti-Semitic dual loyalty charges.

As a rabbi he should be ashamed of himself. So much is encompassed within Judaism (ethics, social consciousness, philosophy, questing to understand God, or what is godliness, etc.), that to reduce it to a mere national status is in itself almost an anti-Semitic act. Yes, we have a sense of peoplehood. So do the Mormons, but it is not a nation by any stretch of the imagination. The American adherents to Greek Orthodoxy have a peoplehood, but that does not make them citizens of Greece.

By religion, I am a proud Jew. By nationality, I am a proud American. America is my nation, not Israel. I care deeply for Israel, as the Irish care for Ireland and myriad other peoples care for their ancestral lands. I practice a wonderful religion in a fantastic country. Gordis has every right to change his nationality. He is now an Israeli and he remains a Jew. I maintain my religion without changing my nationality.

Now onto Gordis's main assertion: Jews can never feel totally secure in the United States. He reminds us that Jews felt secure in Berlin before the rise of Nazism. By inference he cites the anti-Semitism that once existed in this country by reminding us that "there was an era not long ago in which American Jews tiptoed around America, nervously striving to stay beneath the radar." He makes reference to the lack of public outcry from the American Jewish community during the Second World War: "There were no mass protests, no caravans of busses to Washington to demand help for their European kin."

He is correct. But now he admits that the American Jewish community has found its sense of confidence, security and pride as well as its voice. And why do we feel more secure in the United States? Gordis's answer: the State of Israel. He writes: "Much of what fuels American Jewish pride is the existence and the behavior of the State of Israel. In ways we do not sufficiently recognize, Israel has changed the existential conditions of Jews everywhere, even in America. Without the State of Israel, the self-confidence and the sense of belonging that American Jews now take for granted would quickly disappear."

It is truly ludicrous to believe that our sense of belonging in this country depends on Israel. We are accepted today as never before, and our sense of belonging reflects that, because America has changed since the anti-Semitic era of post World War One to the early 1950's. It is now sixty years later. We no longer have Jim Crow laws. We have gone from incarcerating American Japanese to Asians dominating our universities. We have travelled the path from homosexuality being a crime to marriage equality in many states. We have changed from a predominantly white Anglo Saxon country to a nation of minorities, religiously, racially and ethnically. That's why we feel secure in this country, not because of Israel. Any comparison of what could happen here to what happened in Germany shows how out of touch Gordis is with the land of his birth.

Finally, referring to America, Gordis writes: "Without Israel, what would remain to make Jewishness anything more than some anemic form of ethnic memory long since eroded?" In his new-found Israeli nationalism he seems to forget that there is a vibrant Judaism being practiced in America. Of course, Judaism without the existence of Israel would be diminished, but it would still be a robust source of meaning to millions of Jews—because at bottom we are a religion, not an extension of the Israeli nation. We are Americans practicing a religion. Don't try to make me anything else.

Another Challenge to Freedom of the Pulpit
1/9/13

In my last column (December 19th) I wrote about the United Nation's acceptance of Palestine as a non-voting member state. I cited the fact that the UN resolution affirmed a Palestinian state "living side by side in peace and security with Israel, on the basis of the pre-1967 borders." While affirming their own statehood the Palestinians through the UN resolution were also affirming the legitimacy of Israel. I commented that this was a move for peace, not war, not terrorism.

Although this may be a minority opinion among American Jewish leaders and organizations, it is not out of the mainstream. There was a rally in Tel Aviv in support of the UN resolution and the prestigious Americans for Peace Now (APN), the support group of the peace movement in Israel, also enthusiastically supported the resolution.

But in my last column I lamented the fact that many American rabbis believe as I do but are afraid to speak out: "Put bluntly, rabbis and other Jewish community workers fear for their jobs if they do not parrot the official Israeli talking points." I continued: "Being retired I don't have to worry about being fired. I speak for many rabbis who love Israel but are muzzled. I don't blame them. They have kids and mortgages to worry about."

At that point I admitted that a few brave rabbis do show leadership. The three rabbis of B'nai Jeshurun, a historic congregation on the Upper West Side of New York City, supported the UN resolution. This was so unusual that it was reported on the front page of the *New York Times*. At that point I commented, "Not many rabbis have the luxury of working on the liberal Upper West Side."

Well, I was wrong. There is no luxury and no safe haven for rabbis. The *Forward* blasted the news on its front page: "BJ Rabbis Offer Apology as Shul Mulls Next Steps." Although their statement concerning the UN resolution was in an email to the congregation, their apology was delivered from the pulpit on Shabbat morning.

It did not take long for the establishment to crush rabbinic leadership. The ubiquitous hatchet man Alan Dershowitz (who is not a member of BJ) wrote that, "It required incredible chutzpah and insensitivity to the intelligence of the congregants for the rabbis and lay leaders to issue their announcement without first allowing both sides of this issue to be heard and debated." Should rabbis also submit their sermons for consensus consideration before delivering them? Maybe all rabbis should send copies of public statements to Dershowitz before issuing them.

But Dershowitz is a sideshow. The rabbis weren't apologizing to him. He only has words and a modicum of ideas. It's money that counts in the Jewish community. The *Forward* reported that an ad hoc group in the congregation that includes the Manhattan real estate mogul Marvin Davis was formed in protest. An anonymous member described it as an informal "group of wealthy people."

The *Forward* reports that the aim of this ad hoc committee is, "to press the synagogue to establish clear policies on the rabbis' future freedom to speak out unilaterally on public issues." Now this is the nub of the whole controversy, having nothing to do with this particular UN resolution. Issues will come and go, but freedom of the pulpit is an enduring right which must be protected.

One would think that this issue was decided over a hundred years ago. It was the famed Rabbi Stephen Wise who established the "free synagogue" movement. It is ironic that he served as an assistant rabbi at B'nai Jeshurun before establishing his own synagogue in 1907 over the "question whether the pulpit shall be free or whether the pulpit shall not be free, and, by reason of its loss of freedom, reft of its power for good."

Given the context of the current attempt to limit a rabbi's leadership, it is also ironic that Wise was fighting for the right to be a Zionist in an era when the Reform Movement was non-Zionist. He attended the Second Zionist Congress in Basel, Switzerland in 1898 and worked closely with Therodor Herzl, and later with Louis Brandeis and Felix Frankfurter to further the cause of the establishment of the State of Israel. He named his new congregation the "Free Synagogue." It is now named in his honor, The Stephen Wise Free Synagogue. There is also a similarly named major synagogue in Los Angeles.

The question today is do we honor the concept that he championed? Freedom of the pulpit is designed to enrich Judaism, not merely to protect the rabbis. There are many components of Judaism, but surely one of them is to challenge ourselves to confront different opinions in our quest to repair the world, doing Tikun Olam. Today's unpopular opinions often become tomorrow's truths. If we muzzle dialogue and rabbinic leadership we diminish the possibility of our personal growth. That's bad for the individual and it's certainly bad for Judaism.

Both the Reform and the Conservative movements have written guidelines that assure the freedom of the pulpit, but a piece of paper is no weapon against the power of money. When I was a Jewish Federation director we often told this joke: Where does a gorilla sit when he enters the room? Answer: Anywhere he wants. There are too many wealthy gorillas who think that they have the right to set the rules of Jewish discourse and to exclude rabbinic leadership in the dialogue.

Everything You Want to Know About the Jewish Community
10/23/13

Earlier this month the Pew Research Center released its 213-page study of the Jewish community. It made every effort to be comprehensive in both size and scope. Between February and June of this year it contacted 3,475 Jews in all 50 states and the District of Columbia by both land and cell phones. It is a welcome addition to our knowledge base for both Jewish lay leaders and professionals.

But I believe that it made one very serious methodological error that somewhat muddies the analysis. It asked Jews whether they considered themselves religious or non-religious and then proceeded to analyze data for these two separate groups. You don't have to be a Jewish professional to realize that this is a false dichotomy. We all know many Jews who are a vital part of the Jewish community who, if you asked them this question, would answer, "I'm not really religious," simply because they do not go to shul every week or even belong to a congregation.

As I have written in a previous column, I have a close relative who is a devout atheist yet belongs to a Conservative synagogue, keeps kosher and contributes heavily to his local Jewish Federation and other Jewish and secular charities. If asked, he may very well have responded with "non-religious," simply because he does not believe in God. But I know he's a religious Jew in every sense of the word. If asked whether he considered himself a "good Jew," I am sure that he would have replied affirmatively.

But what is being "religious"? When a Christian asks, "What is your religion," he or she is really asking, "What do you believe," meaning do you follow the dogma of the Catholic Church or the Methodists, etc. When a Jew asks the same question he or she is inquiring as to what community you belong to, such as, are you Christian or Jewish. The Jew is not asking for a discussion of belief systems. The stress on belief is a Christian mind-set that the Pew study fell into. If the study was trying to determine the level of commitment to Judaism, it would have been much better to merely ask the Jew whether he/she emotionally feels a part of the Jewish community, not whether he considers himself religious or non-religious.

Having said the above and given the difficulty of analyzing the data because of this pervasive division in the data, the study still has great validity and even presents us with some surprises:

To begin, we have many more Jews in America than we thought—6.8 million (5 million adults and 1.8 children). Some more diverse statistics: Only one-third of Jews belong to synagogues. Fully 10% of American Jews are former Soviet Jews or their children. Jewish rituals still have staying power—70% of Jews participated in a Passover Seder in 2012 and 53% fasted on Yom Kippur.

Here is a shocker: 40% of the total Jewish community believes that Israel was given to the Jewish people by God. I would have expected that of the Modern Orthodox (90%), but 54% of Conservative Jews and 35% of Reform Jews believe that. This fundamentalism within the ranks of liberal Judaism gives me pause. (Of course, 82% of white evangelicals believe this.)

Despite all of the propaganda concerning the rise of Orthodoxy, the study shows that fewer than half of the Jews raised in Orthodox homes have remained Orthodox and more than 20% have left Judaism altogether. It is true that among younger respondents of ages 18 to 29 only 17% have left Orthodoxy, but because of their youth the process is not yet complete. It will be interesting to see the data in another 15 to 20 years.

Here is some very good news: Fully 69% of American Jews feel attached to Israel (30% very attached and 39% somewhat attached), but fully 48% of all respondents doubt that the current Israeli government is sincere in its effort to achieve peace with the Palestinians. This study reflects the fact that we are sophisticated enough to love Israel and still be critical of its government, in spite of the right-wing Jews who brand critics of the Netanyahu coalition as traitors and self-hating Jews.

One odd finding that I find hard to believe—one out of three Jews (34%) feel that believing in Jesus as the Messiah is compatible with being Jewish. Even odder is that the figure for Orthodox is 35%, Conservative 28%, but only 25% for Reform Jews. Maybe I am just talking to the wrong Jews, but I find it difficult to accept this conclusion.

I have read media reports on this study that claim that two-thirds of intermarried Jews are not raising their children as Jews. But I do not find the data to affirm this conclusion. The Table on page 67 of the study shows that only 37% of intermarried couples are not raising their children as Jews. Put another way, 63% of those other intermarried Jews (including the false dichotomy of Jews by religion and by ethnicity, or as they incorrectly denote as no-religion, i.e. all the Jews that you and I know) are raising their kids as Jews. This means that the next generation will produce more Jews, not less. (All we need are 50% of intermarrieds to raise their children as Jews to produce a stable Jewish community for the next generation. Anything over that increases our numbers.)

I am especially heartened by Chapter 6 in the study entitled "Social and Political Views" (pages 98 to 108). It turns out that all that money spent by the Republican Party to convince Jews to become conservatives was wasted. 70% of Jews either consider themselves Democrats or lean in that direction while only 22% consider themselves Republicans or lean that way. Among Reform Jews the Democratic number rises to 77%. As expected, 57% of Orthodox are either Republicans or lean in that direction. Even though we are a small percentage of the population (2.2%) these figures are important because only 10% of Jews are not registered voters compared to 21% of the general public.

I'm especially proud of what I call our "empathy" gauge—how much we think that others are discriminated against: 72% of Jews believe there is discrimination against gays and lesbians as compared to 58% in the general public; 72% of Jews believe the same as to Muslims, as compared to 47% of the general public; against blacks, Jews 64%, general public 47%. Obviously, we have once been there and we understand the plight of the "outsider." 82% of Jews believe that homosexuality should be accepted (rising to 92% of Reform Jews) compared to 57% of the general public and only 30% of white evangelicals.

Finally, fully 88% of Jews (rising to 93% for Orthodox and 92% for Reform) have positive views of their communities compared to 84% of the general public. The conclusion is that we are happy Americans. Not a bad time or place to be Jewish. I could have told you that, but it's nice to hear it from the Pew Research Center.

ANTI-SEMITISM

A History of Anti-Semitism (or Lack Thereof) in America
3/10/10

The actor Jim Brochu brilliantly portrays Zero Mostel in the one man show that is currently off Broadway. I saw the production earlier this year in South Florida. Mostel, who was blacklisted by Hollywood in the 1950's, bitterly declares, "Communist equaled liberal, and liberal equaled Jews." It was "an intellectual final solution."

This sends me back to the record, and Mostel (or Brochu) was absolutely correct. The House un-American Activities Committee (HUAC) was originally chaired by Mississippi Congressman John Rankin who, facing the Jewish Congressman Emanuel Cellar, said on the House floor that "I have no quarrel with any man about his religion . . . any man who believes in the fundamental principles of Christianity."

HUAC reflected the tail end of the worst period of anti-Semitism in our history. The contemporary Jewish community's memory of that period still lingers in our psyches. The American Jewish Committee asked in its annual survey if anti-Semitism was a problem in this country in 2008 (the last time that it asked this question) and the reply is startling. Almost one in four Jews believed it to be a "serious problem," and fully 86 percent believed it is either somewhat of a problem or a serious one.

It's time to go back to the history books. American Jewish history can be divided into four segments, and you may be surprised to learn that in three of the four periods anti-Semitism was not a problem, but rather the country was generally pro-Jewish.

First, the Colonial Period, 1654-1790. Although Jews were prohibited from voting or holding office in most of the colonies, we were included with Catholics and atheists in this ban. It was not specifically anti-Semitism; rather it was an extreme form of the lack of separation of church and state, which was rectified on a national level in the Constitution in 1787.

What is important is that there was not social exclusion that we currently associate with anti-Semitism (exclusion from country clubs or university quotas). Jews were welcomed into the fabric of society. In 1731 when Ben Franklin established his private library company (analogous to the modern country club in many respects) Jews were invited as members. In Boston the Jew Moses Michael Hays became the Grand Master of the Mason's Massachusetts Lodge. He appointed as his deputy an obscure guy by the name of Paul Revere. In 1788 when Mikveh Israel in Philadelphia was about to go bankrupt, prominent Christians raised money to save the congregation. These included Ben Franklin, David Rittenhouse, William Rush (who signed the Declaration of Independence), Charles Biddle (of one of the foremost families of America), and one of the Muhlenbergs (after whom the college in Pennsylvania is named).

The Middle Period or the Period of Jewish Expansion, 1790-1881. In 1790 there were only 1200 to 2000 Jews in this country. By 1880 there were 250,000, primarily as a result of the German-Jewish migration. Jews began to spread out and move west with the rest of the country. Synagogues were founded in Cincinnati (1824), New Orleans (1828), Baltimore (1829), Louisville (1832), St. Louis and Cleveland (1839), Chicago (1847), and finally reaching the West Coast after the Gold Rush in 1850.

During this period Jews were mostly welcomed into their communities. Joseph Jonas, the first Jew in Cincinnati, wrote in his memoir that the people in the territories had never seen a Jew. An old Quaker woman approached him: "Art thou a Jew? Thou art one of God's chosen people. Wilt thou let me examine thee?" She turned him round and round and at last exclaimed, "Well, thou art no different to other people." And to most gentiles we were not. This was a good period for Jews in America.

The Third Period, 1881-1945. With the mass immigration of Eastern European Jews beginning in 1881 we saw the beginning of the modern American Jewish community. We also saw this country turn against immigrations and the final closing of the gates in 1924. We Jews were not the only objects of disdain. The Chinese Exclusion Act of 1882 denied Chinese access to this country and the right to become citizens. It was not repealed until 1943. (I recommend the newly opened Museum of Chinese in America in New York City.) This third period was the only time when Jews faced serious anti-Semitism in America. The HUAC hearings, lasting into the 1950s, were the echoes of a dying era.

Finally, the Modern Era, 1945-2009. Jews began to "make it" in the 1950's. Universities began to open up. Children of shopkeepers became doctors, lawyers and scientists. We even became bankers. And with our success and other changing demographics in America anti-Semitism has dwindled to miniscule proportions. Nearly ten years ago the American Jewish Committee reported that 85 percent of gentiles would welcome a Jewish son or daughter-in-law. While once a Jew could not get accepted into an Ivy League school, nearly every one of them has had a Jewish president.

What other statistics do we need to convince ourselves that we are really an accepted part of America? Yet, fully 86 percent of us think that anti-Semitism is either a somewhat or very serious problem in this country. I believe this is more a reflection of our own victim mentality than it is of reality. I think we need some serious psychiatric counseling.

What About Anti-Semitism in America and Europe?
2/5/14

For the last couple of years I have been receiving emails from Jewish sources that proclaim that anti-Semitism is rampant in Europe and that half of French Jewry is about to emigrate to Israel. This is a reflection of their victim mentality and the mind-set of "us against them," the concept that anti-Semitism will always separate us from the rest of humanity. Now comes Daniel Goldhagen, a controversial academic, with his new book, "The Devil That Never Dies: The Rise and Threat of Global Antisemitism," which puts an academic gloss upon the hysteria.

This is not to deny that there is a rise in anti-Semitism in parts of Europe, especially in Hungary, which I will discuss in this column; but it is a far cry from what the on-line *Tablet* magazine, in its review of the Goldhagen book, declared, "A New Era of Anti-Semitism Is Here."

First let us begin with the United States. For the last two decades studies have been showing a diminution of anti-Semitism in this country, yet many Jewish organizations have been wary of the data. The coup de grace was delivered two years ago by Robert Putnam and David Campbell in their universally acclaimed study of religion in America, "American Grace."

They devised a "feeling thermometer" study in which they asked different religious groups what they thought of other religious communities. Their findings show that Jews were the highest ranked, the most respected and accepted, along with Mainstream Protestants and Catholics.

The fact that we are warmly accepted in American society should not surprise anyone, despite our being bombarded by money-raising scare tactics by the Anti-Defamation League (ADL) and other "defense organizations."

Our prominence in politics, our acceptance through intermarriage, and our entrance into the highest echelons of American business reflect this reality.

Yet within the last decade an American Jewish Committee (AJC) poll showed that 97% of American Jews believed that anti-Semitism was either a very serious problem (37%), or somewhat of a problem (60%), and 49% believed that it was increasing. Thus the perception of the Jewish community did not reflect reality. It appears that American Jews are still traumatized by the history of anti-Semitism in this county in the first half of the 20th century. It may take another couple of generations to cleanse us of this victim mentality.

Now what about Europe? This past November the Institute for Jewish Policy Research (JPR), based in the U.K., published a survey of European anti-Semitism for the European Agency for Fundamental Rights. They canvassed almost six thousand Jews in nine countries, utilizing eleven different languages. It is the largest study ever of Jews in Europe. The study asked Jews of their perceptions of anti-Semitism in their respective countries. Not surprisingly, the memory of the Holocaust in Europe looms larger to them than American Jewish memory of the anti-Semitic 1920's and 1930's in America.

In an introduction to the study, Jonathon Boyd, the executive director of the JPR, writes: "In any assessment of European Jewish life today, we should be cognizant of the extent to which our perspective is clouded by the shadow of this relatively recent history." Given that caveat, the study still does not support the hysteria of my emails or the Goldhagen book.

The study does show that European Jews perceive an increase in anti-Semitism, but it is not of epidemic proportions and neither is it universally rising. Each country has its own story, but Boyd links anti-Semitism with the rise in Europe of antipathy to minorities due to integration of populations as a consequence of the European Union.

He writes: "The integration question is very complex: as the population becomes more mixed and heterogeneous, the character of national identity changes, rendering it both harder to determine what binds one citizen to another and increasing the likelihood of internecine conflict." The conclusion is that anti-Semitism may be rising, at least in the perception of Jews themselves, which is not always accurate, but it is not an exclusive Jewish problem. It is a reflection of a broader societal problem.

This study repudiates Godhagen's thesis that this rise reflects an almost pathological prejudice that spans centuries and cultures, which makes it unique to Jews and impossible to eradicate. His conclusion would reinforce the classic Zionist thesis that negates the Diaspora and that all Jews should make aliyah to Israel for their long-range safety.

The JPR study shows that for Western Europe anti-Semitism is episodic and correlated to events in the Middle East. After the Israeli invasion of Gaza in 2009 (Operation Cast Lead) anti-Semitism increased. By 2011 anti-Semitic incidents had decreased. In Eastern Europe, especially in Hungary, anti-Semitism is not so much linked to the Middle East as to rising nationalism and fear of minorities.

But even in Hungary the study shows that Jews feel very much a part of Hungarian culture. Three percent emigrated and returned, but 48 percent reported that they have considered emigrating, but it is a long distance from thought to action. On the whole, for the entire continent the majority of Jews has never contemplated leaving Europe. This is in contrast to the hysterical emails that claim that half of French Jewry is packing its bags.

Definitely, Europe is not the United States which prides itself on a polyglot, multi-racial, multi-religious and multi-cultural society—so one would expect a more complex situation there concerning anti-Semitism. But Chicken Little is not prancing around and the sky is not falling.

Boyd summarizes the contradictory situation well: "In essence, we have data that indicates life is becoming increasingly uncomfortable for Jews in Europe, and data that indicates that Jewish life remains quite secure."

The real challenge for the communal future of the 1.4 million European Jews is demographics. Death rates are consistently higher than birth rates, and that inevitably leads to population decline. But this is also cloudy since there is no consensus of who is a Jew. As one example, Jewish population estimates for Hungary range from 48,000 to 160,000 depending upon who is included and excluded.

Putting aside the shadow of the Holocaust and misperceived perceptions, but accepting the reality of some uptick in anti-Semitism, the future vitality of European Jewry remains primarily dependent on long-term demographics. However, this is difficult to ascertain. Boyd writes: "There is little empirical basis upon which to develop an educated view."

But European Jews are there and thriving, and according to the data, they intend to remain there. Boyd's final comment on the JPR study reminds Americans: "The Jewish world is not binary, and 'American Jewry' does not equal 'Diaspora Jewry'; indeed, part of the beauty and value of Diaspora is the diversity that exists within it."

Glenn Beck: Jews Killed Jesus
8/18/10

This past month the conservative Fox Network commentator Glenn Beck proclaimed that the Jews killed Jesus. It was a side comment and not a frontal attack upon us, and for all I know Beck is not anti-Semitic. The liberal channel MSNBC immediately replayed the comment, if for no other reason than to show Beck's ignorance.

No matter that the Catholic Church in 1965 definitively concluded that it was not the Jews. I assume that this does not carry much weight with evangelicals and other kinds of Christians. Beck happens to be a Mormon.

This recurring comment is of prime importance to us Jews. If I really believed that Jews killed my savior, I certainly would not be predisposed to liking or even dealing with them. Certainly the charge of deicide has been the basis of anti-Semitism over the centuries.

I covered this topic seven years ago when that noted Hollywood philosopher Mel Gibson produced his movie "The Passion," and I included that column in Volume I of "Provocative Columns." But it seems to rear its head every so many years, so it is important for every Jew to really know the historical facts. (This column is the only reprint from Volume I, which underscores the importance of this topic.) Here are the real facts:

No Jewish Motive

Although killing for power is replete in Jewish history, as unfortunately it is in the history of all peoples, there is no Jewish tradition for killing for theological reasons. Sadly, burning at the stake for the sake of beliefs is a legacy of our daughter religion Christianity.

Jesus, as an ethical teacher, would not have been a threat to the Jewish religious establishment of the First Century even if his teachings radically differed from the Jewish norm (although many scholars seem to indicate that this was not the case).

Indeed there were many strains of Jewish thought at the time of Jesus. The Pharisees, Sadducees, Essenes and Hasidim (not related to modern day Hasidim) were all part of a cauldron of emerging Jewish religious thought. Historically, they did not crucify one another.

Roman Motivation

Continuing our search for motivation, the gospels indicate that Jesus was crucified and that Pilate wrote upon the cross, "Jesus of Nazareth, The King of the Jews." When Pilate asked the Jews, "Shall I crucify your King?" the chief priest protested, "We have no king but Caesar." This questioning reflects Roman concern for the possibility of Jews having a king (i.e. political leader) other than Caesar.

Jesus lived in tumultuous times. The Romans were vigilant against insipient Jewish insurrection. This vigilance was not without good cause. The Jews of the First Century had aspirations to reestablish an independent Jewish state. Merely 36 years after the death of Jesus, the Jews staged a bloody four-year war against Rome that ended in the destruction of Jerusalem and the Second Temple. The last stand of the zealots at Massada is a well-known part of this history. Again in the years 132-135 the Jews staged a second unsuccessful major offensive against Rome.

The Romans were not paranoid. They had every reason to fear the least bit of evidence concerning a challenge to their rule over Judea. The Jews were not a docile subject people. They were a difficult and stiff-necked adversary. It is historically consonant with what scholars know of First Century Judea to believe that Jesus was crucified by the Romans for political reasons, justified or unjustified.

At this point I must say that I believe that individual Jews were involved in the crucifixion of Jesus, Jews who were functionaries of Roman power, but not the Jewish establishment that was busy preparing an insurrection against Rome.

In all occupations there are quislings and corroborators. The term quisling for traitor refers to the Norwegian Vidkun Quisling who facilitated Nazi rule of Norway. Even a covey of quislings would not lead us to the conclusion that Norway or the Norwegian people as a whole had complicity with the loathed Nazis.

So it was in ancient Judea. I do not doubt that the Romans used Jewish agents in the network of rule and those agents were a part of most Roman crucifixions. Having said this, there is no doubt that the crucifixion of Jesus was a Roman act to further the ends of Roman rule.

Wrong Court—Wrong Timing

It is related that Jesus was brought before a religious Sanhedrin (Bet Din). A Sanhedrin composed of 23 members did try capital cases. Most important cities in Judea had a Jewish court of this nature. But the gospels tell us that this Jewish court sentenced Jesus on the eve of Passover or on the day itself. (The gospels differ as to the exact timing.) Jewish sources clearly indicate that no authentic Jewish court would be in session at those times (Mishnah Sanhedrin 4:1). This would be analogous to saying that a Florida court convicted a defendant and sentenced him to death on December 25th. We are aware that no American court is in session on this day.

Any court operating in the middle of the night or at daybreak during the religious season referred to in the gospels could not have been an authentic Jewish court, but would have to have been an illegitimate creature of Roman domination.

Wrong Method

Every nation has its favorite method of capital punishment. Historically England had its gallows, France its guillotine, New York its electric chair, California its gas chamber, etc. Name the method of capital punishment and you can almost isolate the geography and the nationality of the executioner.

Crucifixion was as alien to Judaism as it was common to Roman rule. The fact is that the traditional biblical method of execution was stoning and that a religious Sanhedrin had the right to inflict only four modes of capital punishment: stoning, burning, decapitation and strangling. Jewish law did not permit crucifixion. The fact that Jesus was crucified and not put to death in another fashion indicates that the Romans, not the Jews, killed him. It is as simple as that.

Glenn Beck never apologized for his remark. I am sure there will be people as ignorant as Beck who will continue to utter the charge of deicide. The only defense for Jews is to know the historical truth.

JUDAISM AND SEX

Lots of Abominations in the Bible
9/19/12

Last month Rabbi Robert Silvers wrote a perceptive opinion piece in the *Journal* that caught my attention. (Full disclosure: He usually catches my attention since I am a member of Congregation B'nai Israel in Boca Raton and Bob is my rabbi.)

Rabbi Silvers discussed the meaning of the Hebrew word *toevah*, which most English bibles translate as "abomination," as in Leviticus, chapter 18, verse 22: "Do not lie with a male as one lies with a woman; it is an abomination. He pointed out that the Hebrew word *toevah* is used extensively in the bible regarding food prohibitions, idolatrous practices, magic and ethical violations. His prime example is that eating shrimp (shellfish) is *toevah*. Yet today he knows plenty of Jews who eat shellfish.

I admit that rabbis are an odd lot. Instead of doing something useful, such as helping my wife clean the dishes, I began to ponder the different uses in the bible of the word *toevah*. To begin, the Official *Humash* (Torah commentary) of the Conservative Movement, in a commentary on the above Leviticus verse, indicates that *toevah* is used more than 100 times in the bible. That's a lot of abomination, so I decided to look for myself. The alternative was helping my wife tidy the house. The choice was easy.

I admit that I did not reach 100, but I found some fascinating uses of the word. But before I discuss the various applications, let's discuss the actual meaning of "abomination." According to my second bible, Webster's Third International Dictionary (2,662 oversized pages—one should never leave home without it), that which is abominable is "worthy of causing loathing or hatred; revolting; unnatural; detestable." Pretty heavy stuff. The new Jewish Publication Society bible translates *toavah* as "abhorrent." This is just as bad, since to abhor is "to detest extremely; to loathe; to be full with horror or disgust." This doesn't help too much.

So if *toavah* is translated as abhorrent or an abomination, no wonder that in English speaking lands homosexuals have been detested, loathed and objects of disgust. We humans could be no less judgmental than God himself (or herself, or itself, whatever). Thus it is important to put *toevah* in context and to judge the real severity of the offense of homosexuality. This is to assume that it really is an offense, as they did in the bible, but not in all ancient societies.

Here is a sampling of how the word is used in other sections of the bible: Rabbi Silvers already discussed the *toevah* of eating shellfish. Excluding the ten percent of American Jews who are Orthodox, that alone would wipe out maybe 97 percent of the remaining American Jews. The prophet Ezekiel in one of his hallucinatory dreams (this guy had to be on LSD) used the word to describe practicing the wrong rituals in the Temple sanctuary (involving incense smoke), which was probably a legitimate use of the word since the smoke from incense has always annoyed me.

This one I can't explain: Chapter 24 of Deuteronomy describes the situation where a man divorces his wife. She remarries and the second husband either divorces her or dies. The first husband cannot remarry her because "she has been defiled," and it is a *toevah*. I can't quite figure out the abomination here, but I am only a humble retired Reform rabbi. I'll leave it to the chief Ashkenazi Orthodox rabbi of Israel to explain this one. (Although I am a Litvak, I will also accept an interpretation from the chief Sephardic rabbi.) Please, anybody, make sense of this.

The prophet Malachi said it is a *toevah* to marry a non-Jewish woman. I wonder whether he would allow a woman to intermarry with a non-Jewish male. If this were truly an abomination it would wipe out over 50 percent of our community. Good thing Malachi is not living today; may he rest in peace.

The Book of Proverbs is filled with the word *toevah*. It bandies it about freely. Try this one: "Every haughty person is an abomination to the Lord; assuredly, he will not go unpunished." My trusty Webster's 2,662-page dictionary defines haughty as "Disdainfully proud or overbearing." I am horrified since everyone in my family is overbearing and I fear for their future punishment. As the only humble member of this clan, this is the cross (make that a Star of David) that I have had to bear for over 50 years. But since I now realize that it is an abomination, I tremble to contemplate their fate.

I had a wonderful afternoon discovering many more abominations in the bible (It was a lot more enjoyable than helping the wife), but space limitation denies me the chance to save you good people from committing other abominations.

There is an important lesson to be learned here: There is much good in the bible but also much that reflects the mores of ancient times and is not applicable to today. The bible accepts slavery but labels the remarriage of a divorced woman to her first husband as an abomination, a *toevah*. The bible allows a bride to be stoned to death if she were found not to be a virgin on her wedding night (Deuteronomy, chapter 22, verses 20-21), but brands intermarriage as an abomination, a *toevah*.

I love bible studies. That's why I spent all afternoon thumbing through for *toevot*, plural for *toevah*. But in the end it is the responsibility to use rational thought and modern science to determine what really is moral. Personally, I think that committed love between two individuals is the height of morality, no matter if they are of different or of the same gender.

Let's Talk About Sex and More Sex
7/4/12

With a headline that proclaims sex as the topic I assume that my readership has increased at least 50 percent this week. But I do not mean to be prurient in any manner. What occasions this column is a report in the *New York Times* that the Vatican has censured Sister Margaret Farley for publishing her book, "Just Love: A Framework for Christian Sexual Ethics."

Sister Farley is not just another commentator. She has taught at Yale Divinity School and is the past president of the Catholic Theological Society of America. She argues that we must move away from "taboo morality" in the service of justness and fairness, and she supports gay marriage, female masturbation and remarriage after divorce. No wonder the Vatican went off the wall.

But as non-Catholics we should not make the mistake of believing that Catholicism is monolithic. There are many centers of liberality within the Church that either challenge or ignore pontifical edits. (One example: 99 percent of American Catholic women ignore the Vatican concerning birth control.) In the current case the dean of Yale Divinity School, a Catholic layman, and the president of the Sisters of Mercy (of which Sister Farley is a member) issued statements in support of her.

I was drawn to this news report not because I wish to insert myself into an intra-Catholic dialogue but because this same tension between liberals and fundamentalists exists in Judaism concerning matters sexual. Substitute Orthodoxy for the Vatican and liberal Judaism (Conservative, Reform,

Reconstructionist and Humanistic) for Sister Farley and you have the same debate.

Sister Farley wrote that female masturbation "usually does not raise any moral questions at all." She adds that many women have found "great good in self-pleasuring—perhaps especially in the discovery of their own possibilities for pleasure . . ."

Jewish Talmudic law understood that women should find pleasure in sexual relationships. It stipulated that a wife has certain conjugal rights. She can demand sex from her husband, the frequency depending on his work status: If he is not employed, every night; if he is a worker living in the city, twice a week; if in another city, once a week; donkey drivers, once a week; camel drivers, once every 30 days; a seaman, once every six months.

Understanding the right of women for sexual enjoyment would lead one to believe that Orthodox Judaism would have no trouble with female masturbation. But it does, which mystifies me. Traditional Judaism also prohibits male masturbation based on the story in Chapter 38 of the Book of Genesis where Onan let his seed "spoil on the ground" rather than impregnate the wife of his deceased brother, which was his obligation under the rules of Levirate marriage.

His sin was disobeying a biblical law, not masturbation in itself. And God did not tell him he would go blind if he masturbated. Liberal Judaism, which has progressed a bit from Levirate marriages and thousand year old taboos, is firmly in Sister Farley's camp as concerns masturbation for women and men.

As for same-sex marriage we see the same split between liberals and conservatives in Judaism as in Christianity, with the exception that the vast majority of Jewish religious institutions support same-sex marriage while the reverse is true in Christianity. It's interesting that among lay people there is majority support no matter the position of their official religious bodies. As expected, the Orthodox are still living in the era of the Torah.

Yes, Leviticus, Chapter 20, verse 13 says that if a male has sex with another male, both shall be put to death. (It is an oddity that nowhere in the bible does it prohibit lesbian sex.) But that same chapter (verse 9) says that, "If any man repudiates his father or mother, he shall be put to death." I just don't understand how fundamentalists, including Orthodox Jews, can pick and choose verses in the bible. How do they believe in one statement and ignore another one in the very same chapter?

My stance, which I believe reflects the vast majority of liberal rabbis and lay people, is, as a Southern preacher once said, "God don't make no junk." We are all children of God, and some of us are biologically ordained to be gay, and that is an acceptable variant of nature. My wife is left-handed. In the middle Ages this was considered sinister. In fact the word sinister derives from the original meaning of favoring the left. Today we recognize it as just another legitimate variant of nature. In fact, it could be an advantage if you happen to be a southpaw pitcher in baseball.

On the whole our Jewish hang-ups concerning sex have been more moderate than Christianity's. Our tradition requires our rabbis to be married, not celibate. The Sabbath is the preferred day for sexual relations (with your spouse); it sanctifies the Lord's Day, rather than profaning it. But in all religions, including our own, there are elements that would take us back a few thousand years into a more primitive society.

This is most evident in Israel where the ultra-Orthodox, who are represented in the Knesset and who wield religious authority in the state, are in the process of creating what, if not checked, would be a Medieval theocratic Jewish state. They have succeeded in implementing segregated seating on busses based on gender. They object to mixed choral groups in the Israeli Army because the sound of a woman's voice may instigate a sexual urge in men. (This based on a biblical quote from *Shir Ha Shirim*—Songs of Songs—"Let me hear your voice, for your voice is sweet and your face is beautiful," Chapter 2, verse 14.) And they have succeeded in eradicating pictures of women, even fully clothed, on public billboards and other forms of advertising.

Needless to say that they practice a Judaism vastly different than I and, I suspect, vastly different from the overwhelming majority of American Jews. Personally speaking, I believe that we are not, as the old UJA slogan proclaimed, *Am Echad*—One People. We practice different religions, both of which happen to call themselves Judaism.

There are many differences between these two "Jewish" religions, but sex is a good topic to start with. It certainly keeps people awake. For this I thank Sister Foley for bringing it to my attention and I wish my liberal Catholic friends good luck in their internal struggle to drag the Vatican into the 21st Century. I will be fighting the good fight in my own community.

ISLAMOPHOBIA AND THE JEWS

It's Time to Stop Islam-Bashing
8/5/09

Following the atrocities of 9/11 there has been a campaign to discredit Islam because of the actions of the radical fringe that has distorted that religion. This has not been merely a philosophical dispute. It has played itself out in the political arena. It may have reached its zenith in late 2004 when 44 percent of Americans were in favor of restricting the civil liberties of Muslim-Americans. At that time 27 percent of the respondents to a Cornell University survey supported requiring all Muslim Americans to register where they live with the federal government.

This xenophobia appeared to be waning but has once again intensified after President Obama's speeches at Cairo and before the Parliament of Turkey. As if to repudiate the sentiments expressed in the 2004 Cornell University survey, Obama declared in Ankara: "The United States has been enriched by Muslim-Americans. Many other Americans have Muslims in their family, or have lived in a Muslim-majority country. I know, because I am one of them."

It is not merely xenophobia that produces this spate of hatred. I see three separate motivating factors. First, it is merely the continuation of the millennia-old conflict between Christianity and Islam. Although the pope has implicitly repudiated the crusades when he recently visited Jordan and expressed his "deep respect" for Muslims, the born-again evangelical movement has taken up the cudgels. One recent email I received was entitled, "Allah or Jesus?" The Southwestern Baptist Theological Seminary in Texas has even created a masters degree to train missionaries in the art of converting Muslims.

A second motivation is the use of anti-Muslim rhetoric in American politics. Anti-Muslim animus can be a rallying call as effective as Roe v. Wade or the Terri Schiavo case. One horrific example is the recent diatribes by

Frank Gaffney, Jr. Gaffney was once the Assistant Secretary of Defense in the Reagan administration and is currently a columnist for the *Washington Times* and the *National Review*. He accuses President Obama of the ultimate crime in a column written for the *Jewish World Review* entitled, "America's first Muslim president?" He writes: "There is mounting evidence that the president not only identifies with Muslims, but actually may still be one himself." Note two assumptions inherent in that statement: Obama was once a Muslim and being a Muslim is in itself not acceptable.

The third motivation that I detect is particularly disturbing to me as a Jew. It is the right-wing Jewish attempt to discredit the religion of 1.3 billion people (a religion that taught us Jews philosophy, and a religion that welcomed Jews to the safety of its shores during the dark years of the Inquisition) because they perceive that it will discredit the national aspirations of the Palestinian people. The intent of these Jews is to transform a conflict between two peoples over one piece of land into a conflict between two religions.

The most egregious example of this behavior is when the Orthodox Palm Beach Synagogue hosted the Dutch politician and bigot Geert Wilders where he received a standing ovation. He exclaimed, "Islam is not a religion. Islam is a totalitarian political ideology. Islam's heart lies at the Quran, and the Quran is a book that calls for hatred, that calls for violence, for murder, for terrorism, for war and submission. We should also stop pretending that Islam is a religion." Wilders called for "voluntary repatriation" of Muslims from western countries.

Wilders was also hosted by Florida State Representative Adam Hasner in Delray Beach. Hasner is the majority leader in the Florida House and a prominent Jew. Thus we get the confluence of both right-wing Zionism and right-wing Republicanism in Islam-bashing. Wilders is so repugnant to mainstream religious and political leaders that he was recently denied entrance into Britain as an undesirable person. Even the Anti-Defamation League (not a liberal organization when it comes to Middle East politics) proclaimed: "The ADL strongly condemns Geert Wilders' message of hate against Islam as inflammatory, divisive and antithetical to American democratic ideals." This did not stop the chairwoman of the local chapter of Americans for a Safe Israel from attacking the ADL for "dishonoring itself" by "defaming Wilders."

Another example of Jews Gone Wild is the recent briefing by Steven Emerson, a supposed anti-terrorist expert who is a frequent speaker before Jewish Federation dinners, when he created a new category called "stealth jihad." Not content to condemn the violent distortion of Islam, of which we can all agree, he impugns the humanity and the loyalty of the Muslim-American community by declaring that it has a secret objective of taking over

America, which he calls a "stealth jihad." He labels legitimate political activity, something at which the American Jewish lobby excels, subversive when practiced by Muslims. Emerson's hatred is more vile that Wilders' because it is more sophisticated. I assume that Emerson will continue to be welcomed as a speaker by Jewish organizations to the shame of our community.

It's time that mainstream Christians and Jews and American politicians speak up against those who distort our religions and our political system and agree with President Obama when he stated in his Cairo speech that "the truth (is) that America and Islam are not exclusive and need not be in competition. Instead, they overlap, and share common principles—principle of justice and progress, tolerance and the dignity of all human beings."

A Jewish Problem: Anti-Muslim Hate-Mongers
1/23/13

Three weeks ago a Muslim man was pushed from behind into the tracks of an incoming New York subway meeting instant death. The perpetrator was apprehended and she declared, "I hate Muslims (and Hindus) ever since 2001 when they put down the twin towers. I've been beating them up."

This is just one instance of violence and harassment against Muslims in America among many this past year. In Missouri the Islamic Society of Joplin's building was destroyed by a suspicious fire. The Islamic center of Greater Toledo, Ohio was torched. A New York man was stabbed repeatedly outside a mosque proclaiming, "I don't like Muslims." In Panama City, Florida a mason jar filled with gasoline was thrown at the home of a Muslim family.

The FBI reports that in 2010 there were 160 anti-Muslim hate crimes committed, the last year that FBI statistics are available. The Council on American-Islamic Relations (CAIR), the Muslim equivalent of the ADL, reports that there were 18 attacks specifically against mosques in 2012. The Southern Poverty Law Center reports that in 2011 the number of anti-Muslim groups increased to 30, up from 10 the previous year.

It's not just violence. It's an attempt to "cleanse" America of a Muslim presence. This past year the following organizations were attacked by Anti-Muslim activists: Campbell's Soup for offering halal certified soup; Whole Foods for "whoring itself out to Islam" for offering halal foods during Ramadan; the Boy Scouts of America for having an Islamic Scouting group; the Metropolitan Museum of Art because it opened an exhibit on Islamic Art Treasures; the Family Feud television game for having a Muslim family compete; and Dr. Phil was labeled an "Islamo-panderer" for being sympathetic to Muslim guests.

This Islamophobia and outright hatred has spread to the political arena. The most egregious instance this past year was when Representative Michelle Bachmann declared that the Muslim Brotherhood had "penetrated" the U.S. government, specifically singling out Huma Abedin, a prominent Muslim-American aide to Secretary of State Hillary Clinton. This McCarthy-ite maneuver was mildly criticized by House Speaker John Boehner ("Accusations like this being thrown around are pretty dangerous"), but actually supported by the only Republican Jewish member of Congress, Eric Cantor, when he praised her saying, "Her concern was about the security of the country."

The Republican Party is close to declaring open warfare on Muslims. In 2011 and 2012, 78 bills or amendments aimed at interfering with Islamic religious practices were considered in 31 states and the U.S. Congress. Of these, 73 bills were introduced by Republicans, one by a Democrat in Alabama, and four were bi-partisan.

Most of these bills were aimed at outlawing Sharia law (comparable to Jewish Halacha), a non-existent problem. Muslims do not want to foist Sharia law onto America any more than Orthodox Jews want to foist Halacha onto America. Yet six states actually passed anti-Sharia laws—Arizona, Kansas, South Dakota, Tennessee, Oklahoma and Louisiana.

Representative John King as Chair of the Homeland Security Committee held hearings this past year on Muslims in America. His first hearing was titled, "The Extent of Radicalization in the American Muslim Community and that Community's Response." This was truly a McCarthy witch hunt. A few years back he claimed with absolutely no evidence that "80% to 85% of the mosques in this country are controlled by Islamic fundamentalists." The Leadership Conference on Civil and Human Rights pointed out to King before the first hearing that, "Experts have concluded that mosque attendance is a significant factor in the prevention of extremism."

Now the big question: Who are the major perpetrators of this anti-Muslim hatred? Answer: Jews. Sixty two of the above 78 referenced anti-Muslim laws were based on David Yerushalmi's American Laws for American Courts (ALAC) model legislation. Not all, but a great preponderance, of anti-Muslim hate-mongers are Jews, including the following:

Pamela Geller—known for her leadership in the movement against the proposed mosque near Ground Zero. She has recently started an anti-Muslim billboard campaign on highways and in New York subways. She has attacked a group of Christian, Jewish and Muslim clergy in Denver because they started an interfaith "Love Thy Neighbor" campaign. She called the Christian and Jewish participants "quislings, craven, cowardly, knaves," for participating with Muslims.

Daniel Pipes—has encouraged derogatory cartoons of Muhammad to be published every day "until the Islamists become accustomed to the fact that we turn sacred cows into hamburger."

David Horowitz—who combines anti-Muslim with anti-liberal rhetoric. In his book Horowitz says that both Muslims and progressives abhor America and American values.

What does this rogues gallery of haters have in common? First, they are all staunch supporters of Israel and they believe that delegitimizing Islam somehow helps Israel in its conflict with Palestinians. Of course, they are hurting Israel in that they are turning a conflict over land into a religious war. I do not blame the Israelis. It's a fair generalization to say that Israelis exhibit animosity toward Palestinians, but they do not denigrate their religion. It is these American Jewish zealots that hate Islam, not Israelis.

Second, most, if not all, of the above are welcomed speakers at synagogues (mostly Orthodox) and Jewish Federations, simply because they are pro-Israel. (Pam Geller was invited to speak at the Los Angeles Federation but was disinvited after an outpouring of community outrage.) What does this say about our Jewish sensitivity to bigotry in America? Does being pro-Israel excuse all other sins? Bernie Madoff is pro-Israel. Does that make him fit to be a synagogue or Federation speaker? This is truly a disgrace to our community.

The biggest disgrace is that our rabbinic and lay leaders remain silent. Very few rabbis have preached against anti-Muslim hatred from the pulpit. Most of our national Jewish organizations issue statements weekly on behalf of Israel, but not very often against the increase in hatred in this county against Muslim Americans.

How would you feel if Jews were being pushed onto subway tracks; if 18 synagogues were attacked this past year; if 31 states were to pass laws against Halacha (Jewish law); and if the House Un-American Activities Committee (HUAC) were resurrected and hearings were held to determine if all Jews in Hollywood were communists (we have been there!)? We of all people should empathize with our fellow Americans who happen to be Muslims.

The Muslim writer Sheila Musaji has written: "It takes courage to speak out against Islamophobia (or any bigotry). It takes courage to defend the ideals of America. It takes courage to stand for the principles and values of Judaism, Christianity and Islam. Many of those speaking out in defense of American Muslims have been attacked in articles coming out of the Islamophobic echo chamber."

Yes, it takes courage. And I have seen few rabbis and lay leaders exhibit this courage. Where are you?

It's Time to Stop Islam-Bashing
2/24/10

Some of us who have lived in Florida for a long time may remember Rabbi Leon Kronish of Miami Beach who was one of the foremost rabbis of his generation. Well, the apple doesn't fall very far from the tree. His son, Ron, who is a rabbi and a Ph.D. from Harvard, made aliyah (emigrated to Israel) some 30 years ago. He is the founder and director of the Interreligious Coordinating Council in Jerusalem. Recently I had the pleasure of hearing him speak at Florida Atlantic University.

His organization did something which was very unique. He brought together Imams and Orthodox rabbis to study their respective texts. The Bible was translated into Arabic and the Quran into Hebrew. These clergy studied together. What they learned was that Islam and Judaism taught the same ethical lessons. To many Americans (and many Israelis, for that matter) this is some kind of revelation, since we are currently surfeited with anti-Muslim rhetoric.

To be sure the Quran has some problematic passages. I covered this ground in a column seven years ago, but I feel that I must repeat the message today. The truth is that there are parts of the Bible, New Testament and Quran that make any modern reader cringe. They were products of their times, and all three include fabulously uplifting messages as well as depressingly vindictive diatribes.

Looking at the New Testament, you really do not want to read the anti-Jewish passages in the Gospel of John. An Episcopalian priest once confided to me that he would expunge the book from the cannon if he had the power. Today, hate-mongers are providing us with every dubious passage in the Quran.

But before we Jews become too smug, let us face up to the portions of our Bible that are truly embarrassing. The most egregious example is found in Deuteronomy, Chapter 25, verses 17-19. They enjoin the Jews to "Remember what Amalek did to you on the way as you came out from Egypt, how he attacked you on the way . . . (therefore) you shall blot out the remembrance of Amalek from under the heaven . . ." First Samuel, Chapter 15, verses 1-34 extend these orders to the point of genocide (We can't avoid the word—it's genocide): "Now go and smite Amalek, and utterly destroy all that they have; do not spare them, but kill both man and woman, infant and suckling, ox and sheep, camel and ass." (Verse 3)

To prove that God is serious about this prescription for genocide, When King Saul defeats the Amalekites but allows Agag, their king, to live, as well as some choice cattle (he evidently spared no women or children) God decrees that the crown is not to pass to Saul's children, paving the way for David to found a new dynasty. Jewish commentators have indicated that if you can equate a contemporary enemy as an Amalekite, then you can proceed to genocide.

A significant portion of the settlers on the West Bank have come to this conclusion. A recent book in wide circulation in Israel published by two West Bank rabbis proclaims, "The prohibition 'Thou Shall Not Murder'" applies only "to a Jew who kills a Jew." They maintain that non-Jews are "uncompassionate by nature" and attacks on them "curb their evil inclination." These settler-rabbis also believe that children of Israel's enemies may be killed because "it is clear that they will grow to harm us."

The point of this exercise is to indicate that all three Abrahamic religions can be distorted. Yes, there is a movement in Islam that is dangerous to the West and to Islam itself. But it is not mainstream Muslim philosophy. Less than 20 percent of the 1.3 billion Muslims in this world are Arabs and only an infinitesimal portion of them are terrorists (however you define that term).

Yet anti-Muslim hysteria abounds in this country. In an earlier column I reported that in 2005 a Cornell University study reported that almost every other American (44 percent) is in favor of restricting the civil liberties of Muslim Americans. Fully 27 percent of respondents supported requiring all Muslim Americans to register where they live with the federal government. I cannot prove this, but I believe that this animus has not subsided in the last five years.

Daily, veritably daily, I receive emails trashing anything Muslim. They protest that Islam is a "cult," that Obama is a secret Muslim (as if that were a crime), and that the objective of the two million Muslims living in this country is to destroy Western culture. I received one email that proclaimed that Islam in America endangers our multicultural society. The writer did not see the irony that his exclusion of Islam itself destroys the concept of multiculturalism.

What particularly disturbs me is that right-wing Jewish activists use anti-Muslim rhetoric in the belief that this somehow supports Israel. These Jews who peddle this venom do not realize that they do Israel no favor. They turn a war over nationalism (control over a piece of land) into a war between religions. I prefer that we do not pit 14 million Jews against 1.3 billion Muslims. Beyond the practical considerations, this Islam-bashing diminishes Judaism. We turn ourselves into nothing better than the bigots who have plagued us for millennia.

In the name of Judaism, for our own dignity and wholeness, we must realize that we are not in a war of civilizations, the Judea-Christian West against Islam. We are fighting terrorists, who happen to be Muslims. Let's be a little sophisticated.

Shariah Law and Anti-Islam Animus
1/25/12

The conservative Center for Security Policy recently issued a warning that Shariah law was being implemented in American courts. Its spokesperson said that Islamic religious demands are arriving mostly through rulings involving cases where foreigners are the principals and he commented that "Shariah enters U.S. courts through the practice of comity to foreign law."

I shall discuss comity in a moment, but first let me share with you the reaction to this assertion regarding Shariah law. The wonder of the internet is that it allows reader reaction. There were 237 postings the day that I received this email. Here are some examples: any judge within the United States who invokes the use of any foreign laws should be locked up for treason; wake the hell up America; not only is Shariah not the law of the United States of America, it is the law of the Devil and against the law of God; and my favorite, sent in capital letters—ELIMINATE ALL MUSLIMS THAT ARE FORCING ISLAMIC LAWS AND THEIR DEATH CULT RELIGION.

This hysteria is fueled by conservative politicians. Newt Gingrich has called for a federal law outlawing Shariah law, declaring, "Shariah law is a moral threat to the survival of freedom in the United States and in the world as we know it." Such a law has been proposed in the House of Representatives (H.R. 973). The Tennessee General Assembly recently passed a law that states that Shariah promotes "the destruction of the national existence of the United States." More than a dozen other states are considering a similar law.

Now it's time to discuss the concept of comity to foreign law. The United States has no bilateral treaty, nor is it a signatory to any international convention that requires our courts to recognize or enforce foreign judgments or laws. However, an American court can enforce a foreign judgment if it feels that it is compatible with American standards of fairness and procedural legitimacy. An example: An Israeli couple living in America can enforce a divorce decree from a religious court in Israel based on Jewish law or a Saudi couple can enforce a divorce decree from a religious court in Saudi Arabia based on Shariah law—if, and this is a most important if, the court decides that either divorce decree is reasonable based on American legal standards.

Another way that Shariah law legitimately can be implemented in American courts is through the use of arbitration. Arbitration is often used in business disputes to avoid expensive and time-consuming court litigation.

Both parties agree to be bound by the arbitrator's decision and such decisions can be enforced by a court of law. Two Muslims can decide to use a court that applies Shariah business standards and its decision would be enforceable under the American legal system. There is nothing sinister here. It's their business dispute and it's their American right to decide it as they wish.

I am compelled to share with you a piece written on the blog TPM (Talking Points Memo) by Josh Marshall: "In our investigation into the growth of Sharia Law in the USA we came across some surprising findings. Numerous American cities now have one or more Muslim religious courts in operation where believers go to adjudicate family law disputes, real estate transactions and various other matters according to Sharia Law by binding arbitration. These religious court verdicts can then be enforced by civilian American courts. Various states have also passed laws to codify Muslim dietary laws, though a few of these laws have been struck down. And numerous national corporations now process foods to suit Muslim dietary standards. Finally, one jurisdiction in New York has been settled entirely by devout Muslims: no candidates run for office except those approved by the local imam; road signs in the town are all printed in both English and Arabic; and various local practices have been brought into line with Sharia.

"Actually, there's one detail I didn't mention. The law here isn't Sharia; it's Halakhah, Jewish religious law. And all of the above are true if you change 'Muslim' to 'Jewish' and 'Arabic' to 'Hebrew.' (Actually, Yiddish written in the Hebrew script, to be specific.)"

Marshall then comments: "All true. And yet I think it's a pretty good example of the fact that the kinds of things (with Muslims) that are supposed to make us run around with our hair on fire, are already happening and have been for decades with Jews and no one seems to care because, frankly, why should they?"

The American Muslim community is predominantly middle class, eschews terrorism and votes Democratic. (Maybe that's the reason the Republican conservatives target it) A recent poll by the highly respected Pew Research Center shows that Muslims exhibit the highest level of integration among major American religious groups, expressing greater degrees of tolerance toward people of other faiths than do Protestants, Catholics or Jews. It also indicated that nearly 80 percent of American Muslims rate their communities a good place to live, despite the existence of anti-Islamic rhetoric. This highlights the absurdity of anti-Shariah law agitation.

Not only do we do an injustice to American Muslims, but we do harm to America. The Yale historian Eliyahu Stern has written: "In the 20th century we thrived by promoting a Judaic-Christian ethic, respecting differences and accentuating commonalities among Jews, Catholics and Protestants. Today, we need an Abrahamic ethic that welcomes Islam into the religious tapestry of American life. Anti-Shariah legislation fosters a hostile environment that will stymie the growth of America's tolerant strand of Islam. The continuation of America's pluralistic religious tradition depends on the ability to distinguish between punishing groups that support terror and blaming terrorist activities on a faith that represents roughly a quarter of the world's population."

In less academic and more visceral terms this sentiment was expressed by a local Muslim, as reported by the *Sun Sentinel*, in response to Congressman Alan West's attack on Islam: "It's sleazy politics to whip up fear of Muslims. It's a dirty, sleazy tactic to attack a religion."

Since I am writing in a Jewish newspaper, I cannot conclude without mentioning a recent study by the Center for American Progress which shows that seven foundations have spent more than $40 million in the last 10 years to spread misinformation about Muslim Americans. The *Forward* editorially commented, "And who leads those efforts? Far too many Jews." It goes on to name Pamela Geller, David Yerushalmi, Daniel Pipes and Steven Emerson, who even criticized President George W. Bush and New Jersey Governor Chris Christie for being soft on Muslims.

Neocon Jews, a small percentage of our community, bring disgrace upon our liberal Jewish traditions, and they do so under the misguided belief that by denigrating Islam they somehow support Israel. And yet these people are invited to speak in synagogues (primarily Orthodox) and at Jewish Federation functions and are accorded respect. They should be labeled what they actually are: Hate Mongers. There is no place in Judaism for that.

Committee on Homeland Security to Investigate Muslims
1/5/11

One of the major consequences of the Republican control of the House of Representatives is that right wing elements in that party now have control of the investigative process, the same power that the disgraced House Un-American Activities Committee (HUAC) wielded in the 1940's and 1950's.

Representative Peter King, the Chairman of the Committee on Homeland Security has announced that he will hold hearings on the "radicalization" of American Muslims. Of course, there are individual Muslims, both foreign-born and native Americans, who are attracted to the terrorist Al Qaeda doctrines, just as there were individual Jews who were attracted to communism in the 40's and the 50's.

That didn't make the Jewish community a radical threat. In fact, it was a liberal but fiercely patriotic community. So it is with Muslim Americans.

They are a striving, successful (on the whole) immigrant group in the best tradition of this country of immigrants—middle class and patriotic.

Why, then, the need for an investigation? It seems that Americans need an enemy to fear, and Representative King, who has exhibited anti-Muslim leanings in the past, intends to play upon these fears and to curry to those disaffected populists that comprise the Tea Party wing of Republicanism. This will also find favor among the fundamentalist Christian right who are still fighting the crusades in their unrelenting competition with Islam to save the world through Jesus Christ.

Ibrahim Hooper, a spokesman for The Council on American-Islamic Relations has issued a statement that "we're concerned that it'll become a new McCarthy-type hearing." Islamic organizations are wary of cooperating with the Committee, as they should be. The comparison is really not with McCarthy as much as with the history of HUAC. That committee used the guise of looking for communists to propagate anti-Semitism. There is every reason to believe that King's Committee on Homeland Security will fan the anti-Muslim rhetoric that is so prevalent in America today and is spreading like wildfire on the internet.

We can learn from history, or, at least, we should learn from history. In 1944 Mississippi Congressman John Rankin chaired the House Committee on Un-American Activities. One of the first witnesses that he called was the Reverend Gerald L. K. Smith, a rabid anti-Semite who headed the American First Party that advocated as late as 1944 for a compromise with Hitler. He testified that, "There is a general belief that Russian Jews control too much of Hollywood propaganda and they are trying to popularize Russian communism in America through that instrumentality. Personally I believe that is the case." (This was absurd since the Russian immigrant Hollywood moguls were all conservative Republicans with the exception of the Warner brothers, who were liberal Democrats, not communists.)

Smith was one of the "experts" that Chairman Rankin relied upon. Chairman King has indicated he will call "experts" on Islam to appear before his committee. I shudder to think of what his definition of an expert is. Will it be an updated version of Gerald L.K. Smith?

HUAC Chairman Rankin declared: "I am talking about the communism of Leon Trotsky that is based upon hatred for Christianity. Remember that communism and Christianity can never live in the same atmosphere. Communism is older than Christianity. It is the curse of the ages. It hounded and persecuted the Savior during his earthly ministry, inspired his crucifixion, derided him in his dying agony, and then gambled for his garments at the foot of the cross; and has spent more than 1,900 years trying to destroy Christianity and everything based on Christian principles."

At this point—STOP. Go back and read the previous paragraph and insert the word "Judaism" wherever Rankin used the word communism, and you have the real meaning of his statement, which motivated his committee hearings. This happened once in America to us Jews. I hope that it does not happen again with Muslims as the boogeyman, rather than Jews.

In 1946 the Republicans took control of the House (as well as the Senate) and this further increased the activities of HUAC. Its new chairman was a Neanderthal from New Jersey (which proves that not all bigots come from the South) John Parnell Thomas. He was an Irish Catholic who changed his name from Feeney to Thomas and began attending Baptist services. Thomas once testified before HUAC when it was under the chairmanship of Martin Dies that, "The New Deal is either for the Communist Party, or is playing into the hands of the Communist Party."

Under Thomas' guidance this country was feted to the spectacle of the jailing of the Hollywood Ten. Immediately after their indictment Hollywood responded with the infamous blacklist which lasted for almost ten years, denying many liberals and naïve activists (who joined the party in the 1930's as an answer to rising fascism) the ability to make a living.

Hysteria ruled, and it wasn't from McCarthy, although he did his share. It emanated from a committee of the House of Representatives under Republican control. Let us hope that history does not repeat itself for the sake of the Muslims amongst us and for the sake of America.

Shame on America, Jews & the ADL
Ground Zero Mosque Controversy
9/8/10

To begin, the mosque controversy does not involve a mosque. It is planned as a 13-story community center encompassing a swimming pool, 500-seat performing arts center, gym, culinary school, restaurant and, yes, a prayer space for Muslims, which already exists in the current building. A formal mosque would forbid eating or the playing of music on the premises. I guess that we are now at the point in America where Jews can have our JCC's and Christians their YMCA's, but Muslims are not wanted.

There is also the controversy over the proposed name, Cordoba House. The hate-mongers have described this as a reference to Muslim designs to attack western culture, hearkening back to the Muslim-Christian wars of domination in medieval Spain. The name was chosen for precisely the opposite reason. In the tenth century Cordoba was the center of the most liberal and sophisticated Caliphate in the Islamic world. All religions were not merely tolerated but respected.

The caliph, Abd al-Rahman III, had a Jew as his foreign minister and a Greek bishop in his diplomatic corps. He also had a library of 400,000 volumes at a time when the largest library in Christian Europe numbered merely 400 manuscripts. There were also 70 other smaller libraries in Cordoba. The very reference to Cordoba reflects the sophistication and liberality of the Muslims behind this project. They have changed the name of the center to the address of the building, Park 51, to deflect criticism. This was unfortunate, since nothing will quiet a hate-monger.

Feisal Abdul Rauf, the Imam behind the proposed community center, has been attacked as an Islamic terrorist, even though he is a practitioner of Sufi Islam, which reaches out to all other religions as manifestations of the Divine. My God, the conservative Bush administration utilized Rauf as part of an outreach to the Muslim world. You can bet your life that he was thoroughly vetted by our government. He is currently being used by the Clinton State Department as well in the same capacity. Fareed Zakaria of *Newsweek* and CNN succinctly put it, "His vision of Islam is bin Laden's nightmare."

And what is Rauf's sin? He will build a Muslim community center two blocks away from Ground Zero, variously described as a "hallowed battlefield," "holy ground," and a "war memorial." Even President Obama in his defense of religious freedom commented that, "Ground zero is, indeed, hallowed ground." I beg to differ.

If Ground Zero is holy ground, then the railroad station in Madrid, the Underground in London, the federal building in Oklahoma City, the Pentagon (where there is presently a prayer space for Muslims—yes, patriotic, religious Muslim Americans work at the Pentagon) and every other physical location that has been the object of terrorism is holy ground. If Ground Zero is holy space why plan for it to be developed with office buildings (in which the object will be to amass money—obviously a holy pursuit), a shopping center (in which consumer goods will be peddled to continue to gorge the American appetite for material possessions), and with a theater for modern dance (a project to which I personally look forward as a devotee of the Joyce, the modern dance Mecca of New York)? I'm sorry, but someone has to tell America that this designation of holy space is merely part of a mass hysteria that really scares me.

The question which must be asked is why this hysteria? The impetus comes from a triumvirate of right-wing Christians, Jews and politicians. Fundamentalist Christians are still fighting the crusades, still vying to convert the world to their truths. Islam is the fastest growing religion in the world, to the distress of these Christian proselytizers. What better way to win this battle than to brand all Muslims as terrorists?

Right-wing Jews think that they are doing Israel a favor by painting Islam as a terrorist religion thereby proving that Israel need not negotiate with the Palestinians. The idea is to project the concept that we are civilized and they are not. This theme is picked up in the right-wing press of Israel. Commenting on the New York proposed "mosque," a columnist in the *Jerusalem Post* declares that "Islamism is a modern political tendency which arose in a spirit of fraternal harmony with the fascists of Europe in the 1930's and '40's." Ground Zero isn't Israel's "holy ground." Why would he be involved with this discussion? Simply because right-wing Jews in Israel as well as the United States believe that demonizing the religion of 1.3 billion people is good for Israel. God help us.

Right-wing politicians join the fray. On Fox News Newt Gingrich compares a mosque at Ground Zero to Nazis protesting at the United States Holocaust Memorial. The Democrats are cowed by the American outpouring of hate and even Harry Reid voices disapproval of the Park 51 site. It's a perfect storm of hate.

Periodically we go through this in America. The anti-Catholic No-Nothing party ran ex-President Millard Fillmore in the presidential election of 1856 and garnered 27 percent of the votes. We deported over 10,000 people during the First World War because they opposed our entry into that war and we incarcerated loyal Japanese Americans during the Second World War. Now during this "war on terror" I shudder to think where we are headed.

The tool used in this hate campaign is the concept of collective guilt. Based on that, all Jews are traitors since Ethel and Julius Rosenberg sold out this country. All Christians are terrorists since Timothy McVeigh attacked the federal building in Oklahoma City. Neither are all Muslims traitors nor terrorists. Islam is not monolithic. Its forms are as varied as Judaism or Christianity. I do not practice Judaism the same as a Satmar Hasidic Jew. A Catholic does not practice Christianity the same as a Jehovah Witness. Imam Rauf does not share the same Islamic beliefs as bin Laden.

Of all people Jews should beware of collective guilt since we have suffered from it for millennia. Yet the organization that started this hysteria is headed by a right-wing Jewish supporter of Israel by the name of Pam Geller. She is quoted in the mainstream media (including the *Jewish Journal*) as if she is a legitimate political voice. Yet on her blog, Atlas Shrugs, she has declared that "Obama is the illegitimate son of Malcom X." She has written that we have "an American-hater for president." She has proposed that devout Muslims should be prohibited from military service. She asks, "Would Patton have recruited

Nazis into his army?" To all of the rabbis quoted in the *Jewish Journal* urging that the "mosque" be moved, know who is pulling your strings.

Finally, to the role of the Anti-Defamation League and its director, Abe Foxman. The world was literally "shocked," that's the word used by the Associated Press, by ADL's call for the mosque to be moved. Fareed Zakaria called it a "bizarre decision." Foxman, a Holocaust survivor, said, "Survivors of the Holocaust are entitled to feelings that are irrational." Referring to loved ones of the September 11 victims, he continued: "Their anguish entitles them to positions that others would categorize as irrational or bigoted."

How dare Foxman use the Holocaust to justify prejudice. He does blasphemy to the memory of Jews and other oppressed minorities whose lives were sacrificed on the altar of bigotry. Zakaria responds: "Does Foxman believe that bigotry is OK if people think they're victims? Does the anguish of Palestinians, then, entitle them to be anti-Semitic?"

Five years ago the ADL honored Zakaria with the Hubert H. Humphrey First Amendment Freedoms Prize. Incensed over ADL's succumbing to bigotry, he has returned the award with the $10,000 honorarium that came with it. It takes an honest non-Jew to bring us to our Jewish senses.

The last word was recently written by Daniel Luban, a doctoral student at the University of Chicago, in *Tablet Magazine*: "While activists like Pam Geller have led the anti-mosque campaign and the broader demonization of Muslims that has accompanied it, leaders like Abe Foxman have acquiesced in it. In doing so they risk providing an ugly and ironic illustration of the extent of Jewish assimilation in 21st-century America. We know that Jews can grow up to be senators and Supreme Court justices. Let's not also discover that they can grow up to incite a pogrom."

Learning Humanity from Muslim Emails
10/6/10

What do the following have in common: Switzerland, France, UK, New Zealand, Australia, Jordan, Russia, Canada, Saudi Arabia, India, Morocco, Botswana, Brazil and Dubai? Second question: What do these American cities have in common: Honolulu, Buffalo, San Antonio, Trumansburg, N.Y. (where is that?), Bronx, N.Y. (OK, I could go on and list another 20 cities, but you get the idea)?

The answer is that the over 50 emails that I received in response to my column on the Muslim community center two blocks from Ground Zero came from the above locations. It seems that in the age of the internet a column can go viral. Ninety percent of the emails were from Muslims who thanked me for understanding that Islam is a great religion and should not be judged by the extremists who distort it. The column was also republished with my permission in the *American Muslim* and the *Gulf News* in Dubai.

Let me share with you some of these responses. A retired American Admiral wrote: "I am a Jew, and I am a Christian because I am a Muslim. Moses and Christ are prophets of Islam, as are Mohammed and all 125,000 prophets mentioned in the Quran."

Referring to the name "Cordoba House" which has been misrepresented in the American press, one person wrote, "I have always looked at the period in Muslim Spain, when Christians, Jews, and Muslims lived together in absolute harmony, as an example for our time, and I appreciate your reference to it." To this Muslim Cordoba does not signify conquest as right-wing Americans proclaim.

If you think that Islam is monolithic it is refuted by an email that I received from the president of the Arab-American Secular Coalition. I have no idea how large this organization is, but it does highlight the fact that there are humanistic non-theocratic Muslims as there are comparable Jews.

Many of the emails reflected the great pain that the current outburst of hate has inflicted on the American Muslim community. The past president of the Interfaith alliance in Indiana wrote: "To Islamophobes I ask these questions. Do you give us the same rights as Americans as you do to yourselves? Do you treat all Muslims, extremists and moderate, as terrorists? Do I tell my four children and six grandchildren, all born in the USA, that this is not your home as you cannot build a mosque here?"

The responses reflect the fact that it really boils down to the fact that prejudice comes from not knowing the other person on a personal level. It takes me back to my childhood in a small coal town in Pennsylvania when I met Christians who had never met a Jew before, as strange as that sounds. It's easy to hate someone who is an abstraction to you.

A journalist from India wrote me: "I was at the East-West Center in Hawaii a few years ago for a faith-media seminar. On Friday, our very considerate hosts offered Muslim participants a chance to join a local congregation for noon prayers . . . Some non-Muslim colleagues came along because they had never seen a Friday prayer. We were all convivial, but I daresay at least one or two of them were relieved that the Imam had not declared war on the West and we had not unsheathed scimitars as part of ritual."

In this same vein, a Christian respondent from the UK wrote: "My own view of Islam is colored by living in Pakistan, where on occasions Muslim friends would ask my wife or me to pray for them, and when they knew we were in trouble, would tell us that they were praying for us." A Muslim physician wrote: "I beseech you to spread the word that all Muslims are not anti-Semitic. Islam is derived from Judaism. I have had the pleasure of having many great teachers who happened to be Jewish and a few good friends who are Jewish. We need to start talking before bigots on both sides trigger something."

It's not all kumbaya around a bonfire. There are some real differences of opinion between Muslims and Jews, especially concerning Israel. A Muslim from Fort Myers, Florida wrote: "I am very critical of the brutal Israeli policies in the Occupied Territories," but he went on to say, "I am also very critical of radical militants that had tarnished my religion, Islam. Unfortunately Israeli supporters tend to label people like myself as anti-Semitic."

Another respondent wrote: "I am a Palestinian with grudges against those Jews who usurped my home in Jaffa. But you remind me of Mr. Makhover who gave me a summer job in Tel Aviv, treated me like a son and guided me when I was 12." He concluded, "The list of good Jews in my life is long." Compare this understanding of the "other" by a practicing Muslim with right-wing Jews who feel compelled to demonize all Muslims because they think that it is good for Israel. Not only is it not good for Israel, but their distorted version of Zionism makes a mockery of Judaism, just as Osama bin Laden makes a mockery of Islam.

One Muslim reader of my column shared with me a piece that he wrote for his hometown newspaper in Buffalo. He explained how in America the concept of the "melting pot" of cultures has been largely supplanted by the concept of what our Canadian neighbors call the "Mosaic of Cultures." He writes: "This characterization implies that, like tiles in a mosaic, diverse cultures retain their individual identity to collectively create something more beautiful than the individual elements."

Finally, he rejects the mosaic concept because it implies closeness without bonding of tiles. He prefers the concept of "Tapestry of Cultures—a blend of colorful fibers and threads of ethnic and cultural diversity." He continues, "Each unique group contributes its own rich color and texture to create a strong and beautiful whole. The threads are bound together for strength, but they do not lose their fine qualities in the process." This concept speaks to the very core of the American Jewish experience.

It is this Tapestry of Cultures that is and should continue to be the strength of this country. The current spate of hate against our Muslim fellow citizens threatens to loosen the bonds of that tapestry.

MUSINGS

Lesson to be learned from Myanmar
1/22/14

All religions can be perverted, but there are certain oxymorons that are hard to contemplate, such as a war-mongering Quaker, a religiously zealot Unitarian or a violent Buddhist.

It is Buddhism, a religion that teaches avoidance of harm to any living creature, that I want to focus on today. Buddhism is best known in this country through the teachings of the Dalai Lama, a universally respected religious leader who promotes love and compassion and supports inter-religious harmony. Although Buddhism, like all religions, is not monolithic, it is fair to say that the Dalai Lama reflects the Buddhist ethos.

And then there is Myanmar (formally called Burma), a country of 55 million people comprised of 90 percent Buddhists. Since June of 2012 violence against its Muslim minority has increased, spurred by a radical monk leading a movement called 969. It began in the western state of Rakhine where Buddhists and Muslims had a kind of caste system in which Muslims performed menial work overseen by Buddhist bosses. It soon spread throughout the country.

To date over 240 people have been killed and 140,000 Muslims have fled their homes. Buddhists are advocating that Muslims who cannot prove three generations of legal residence, a large part of the nearly one million Muslims in Rakhine state, should be put into camps and deported from the country.

What is most disturbing is that the impetus for this anti-Muslim campaign comes primarily from Buddhist clergy, not from political leaders. This past April the Myanmar Buddhist journalist Swe Win published a column in the *New York Times* entitled, "Monks Gone Mad." He reports that the much venerated Buddhist order, the Sangha, has become largely corrupt.

Win was reared in a conservative Buddhist family and spent every summer after the fifth grade studying at monasteries. He wrote that rather than focusing on meditation the monks practiced astrology to attract donations and many monks own luxury cars and LCD television sets. "Only when you grow old do you seek the path of spirituality," one abbot told him.

The anti-Muslim animus is not new. In 2001 when Win was in prison serving time as a student dissident, a fellow incarcerated monk proudly told him that he had defended Buddhism by torching Muslim properties.

This past November the *Times* reported, in a nearly full page story befitting its importance, a shocking incident where a Buddhist mob stormed through a farming village and hacked to death a 94-year old Muslim woman with machetes, ignoring her pleas for mercy. Richard Horsey, a former United Nations official in the country, commented: "For a culture that has such great respect for the elderly, the killing of this old lady should have been a turning point, a moment of national soul searching. The fact that this has not happened is almost as disturbing as the killing itself."

Contrast this to the reaction to the newspaper photo of the Police Chief, Bull Conner, using attack dogs against peaceful demonstrators, including children, in Birmingham, Alabama in 1963. Racism marched one bridge too far. The truism that a picture is worth a thousand words spurred a national revulsion that helped assure passage of the Civil Rights Act of 1964.

To the contrary, subsequent to the horrific death of this woman there has been either increased political anti-Muslim rhetoric or indifference. Myanmar President Thein Sein actually endorsed the ethnic cleansing of Muslims who have not been in Myanmar for at least three generations, labeling them a "threat to the peace of the nation." (Under international diplomatic pressure he finally retreated from that position.) Daw Aung San Suu Kyi, the leading civil rights activist and Member of Parliament, has not condemned this anti-Muslim hysteria. She spent 15 years under house arrest and received a Nobel Peace Prize for her commitment to civil rights, yet she has remained silent.

How could this happen in a Buddhist country? I can't tell you *why* it happened, but I can isolate *how* it happened. It involves what I call the three tools of hatred. First, it builds upon segregation. Referring to Muslims, a Buddhist woman told a *Times* reporter, "We lived side by side but we never talked to each other." When asked if their children played together, a group of Buddhist women burst out laughing, "Even a small boy knows that he should not play with (a pejorative term for Muslims)." It's easier to hate someone you don't know.

Segregation leads to the second and third tools of hatred, dehumanization and scapegoating.

A Buddhist monk in saffron robes proclaims that Muslims are "vipers in our laps" and do not "practice human morals." Ergo, they must be inhuman. This brings to mind the famous incident when the racist Rabbi Meir Kahane welcomed Jewish and Arab Hebrew University students with the greeting, "Welcome Jews and dogs." Never forget that it is permissible to kill animals. Given segregation and dehumanization, scapegoating is inevitable, witness our Jewish experience in Europe. Recently, in one village in Myanmar violence broke out after the rape and murder of a Buddhist girl for which Muslims were immediately blamed without any apparent evidence.

Why am I so interested in Myanmar? The answer is that I want to learn from this. First, if this hatred can flourish in a Buddhist country, it could happen anywhere. Human frailty is universal. No religion, no nationality, is exempt. The Talmudic rabbis taught that each of us has within us the *yetzer tov*, the good inclination, and the *yetzer ra*, the evil inclination. It is a constant personal struggle to have good overcome evil. So it is with civilizations and religions.

This realization reminds us that all religions, even Buddhism, can, and have been corrupted. I need not recite the medieval experience of Christianity with the wanton killing of non-Christians, or the current experience of al Qaeda or Taliban distortions of Islam, or the fanatical rabbis on the West Bank who proclaim that it is moral to kill Palestinian children because they will someday be grown, and thus your enemy.

The most important lesson for me to remember is that the Myanmar experience does not represent normative Buddhism, any more than Middle East terrorists reflect on the 1.3 billion Muslims world-wide and the sophistication of Islam. And certainly, the Jewish fanatics do not speak for normative Judaism.

The lesson is not to generalize; otherwise we fall into the trap of dehumanization and hatred of fellow human beings.

Choose One but Not Two Religions
11/9/11

The Pew Forum on Religion and Public Life reports that one in four American adults who are married or living with a partner are in a bi-religious relationship. The most difficult decision for these couples who have children is to decide in which religion to rear their offspring.

The *Tablet*, an on-line Jewish magazine, recently reported on one response to this dilemma. It is an organization entitled Interfaith Community, which was founded 25 years ago in New York City by two intermarried women.

Its aim is to rear children in both Christianity and Judaism from the ages of 4 to 13 in preparation for them to choose their religious identity when they mature. It now has seven nationwide chapters. There are other such organizations in Washington, D.C., and Chicago.

One of the founders of Interfaith Community, Lee Gruzen, was quoted in the *Tablet* article: "I felt strongly that the children of mixed marriage had this special big gift handed them, not something that was going to be in conflict but something that was just a profound enrichment."

I'm not sure that it is such a special big gift. Let me reflect on my own experience with children reared in such a manner. I was the Reform rabbi in Ann Arbor, Michigan in the late 1960's and early 1970's. For three years I taught the conversion class at the University of Michigan Hillel Foundation. At that time the Hillel rabbi was Orthodox and he felt more comfortable if I taught the class. Being committed to outreach, I jumped at the opportunity to contribute my services.

My classes ran according to the university's calendar, one each semester. At the beginning of the semester I asked each student to explain his or her Christian upbringing. Invariably, at least one student would report that he or she was a graduate of a synagogue religious school. I would then ask why he wanted to be in my class. The answer was always the same. He was also a graduate of the local Baptist, Methodist, etc. Sunday school.

They explained that their parents solved their problem by creating an identity problem for them. Just as invariably, they were seeing psychologists or psychiatrists. They felt neither authentically Jewish nor Christian. These college students reported that they felt pressure to pick a religion but could not because the process of choosing was an implicit rejection of one of the parents.

I admit that my sample represents an anecdotal response rather than a scientific finding, but I know of no study that shows that a dual upbringing is emotionally healthy (or for that matter, showing the reverse) so I tend to stick with my own experience.

The Interfaith Community was highlighted in a Columbia University College of Journalism Report that quoted Samuel Heilman, Professor of Sociology at the City University of New York, to the effect that this may be more acceptable today than 30 years ago: "In the post-modern world where multiple identities—racial, religious, ethnic—is a given . . . this is a whole new question."

I'm not sure that he is correct. It is one thing to say I am half Irish and half Italian, because I know that I am one hundred percent American. There is no real split identity here. There is no philosophy in being white or black and neither parent can ask the child to be his or her color—the child has no choice other than being what genetically he is. There may be tension outside of the family (and hopefully that is diminishing) but there is none within.

One of my intermarried correspondents indicated that he was against teaching both Christian and Jewish *beliefs* to his children (they are being reared as Jews) but that they blend *rituals* within the home, celebrating with a Christmas tree and Easter egg hunt "without religious significance, kinda like July 4th." If it works for them I have no objection, but it would not be my choice.

Please understand that I believe that a child of intermarried parents should not be shielded from Christianity. He or she should enjoy the beauty and significance of Christian symbols and simchas (Christmas dinner and Easter egg hunts etc.) at their grandparents' home or at the homes of their Christian first cousins. In doing this they have the joys of both religions but with the knowledge that they are not "half and half," that they come from a wholly Jewish environment.

But Lee Gruzen's quote that children of mixed marriages were handed a "special big gift . . . that was a profound enrichment" was not entirely wrong. These children, being raised as Jews, have a broader understanding of humanity than the child of two Jewish parents. They have grandparents, aunts and uncles and cousins who are not Jewish, and this broadens their perspective on life. They do not have to be taught the humanity of those who practice another religion. They live this humanity daily. Their existence within Judaism enriches our culture and is ballast against those xenophobic Jews who would exclude as irrelevant anyone who is not Jewish.

My conclusion is that unless I see some serious studies to the contrary, I will continue to advise young people contemplating marriage or cohabitation to make a decision one way or the other, but don't rear your children in both.

Learning to Forget and to Forgive
12/23/09

I try to avoid writing incessantly about Israel since that is but one part of the Jewish experience. Also, I try to limit my comments on the political process since there is a plethora of competent commentators to do that job. My wife constantly reminds me that I'm a rabbi and I should write on "religion" more often, whatever that may mean.

So, as I was sitting at my computer contemplating what to write my problem was solved when I received a call from a close relative asking for some rabbinic advice. His problem is that he cannot either forgive or forget the fact that some of his close friends are oblivious to the poverty that exists among us and do not give *tzedaka*; rather they blithely spend their money on their own creature comforts. Referring to a recent sermon that I gave on the High Holy Days, he said, "I know that I have to forget and forgive, but it's hard."

Ah, someone actually listened to my sermon. Inspired by this thought, I want to share with you the thrust of that sermon. At the end of Yom Kippur we wish each other a good year ahead. But a good year does not come from God. It is a proactive process that we control by our own actions. My thesis is that to have a good year we have to learn to forget and to forgive.

Learning to forget is difficult, particularly for Jews. We are specialists in remembering. We remember our history. We remember the Holocaust. We attend Yizkor services. The Hebrew word *yizkor* means remembrance. And Remembering is good, but it has its limitations, especially in interpersonal relations.

The story is told of a man who said, "Every time that we have a fight my wife gets historical." A friend thought he meant "hysterical," but he said, "No, I mean historical. She says to me, 'Do you remember what you did to me ten years ago, and do you remember what you did to me 20 years ago?' Every time we have a fight she gets historical."

If we can't learn to forget, every slight, every harsh word uttered by someone we love or trust will haunt us our entire lives. If we can't let go, we live a life of grudges. My favorite aphorism is: "To hold a grudge is to allow someone to live in your head without paying rent." Not forgetting hurts us more than the other person. One of those church bulletin signs that one reads from the street put this thought succinctly: "The best way to get even is to forget." The medieval Jewish philosopher, Bahya, said it best: "Were it not for the ability to forget, a man would never be free from melancholy."

The act of forgetting was understood as crucial for mental health by our rabbis almost two thousand years ago. An interesting passage in the Talmud involves two great rabbis, Eliezer and Akiba. There was a drought and the people were summoned to the synagogue. Rabbi Eliezer stood before the congregation and prayed hard and long for rain—but none came. Then Rabbi Akiba stepped up to the bima and offered a brief and simple prayer—and the rains began to fall.

Suddenly a voice from heaven came forth and said: "It is not that Rabbi Akiba is greater than Rabbi Eliezer. But Eliezer remembers the wrongs done to him and Akiba forgets them." The Talmud is saying that Rabbi Akiba is more blessed and his prayers are answered because he has the ability to forget the little insults and sleights that all of us collect during life. The ability to forget is truly a blessing.

If we cannot forget, we must learn to forgive. Forgiveness is not merely a psychological imperative, but it is the philosophical basis of Yom Kippur. How can we expect God to forgive us, if we cannot forgive others? Forgiveness is the ability to understand that people change and mature, that people are not all bad or all good. Judaism teaches that within each of us are the *Yetzer HaRa* and the *Yetzer Tov*, the evil inclination and the good inclination. Understanding that we struggle for the good to predominate over the bad in ourselves, how can we not forgive others when they are not perfect?

Judaism teaches that mankind is made in the image of God, meaning that the very concept of God presents to us the paradigm of perfection to which we strive, even though we are doomed to never actually reach it. But the image of God concept presupposes the ability of mankind to change, to grow, to strive toward God. The inability to forgive past wrongs negates the possibility of growth and repentance and denies the image of God formula. The inability to forgive holds time constant and denies the capability of human beings to grow.

We all know stories of relatives who have not spoken for years and after one of them dies the other is full of remorse that he or she did not reconcile before it was too late. Must we wait until it is too late to recognize that for our own mental health we should forget and/or forgive? It is the Jewish way.

As my relative who occasioned this column by his phone call said, "I know that I have to forget and forgive, but it's hard." It is hard, but who said that striving to be a good Jew is easy?

The Perennial Question—Why Jews are Liberal?
3/24/10

This past fall Norman Podhoretz published his latest book, "Why Are Jews Liberals?" in which he bewailed this peculiar phenomenon. The fact that we are overwhelmingly liberal is an incontrovertible fact acknowledged by conservatives and liberals alike. Since 1928 Jews have voted for the Democratic candidate for president on average at 75 percent. This past election 78 percent of us voted for Obama in spite of heavy Republican advertising in the Jewish press claiming that he was anti-Israel, anti-Semitic and generally a miscreant.

Everyone quotes Milton Himmelfarb's famous quip in the 1950's that "Jews earn like Episcopalians and vote like Puerto Ricans," (the richest and the poorest ethnic groups in America at that time). The usual social pattern is that when a group gets richer it tends to become more conservative, moving from the Democratic Party to the Republicans. Obviously, we Jews are an anomaly.

Why? That is the question that plagues conservatives. Podhoretz, who was the editor of Commentary from 1960 to 1995, is not the first, nor will he be the last, to ponder this question. To be honest, I try not to waste my time reading Norman Podhoretz. I did not read the book, especially on the recommendation of Leon Wieseltier, the literary editor of the *New Republic*, who reviewed it in the *New York Times*. He called it a "dreary book," adding, "His perspective is so settled, so confirmed, that it is a wonder he is not too bored to write."

I did read Podhoretz's follow-up opinion piece in the *Wall Street Journal*. I will give him that much time. There he presents three arguments as to why we are foolish to remain liberals. First, we liberal Jews are not authentic Jews. He points to the fact that Orthodox Jews are overwhelmingly Republican because they reflect true Jewish values. He is statistically correct but philosophically naïve.

What he doesn't understand is that other liberal Jews and I practice a different religion from the Orthodox Jews of Borough Park or Monsey. Judaism is not monolithic and there is no authentic Judaism. There are only different Judaisms that share certain rituals and history, but not necessarily the same beliefs. I would not expect Podhoretz, who wrote a book that proclaimed the biblical prophets to be neoconservatives, to understand this.

Second, Podhoretz believes that being pro-peace and pro-Israel, (i.e., being liberal) is deleterious to Israel. If you believe that the peace process is wrong, it is an easy polemic to declare that Jewish liberals are anti-Israel. There is no room in Podhoretz's psyche to fathom that someone who disagrees with him could also love Israel. This is an intellectual arrogance that is shared by most of the conservative think-tankers.

Third, Podhoretz just can't understand why we liberals would want to change a society that has been so good to us. This theme was recently elaborated on by Ron Lipsman, a professor at the University of Maryland. In arguing against the liberal stance of demanding a high wall of separation between church and state, he wrote: "The strongly Christian society that America was, and which Jewish voters are helping to destroy, laid out the greatest welcome mat ever seen in world history for the Jewish people."

Leaving aside the fact that liberals are not trying to destroy Christianity but merely want religion to thrive, divorced from government, Lipsman and Podhoretz misread history. There was no welcome mat in the period between 1881 and 1945/1950. There was anti-Semitism, job discrimination, university quotas and restrictive covenants that guaranteed that we Jews would not be able to live near gentiles. It was liberals who fought these practices and in the process made this country better for us and for other minorities. And it is the liberal tradition that will continue to make this country live up to its potential.

Why? Why are we Jews still voting like Puerto Ricans when we should be sitting in our country clubs contentedly smoking our Havanas? In response to the publication of Podhoretz's book the *Tablet*, an on-line Jewish magazine, published a symposium on this question. The conservative contributors echoed Podhoretz's arguments.

The liberal writer Morris Dickstein had a different answer: "Strangely (Jews) remember where they came from, and even more strangely, they empathize with others who are still struggling. Their subliminal memories go back not only to the ghetto and the tenement but to the condition of being despised outsiders, humiliated, persecuted, even killed." He added, "The memory of oppression is built into their DNA, like the adjuration in the Torah and the Haggadah never to forget that they were once slaves in Egypt."

Another liberal contributor, Todd Gittin, a Columbia University professor, opines: "I know no better hypothesis than the following: Jews pride themselves on defying self interest. They rejoice in the anomaly. This is in no small part because the theological foundation of Judaism is the belief that one's people were chosen to carry out a unique relation to divine purpose. Jews may not be more devout than others, but somehow—and I do not understand *quite* how—we relish the opportunity to answer the question, 'If I am for myself alone, what do I amount to?' with liberalism's great appeal, which is to self-transcendence."

I agree with both Dickstein and Gitten, but I take exception to Gittin's belief that we are "defying self interest." I believe that we act out of our history and our subliminal religious commitments, but I also think that in the long run liberalism is the better protector of Jews in America. If this country abandons the needs of the poor; if we decimate the middle class; if we end up with a two-tiered society, the rich and the poor, with no middle class— and that's where the conservatives would take us, then we Jews and all other minorities would face a hostile environment.

I don't think that Jews think that way when they support liberal causes. I think that they just vote like Jews. (One conservative griped that "They act as if God would strike them dead should they pull the lever on Election Day for a Republican candidate.") But in the long run, to answer another perennial question: Yes, being liberal is good for the Jews.

The Downfall of a Kosher Food Empire
1/6/09

For the last two years we have witnessed the saga of Agripocessors, the giant kosher meat conglomerate, and the Rubashkin family that owns it. It all began with an expose by the *Forward* that revealed the despicable working conditions in its slaughtering plant in Postville, Iowa. It culminated recently in a federal immigration raid on the plant that revealed that not only was the Rubashkin family consciously hiring illegal immigrants whom they were exploiting, but that many of them were children.

It is ironic that a Bush administration ploy that has harassed many poor illegals who were just trying to feed their families has resulted in some good. The increased interest in Agriprocessors resulted in the arrest of Shalom Rubashkin and the bankruptcy of the firm. Personal confession: We keep a kosher home and we have refused to purchase Agriprocessors products for the last two years. I would rather eat fish for the rest of my life than support a company that exploits its workers through subhuman working conditions and substandard wages. So it is not without some sense of pleasure that I view the downfall of the company and the family.

Recently the *Forward* ran an end of the year reflection on Aaron Rubashkin, the patriarch, and the extended family. The *Forward* reports that Aaron Rubashkin "has done Jewish charitable work that has made him an almost saintly figure in the world of Chabad-Lubavitch, the ultra-Orthodox sect to which he and his family belong. He is often referred to as a *tzadik*, or holy man, by Orthodox rabbis."

The question is: how can a person who is family oriented, loves his fellow Jews and gives generously to Chabad charities wantonly exploit poor immigrant workers to enrich the bottom line? Is there not a cognitive disconnect here? The answer is no, if you define the rest of humanity as something other than the humanity of Jews. The fact is that there is a strain in Jewish literature that states that Torah's proscription that you should treat the stranger with the same care and love as yourself applies only to a Jewish stranger. Worse yet, a Jew does not owe the non-Jew the obligation to act honestly toward him. Of course, this is repudiated by modern Judaism as a relic from the past, but it is in our literature, and not always has it been the minority opinion.

The fact is that the Rubashkins are a product of this insular us-against-them environment that is a carry-over from medieval times. In the *Forward* article, Rabbi Yossi Jacobson described this life-style: "In Crown Heights or in Boro Park or in Flatbush, it's always the goyim and the *yidden*. That's how it is, you know? We don't do nothing with the goyim. We don't even go to their schools. We don't wave to them, because we don't even know them, and they don't want to know us."

It is this isolation that allowed them to exploit their non-Jewish workers while being righteous in their own community. There are two other motivating factors. First, the Rubashkins are mired in the Jewish victimization syndrome. When they first arrived in Postville there was tension between the family and the city fathers. Then Mayor John Hyman recalls being lectured to by Aaron Rubashkin: "Aaron proceeded to give me a history lesson—a history of the persecution of the Jews. He said he had a background of persecution and he wasn't about to let this persecution happen again in Postville." Victimization leads not only to the belief that there is rampant anti-Semitism out there, but also to the conclusion that the "other" is in some way your enemy and not worthy of respect, in business or otherwise.

Second, Shalom Rubashkin summarized his religious philosophy that inevitably led to the dehumanization of his non-Jewish employees: "We have stayed on this planet longer than anyone else because we believe our way is the right way. You start slipping, making changes here and there, and then you have nothing. We live by our own rules here, and they've got to understand that."

The refusal to change, the refusal to understand that there are competing systems that are true for others and are as valid for them as yours are for you, the belief that you have the only truth, lead to dehumanization of the "other." This paradigm applies to all fundamentalisms, whether it is Jewish, Christian or Muslim. Shalom Rubashkin and his entire family are products of this type of thinking and in the end are victims of its consequences.

PART TWO—ISRAEL
CRITICISM OF ISRAEL

The Legitimacy of Criticizing Israel
1/19/11

At the end of each column I publish my email address because I appreciate a certain amount of dialogue with my readers. The feedback also helps me gauge the feelings in the Jewish community.

One person who emailed me made the comment that when I finally write a piece that praises Israel she will frame it and put it on her wall. She has a point. Apropos to her point, a good friend of mine who shares my concern for Israel asked if I would also criticize the Palestinians for their behavior, the same way that I comment on Israel.

Let me answer this question because it not only applies to me but has universal application to all liberal columnists.

My answer is that every rabbi who wants adulation from his congregation praises Israel. It is a standard High Holy Day sermon. The Jewish press is replete with commentators who mouth the usual talking points of the AIPAC/ADL/ Jewish Federations/Israel Consulate Jewish establishment. You don't need me to join the chorus. I write to enlighten, not to be loved.

There are many Arab commentators now criticizing the tactics of Hamas, Hezbollah and even Fatah. I don't have to join that bandwagon either, even though it would be easy to do so. That must come from their own people to have any real effect, just as we Jews do not accept criticism from outsiders. In fact, when non-Jews do criticize we label them anti-Semitic.

I am reminded of the opening chapter of the Book of Amos, maybe my favorite prophet in the bible. He begins by having God damn the leaders of Damascus (you could just hear the Jews applauding). Next God declares that the Philistines in Gaza shall perish for their sins (more applauding by the Jews). God, through the voice of Amos, then calls out the Phoenicians, Edomites, Ammonites and Moabites for their sins.

Up to this point Amos is very popular. He then hits them between the eyes. He speaks of the transgressions of Israel: "Because they sell the righteous for silver, and the needy for a pair of shoes. They trample the head of the poor into the dust of the earth, and turn aside the way of the afflicted." All of a sudden Amos was not too popular with his fellow Jews. The Book of Amos teaches us that it is easy to criticize the enemy, but very difficult to critique one's own people. But Amos is revered simply because he loved Israel enough to confront its failings.

I'm no prophet, but I'm inspired by their examples. Praise without criticism does Israel no good. There are many Israelis who would agree with that statement. This past year Ami Ayalon toured the United States on a 6-city speaking tour sponsored by J-Street. He is a former Commander of the Israeli Navy and Shin Bet (Israel's internal security service). To support Israel in the past, we American Jews were asked to send money. Now Ayalon proclaimed that it is imperative for friends of Israel "to tell us the truth—even if it is painful," because Israel is finding it harder to see for itself what is happening—how its isolation is increasing and the chances of maintaining both a Jewish and democratic Israel are diminishing.

It is hard enough for Jews to accept criticism of Israel by another Jew, but as I mentioned above, it is still harder to hear the opinions of non-Jewish critics. One reader asked why the western world focuses on Israel and ignores the human rights violations of nations in Africa and Asia. Ed Koch writes: "When Israel is singled out for special criticism that would never be directed at another country taking the same course of action, it is a disguised act of anti-Semitism."

What Koch ignores is the human tendency to focus on family and country before worrying about the rest of the world. We Americans are still concerned for the welfare of New Orleans in the aftermath of Katrina, but we quickly forget the fate of other cities throughout the world that were devastated by earthquakes and other natural disasters—if we even thought about them to begin with.

Family and friends: Whether we like it or not, Israel is part of the family of western culture. It is the birthplace of Jesus and the bible of the Jews is part of the foundation of our culture. We like this when it benefits us. Israel receives more foreign aid from the United States than any other country, excluding the war aid to Afghanistan and Pakistan. Only Israel is allowed to spend 25 percent of its military aid in its own country, rather than with American suppliers. Why? Because it's part of the family. We expect more from Israel than some under-developed country whose name we can hardly pronounce and whose fate we rarely ponder.

Prejudice, but not against Israel, does enter into this. Americans and Europeans look down on Africans and thus do not expect them to act in the same civilized way that is expected of Israel. A reverse prejudice toward Jews is operative here. The fears about anti-Semitism aside, the western nations look upon Jews as a superior people—maybe not loved, but certainly superior. If we were not so advanced, how else would we be able to control the banks, Wall Street, the entertainment world, etc. We Jews reinforce these beliefs by circulating lists of Jewish Nobel Prize winners and other such self-laudatory garbage.

The bottom line is that we can't have it both ways. Israel will always be held to the same high standards we hold for our own nations (both in Europe and America). For the most part, it's not anti-Semitism that motivates the criticism coming from non-Jewish sources. Much of it comes from people who deeply respect the Jewish peoplehood, and are reacting to our own failure to meet their high expectations.

As a columnist and as a rabbi I can only ask that my readers do not have a Pavlovian response of defending everything Israel does. The motto "My country, right or wrong," leads to disaster, as does "My people right or wrong." I take no joy in criticizing Israel, but the Netanyahu government leaves me little choice.

The Perils of Criticizing Israel
3/10/09

Beware if you intend to criticize Israel. You may find yourself de-legitimatized by the American Jewish community. You may even lose invitations to dinner parties.

Here's the back story: In January and early February I wrote a series of three columns that criticized Israel, that, in short, accused Israel of over-reaction and choosing the Gaza invasion as an alternative to seeking a continuation of the ceasefire with Hamas. I quoted the head of the Israeli Shin Bet as well as the former head of the Mossad. My thesis was that it was a voluntary war that needlessly killed 1300 Palestinians, including 400 to 500 children. Finally, I wrote that Israel should negotiate with Hamas, given that everyone either is or was a terrorist, including Begin and Shamir during the formative years of Israel. (These columns are reprinted in this book.)

I am aware that this is not the majority opinion of the American Jewish community and I expected that there would be columns written to answer my substantive allegations. What interests me is the personal attacks that I received both by email and in the columns of the *Jewish Journal*. One letter to the editor urged: "Please check the credentials of your columnists, particularly Rabbi Bruce Warshal and Leonard Fein. It appears that they are undercover agents for Al Jazirah and/or the Arabic Press. One thing that appears to be evident is that they must have been writers for the "Daily Worker.""

I won't defend myself, but it is absurd to attack Leonard Fein, the founder of *Moment Magazine* as well as Mazon, the Jewish Response to Hunger, and one of the most respected Jewish voices in America.

The Consul General of Israel for Florida and Puerto Rico attacked me in the *Journal*. He wrote that I exhibit "hatred and scorn" toward Israel and that I am "self-loathing." The latest personal attack (as of this writing) was in a column in the *Journal* by the regional director of the Anti-Defamation League. He accused me of employing the "techniques of a demagogue" and of not being interested in "civil discourse." He ominously stated, "I don't know what is deep in the heart of Rabbi Warshal." What irony! He accused me of a lack of civil discourse.

He showed his true colors when he writes: "While (Warshal) claims that he is just looking at the facts, the individuals he cites as sources, such as Uri Avnery and Henry Siegman, have long and consistent records of anti-Israel biases." How absurd! Avnery is a respected Israeli critic who has served as a member of the Knesset. To label him as anti-Israel is beyond absurd, it is ludicrous. It takes me back to the slogans of the American right-wingers when they told Vietnam War protestors that they should love this country or leave it.

No one should have to defend Rabbi Henry Siegman. He is an ordained Orthodox rabbi from Yeshiva University who was the executive director of the American Jewish Congress for 26 years and the executive director of the Synagogue Council of American Rabbis. Presently he is a senior fellow at the Council on Foreign Affairs and a visiting professor at the University of London.

The local spokesperson should not be held up to ridicule. He is merely following the party line of Abe Foxman, his boss at ADL. Foxman has attacked President Obama's choice of former Senator George Mitchell as the administration's peace envoy to the Middle East because—hold on to your seats—he is "meticulously even-handed" and "fair." Foxman is "not sure the situation requires that kind of approach."

That's the problem in a nutshell. The Jewish establishment doesn't want a serious discussion of Israeli issues any more than it wants an unbiased peace negotiator. It wants America to be a cheerleader for Israeli excesses, such as the continued expansion of the West Bank settlements, and it wants all

American Jews to step in line with the approved talking points as distributed by AIPAC and the ADL.

To differ is to be branded anti-Israel if you are a Jew, or worse yet, "self-loathing." If you are non-Jewish you are banded an anti-Semite. Foxman and company have already attacked Bill Moyers and Bob Simon of CBS's "60 Minutes" for reporting that was not sufficiently "pro-Israel." (Incidentally, Simon is Jewish, a Brandeis graduate, and has lived in Israel.)

The Jewish establishment has successfully demonized President Carter as anti-Semitic because he wrote a book entitled "Palestine, Peace Not Apartheid" in which he accurately described conditions on the West Bank. I meet many Jews and not one of them has read the book but they are convinced that Carter hates Jews. That's how formidable and effective the Jewish establishment can be. It's a pity that a supposedly intelligent community can be led around like sheep.

I don't expect everyone to agree with President Carter or with anything that I write, but I take exception to "group think" and to the herd mentality that is pervasive in our community.

Silencing Dialogue in the Jewish Community
6/20/12

December 14, 2011: Jeremy Ben-Ami, the founder of the pro Israel liberal lobby J-Street, spoke at the JCC in Boynton Beach to a packed audience of approximately 500 people.

I was seated in the last row next to a large dour man who, I could tell by his countenance, wasn't happy with the message that Ben-Ami was presenting. Next to him was a small intense man who held a camcorder in his hand the way one fondles a pistol or a shotgun.

At the end of the speech there were questions and answers. After a few friendly and even critical questions, all civil, the large man rose from the very back of the hall and began to bellow invectives against the speaker, basically claiming that he and liberals in general were anti-Israel. He didn't just make the statement; he continued to rant on.

The moderator asked him to stop but he ignored her, and the police were asked to escort him from the hall. At that point the small intense man whips out his camcorder with the expertise of a professional cameraman and records the dramatic scene of the protestor being physically removed, against his will, shouting that liberals are taking free speech away from Jews. It was a perfect setup. I am sure that it was later spread all over YouTube.

May 10, 2012: Susan Rice, United States Ambassador to the United Nations, was scheduled to speak at Congregation B'nai Torah in Boca Raton. Her speech was co-sponsored by the Jewish Federation of South Palm Beach County, the Anti-Defamation League (ADL) and the American Jewish Committee (AJC). Prior to the event the synagogue was warned that a group of right-wing Jews would try to disrupt her speech. The identities of the potential disruptors were known to the authorities.

The security advisors to Ambassador Rice and the synagogue decided to deny them entrance to protect both the dignity of the Ambassador and of the sanctuary. Enters one Alan Bergstein, trailed by his trusty videographer. When asked to leave, along with his entourage, he repeatedly protests, "Why are you asking me to leave," as if he didn't know the answer.

All of this is duly recorded and within five days a very slick professional five minute propaganda video produced by or for Bergstein was released on YouTube. (His name appears at the top of the YouTube video, connoting that he is the producer.) As of this past week Bergstein proudly emailed that it has been seen by almost 30,000 people.

It's worth a few words to review what the video proclaims. It brands B'nai Torah's co-sponsors, the Jewish Federation, ADL and the AJC as "left wing organizations." Where are these people coming from? This is not just a right-wing cabal; it is outright lunacy.

The video shows Ambassador Rice presenting the United States' position that we "do not accept the legitimacy of continued settlements." It then proclaims that President Obama has "thrown Israel under the bus." Nowhere does it show that after having made the American position clear, Ambassador Rice proceeded to veto the admission of Palestine as a United Nations state, or that this administration has used its veto power in the Security Council to kill many U.N. anti-Israel proposals as well.

As a postscript, it is worth noting that a few of the protestors did get through to the main sanctuary and they did interrupt the Ambassador by turning their backs to her and walking out while she attempted to speak.

Talking about the lunatic right wing, in a subsequent *Jewish Journal* opinion piece that Bergstein parlayed after the B'nai Torah incident he bewailed the fact that many South Florida synagogues under the influence of the Democratic Party "learn at the feet of those hand-picked demonizers of Israel." Who are these demonizers? He lists Vice President Joe Biden, Ambassador Susan Rice and Congresswoman Debbie Wasserman Schultz.

One could disagree with their politics (and I would expect Bergstein to do so since he is an active part of the Republican Party), but to brand them demonizers is an act of lunacy. Actually, one should have expected this since in 2008 he spoke out against Rabbis for Human Rights and the Jewish World Service, two eminently respected organizations.

May 25, 2012: Congresswoman Debbie Wasserman Schultz was scheduled to speak at Temple Israel in Miami. There were no protestors or video cameras and hence no YouTube follow-ups because a single member, ex-synagogue president Stanley Tate, the wealthy chair of the Miami-Dade Romney campaign, demanded the right of rebuttal immediately after the Congresswoman's presentation. (It would be perfectly legitimate to ask for the right to "correct" any statements with which he disagreed at a subsequent service.)

The synagogue cancelled the invitation immediately citing "potential security and safety concerns and the dignity of the temple, our member and guests." Did they expect Bergstein and company to show up? The Congresswoman issued this statement: "I believe strongly that in a democracy people should be able to hear from and interact with their elected officials." Evidently not so, if one member has enough money to dictate the programming of the synagogue.

What do these three incidents have in common? The crazies along with Republican operatives (sometimes combined in one person) have been stifling liberal voices within the Jewish community in their distorted view of what is good for Israel and in their pathological hatred of our president (that foreign born, secret Muslim). Our synagogues have always been forums for speakers on social issues important to Judaism (hearkening back to the biblical prophets) and for speakers on Israel from people representing the full spectrum of opinions.

The result of the tumult being caused by incidents like the above—in the words of J.J. Goldberg, writing in the *Forward*, "We've allowed noisy minorities to censor our voices." I quote Goldberg because he is writing in a national publication which reflects the reality that this is not just a South Florida phenomenon. It's a national pattern. Rabbis and congregational presidents are cowed and liberal thought in the Jewish community is being silenced.

According to these censors, even the ADL, Jewish Federations and the AJC would not be allowed to speak. Being a little to the left of those organizations, God only knows where that would leave me.

It's J Street Over Dershowitz by a Knockout
5/5/10

There's a nasty war of words being waged between the Harvard law professor Alan Dershowitz and the supporters of J Street, an upstart "Pro Israel-Pro Peace" lobby in Washington. I use the word upstart to distinguish it from AIPAC, the traditional powerhouse Jewish establishment lobby in Washington that many Jews consider too conservative in its uncritical support of the current right wing Netanyahu government.

In his usual style Dershowitz went beyond civil discourse and attacked J Street for going over to the "dark side." He wrote that "J Street can no longer claim to be pro Israel." He accused J Street of statements that are dangerous because the "implication is that Israel must cease to exist," and that "the reality (is) that many of its members, supporters, speakers and invited guests are virulently anti-Israel." Invoking the ghost of Joe McCarthy, I'm glad that he didn't throw in the argument that all the J Street supporters are a bunch of communists.

Dershowitz accused Jeremy Ben-Ami, the executive director of J Street, of writing that Israel is to blame for American deaths by Islamic extremists in Iraq and Afghanistan. He didn't say that, but more on that later. Here's the background on the whole argument. Before a Senate committee General David Petraeus listed six reasons why the United States needs an Israeli-Palestinian peace agreement. I will quote him directly but I will insert the numerals to clearly distinguish the points (as I did in a column in early April):

He testified: "The enduring hostilities between Israel and some of its neighbors present distinct challenges to our ability to advance our interests in the AOR (area of responsibility). (1) Israeli-Palestinian tensions often flair into violence and large-scale armed confrontations. (2) The conflict foments anti-American sentiment, due to a perception of U.S. favoritism for Israel. (3) Arab anger over the Palestinian question limits the strength and depth of U.S. partnerships with governments and people in the AOR and (4) weakens the legitimacy of moderate regimes in the Arab world. (5) Meanwhile, al-Qaeda and other militant groups exploit the anger to mobilize support. (6) The conflict also gives Iran influence in the Arab world through its clients, Lebanese Hisballah and Hamas."

Subsequent to Petraeus' testimony, President Obama, speaking at the nuclear summit in Washington, said, "It is a vital national security interest of the United States to reduce these conflicts because whether we like it or not, we remain the dominant military superpower, and when conflicts break out, one way or another we get pulled into them. And that ends up costing us significantly in terms of both blood and treasure."

So far, so civil. One can agree with this assessment, as do I, or one can disagree by intelligently parsing the arguments. Or one can do what Dershowitz does. He sets up a straw man by falsely claiming that Petraeus and the President believe that our troops are dying in Iraq and Afghanistan directly because of Israel. He then accuses Jeremy Ben-Ami of J Street of supporting this contention.

But here's what Ben-Ami wrote in the *New York Times*: "An analysis of the Obama administration's calculus on Middle East policy should reflect that many in the Jewish community recognize that resolving the conflict is not only necessary to secure Israel's future, but also critical to regional stability and American strategic interests." Nothing about Israel causing American deaths, etc.

But Dershowitz argues that using the phrase "critical to . . . America's strategic interest" is a "well-known code" to connect Israeli actions with American casualties. To which Ben-Ami responds in the *Huffington Post*, "Really? Code? Who's got the codebook, Alan? My words stand for themselves. If you disagree with President Obama and with J Street that it's an American strategic interest to end the conflict, just say so. But because you know that argument won't fly doesn't give you license to put words into my mouth."

Ben-Ami further writes: "It's precisely this kind of slanderous campaign that you regularly run against anyone who disagrees with you." Well Ben-Ami isn't telling us anything new about Dershowitz, the hatchet man for the Jewish establishment. Years ago I wrote that Dershowitz is to the Jewish establishment what Nixon was to Eisenhower. The power people hire him to discredit anyone who dares to stray from the AIPAC talking points.

The well-respected commentator, MJ Rosenberg, agrees: "Dershowitz will say anything in the effort to smear anyone he does not like . . . I suppose he cares about Israel in his own way. But his main concern is always the game. He seems to view the Israeli government as his client and, as in the courtroom, 'truth' is irrelevant. The only thing that matters is destroying the other side."

In truth, Dershowitz does have a client. Two years ago I called a Federation director and asked a simple question—what is Dershowitz's current speaking fee? He replied that it was between $55,000 and $60,000. He gets this from Federations and other large Jewish organizations. It's pretty obvious to me that he earns much more than his Harvard salary from the Jewish establishment. If I am wrong, let him show the world his income tax return. It's also pretty obvious that Dershowitz is the paid "enforcer," to use a term that Ben-Ami uses to refer to him. Like all thugs, the enforcer does not pay attention to nuance. It's much easier for him to shout his opposition out of the Jewish community.

Except this time it won't work. J Street is here to stay and to be a vital "pro Israel-pro peace" advocate in Washington.

Pity Our Ignorant and Paranoid Community
5/9/12

This is a column that I did not intend to write. In late April I picked up my weekly *Jewish Journal* and read a front page article concerning an incident at Florida Atlantic University. But before I get to the FAU incident you should know that according to an Israeli human rights organization Israel has demolished approximately 25,000 homes of Arabs in the West Bank and East Jerusalem as part of its effort to create a Greater Israel from the Mediterranean Sea to the Jordan River. It is a particularly cruel action that wreaks havoc upon families and has been severely criticized by Israeli civil rights organizations as well as international agencies.

Now we can get to what happened at FAU. Students for Justice in Palestine (SJP) posted fake eviction notices on the dorm room doors of more than 200 students. This was done to show students what it would feel like to be evicted from your home (a prerequisite to Israeli demolition). It was a political statement in criticism of Israel. God forbid that anyone should do that. All hell broke loose with vociferous Jewish reaction.

FAU investigated and found that the notices were randomly distributed and Jews were not targeted. This is very important. The intent was to educate all students, not to intimidate Jews in any way. Actually, the poster was a very clever polemic. It included source material from B'Tselem, the respected Israeli human rights organization, as well as Amnesty International, Human Rights Watch and the Israeli Committee Against House Demolitions. One may argue with its conclusions, but it was a worthy addition to civil dialogue on the Israeli-Palestinian question.

Crucial fact: It was meant to catch the attention of students, but it was not deceptive. In bold capital letters it read: "NOT A REAL EVICTION NOTICE." It went on to say: "This notice is meant to spread awareness for the plight of the Palestinian people." Yet, the first of two *Jewish Journal* front page articles blared the headline "Eviction notices scare students," quoting a few Jewish students from the Hillel Organization. Let me be blunt. If students actually thought that they were being evicted I would check their IQ scores and wonder how they were accepted in FAU in the first place. If you can't read, you shouldn't be in college.

The bottom line is that these are pro-Palestinian students who under the First Amendment free speech clause have every right to criticize Israel, right or wrong. In this case, concerning demolitions, a couple million Israelis as well as most liberal American Jews would agree with their message.

Now comes the Jewish response. The local executive director of the Zionist Organization of America, an organization that supports the concept of a Greater Israel and denies the legitimacy of a two-state solution, screams: "What we want is for the university to call this by name. This group SJP did put out a message that was anti-Semitic in nature . . . (The notice) contained a modern blood libel . . ."

Not to be upstaged in its protection of Israel and the Jewish community the local executive director of the Anti-Defamation League called the eviction notices "intimidation tactics," and suggested that one consequence could be the university "suspending SJP members from participation in the campus organization." Translation: Put Students for Justice for Palestine (SJP) out of business and silence any criticism of Israel. I wonder what our reaction would be if an Arab were to suggest that FAU ban the Hillel chapter from campus?

As an ex-board member of Hillel and now a member of the Honorary Board I was saddened to read that its executive director jumped on the bandwagon when he commented, "There are limits to free speech. My goal isn't to shut them (SJP) up. My goal is to expose them for who they are. They are a wolf in sheep's clothing. They say they are a human rights organization but their real end game is to delegitimize and demonize Israel." Since when is criticism of Israeli demolition tactics reaching the level of delegitimization or demonization?

The Jewish public outcry is then fed to the non-Jewish press where a letter to the editor of the *Sun Sentinel* decries that SJP "does not have the right to cross the line into creating a manifestly hostile environment for Jewish fellow students. Responding vigorously and effectively against this latest anti-Semitic outrage is a test that FAU does dare not fail." What does this mean? Are we going to throw our financial weight around? Are we not going to go to their football games? Are we going to declare FAU as the bastion of anti-Semitism?

Here is the crux of my criticism of the American Jewish community. First, as a whole we are ignorant of what is happening in Israel and we are ignorant of the specific points of contention between Palestinians and Israelis. On the whole (probably 99 percent) we do not read Israeli newspapers, even though they are on the internet in English.

When we visit Israel we go on guided tours that present Israel as a wonderful Jewish Disney World with no reference to the legitimate national aspirations of 4.5 million Palestinians. We do not visit the West bank and learn first-hand what it is like to live under an occupation that robs them of dignity and hardens the hearts of the occupying power.

In short, we are an ignorant community (not dumb, we're very bright—just ignorant of basic facts concerning the Israeli-Palestinian struggle), and out of our ignorance we fall prey to the well-funded "Jewish leaders" who tell us what is anti-Semitic and what is legitimate dialogue. And these leaders use our inherited victim mentality (We Jews remember every pogrom, every detail of the Holocaust, every quota that kept a relative out of an exclusive college) to convince us that an anti-Semite lurks around every corner.

Thus in our paranoid world, it is very easy for the ADL or the ZOA to tell us that a couple of FAU kids with a legitimate message and a creative delivery system demonizes Israel and, in the words of the ZOA spokesperson, is "a modern blood libel."

Pity our community.

BDS—Let's Keep Our Heads Cool
4/17/13

Criticism of Israel takes many forms, from mild rebuke to tough love from pro-Israel friends to the more drastic BDS movement. BDS—Boycott, Divestment and Sanctions—is a most aggressive tactic to force Israel into a peace settlement with the Palestinians. The Anti-Defamation League (ADL) in a full page ad in the *New York Times* has declared BDS anti-Semitic. But is it?

Up front, let me state that although I am a tough critic of the Netanyahu government I do not support the BDS movement—at least not at this point. If Israel were to annex the West Bank and suppress the Palestinians into an apartheid state, I expect a good portion of liberal American Jews as well as I, would join the BDS movement.

Boycotts are as American as apple pie and as Jewish as chicken soup. Every other day I'm asked by some Jewish organization to boycott something. It's either Mel Gibson's movies or the *New York Times* (It's anti-Jewish because it prints articles critical of Israel, as some right-wingers believe!). I have been a proponent of BDS against South Africa during the apartheid era, and history has shown that it is an effective tool. But when a pro-Palestinian group uses it against Israel, according to some Jews it morphs into hate speech.

I did not support BDS against South Africa out of hatred. I wanted to change its policies so that it could become a more humane country. I believe that the vast majority of supporters of BDS against Israel do not want to destroy Israel, nor are they anti-Semitic. They merely want Israel to make peace with its neighbors. Even though I do not agree with the need for this tactic at this point in history, I do respect the integrity and motivations of its proponents.

But a spokesman for the Consulate General of Israel in New York wrote in the *Times* that BDS "is not a call for peace, but rather a call for a 'one-state solution,' which is a euphemism for the annihilation of Israel." I am sure that there are some supporters of BDS who believe in a one-state solution (which I vehemently oppose), but it should be noted that the Minister of Housing and Construction and the Minister of Interior in the current Israeli government are proponents of a Greater Israel from the Mediterranean Sea to the Jordan River, i.e. a one-state solution. It is also ironic that many of the far right-wing supporters of Israel, including the Zionist Organization of America (ZOA) and Sheldon Adelson, support a one-state solution.

This whole issue is being played out on college campuses. There has been much press recently concerning both Brooklyn College and Florida Atlantic University. In New York, conservative members of City Council demanded that Brooklyn College cancel a BDS event. Assemblyman Alan Maisel of Brooklyn hysterically commented, "We're talking about the potential for a second Holocaust here." Mayor Bloomberg responded that although he "couldn't disagree more violently" with BDS, "If you want to go to a university where the government decides what kind of subjects are fit for discussion, I suggest you apply to a school in North Korea."

Locally, the opposition to the BDS movement at FAU and its prime proponent, Students for Justice in Palestine (SJP), has been highjacked by Jewish hate-mongers who are committed to attacking Islam, having nothing to do with the specifics of the BDS movement. I have received hysterical emails from prominent local Jews. One declares that "Islam is on the rise at FAU," while another declares the campus is "under siege."

One Howard Zipper, a Boca Raton physician, in a letter to the FAU president, writes: "The SJP, affiliated and aided by radical Muslim groups, has run unfettered . . . the FAU administration . . . has been lax and unresponsive to the shockingly brazen displays of anti-semetic (sic) racial bigotry rampant on your campus permitted under the guise of 'academic freedom of expression'." (My God, he's a medical doctor. One would assume that he could spell "anti-Semitism.")

I have met with the three leaders of Students for Justice in Palestine at FAU. They are bright, committed and certainly not anti-Semitic. One is Christian, one Jewish and the third is an American-born Muslim of Palestinian parentage. As leaders of a recognized student organization, they have every right to present the Palestinian narrative, just as Hillel (on which I serve on its Honorary Board of Directors) has the right and obligation to present the Israeli narrative. It's a university where issues should be vigorously debated.

I don't have to agree with every tactic or assertion of SJP, but I respect their commitment to truth as they see it.

It is sad that anti-Islam hate-mongers have attacked the FAU administration, for which I have great sympathy. Here is a university situated in a city that is 50 percent Jewish, accused of being soft on anti-Semitism and not hard enough on the plague of Sharia law, the Muslim onslaught and everything short of a Soviet invasion, ala the Russians are coming, the Russians are coming. It has gotten so bad that the President and CEO of the Jewish Federation in Boca Raton has had to issue a statement in which he makes reference to the right-wing crazies and writes; "I'm particularly disturbed by this element's unfounded allegations of anti-Semitism against the FAU administration."

The Board of Directors of Hillel of Broward and Palm Beach, with its headquarters on the FAU campus, issued a statement putting this whole fabricated crisis in perspective. It commented that Hillel was "on the ground," and proceeded to describe the many pro-Israel programs that it sponsors. As regards Students for Palestinian Justice it commented: "It is important for us to all understand that free speech is protected regardless of how vehemently we may disagree with its content." Most important it emphasized that, "Our students have been trained to respond with their own brand of positive programming to counter any negativity."

Both Hillel and the Jewish Federation reject the anti-Islamic flame-throwers who are distorting the situation at FAU, including vigorous dialogue that comes with campus life. They are the voices of reason and moderation. We are not living in North Korea.

THE PEACE PROCESS

Netanyahu's Deceptive Speech that Killed Peace
6/22/11

At the invitation of House Speaker John Boehner, Benjamin Netanyahu addressed Congress. Immediately before that event President Obama presented his formula for an Israeli-Palestinian peace based on the 1967 borders with land swaps to accommodate Israeli settlements that will be included within Israel.

Even though this has been United States policy for the last 20 years or so, even if it was not verbalized by a president, Netanyahu jumped upon this position as effectively advocating the annihilation of Israel. Mitt Romney immediately declared that Obama had "thrown Israel under a bus," and one Likud member of the Knesset decried that it was "a plan for Israel's destruction."

In Netanyahu's speech before Congress, in which he received approximately 30 standing ovations, he elaborated on the Israeli security issue in the first of his five points that he required for a peace agreement. Let's review these five points.

Security—Not only can Netanyahu not live with modified 1967 borders, but he would require a long-term Israeli military presence along the Jordan River to protect Israel's eastern border from countries like Iraq and Iran.

I recently had an argument with a young man who declared that Israel could not return the Golan Heights because that would allow Syria to control the high land over the Hula Valley. I can remember when 30 years ago as a Jewish Federation executive director I would shepherd American Jews up the Heights and show them the view and argue the same position. It had some validity then, but not now. In an age of sophisticated missiles, Syria, or any country (including Iraq and Iran) does not need contiguous land. Syria and

87

Iran have missiles that are capable of annihilating a specific house in Tel Aviv, not merely a farm in the Hula Valley.

This has relevance to the supposed need for a continual military presence on the Jordan River in the West Bank. If Iraq or Iran were to attack Israel it would be by missiles, not a land invasion from the east. Even if they thought to do so, in the age of satellite reconnaissance Israel would be able to detect such a military build-up long before it became dangerous or even close to its borders.

Land is no security these days, only peace is real security. This was brought home to me many years ago by General Shlomo Gazit, who was the chief of military intelligence and responsible for the Entebbe rescue of 1976. Under Menachem Begin he was involved with the aborted peace negotiations with Syria. He proposed Israeli early warning electronic monitoring stations in the Golan so that Israel would have advance notice of any Syrian military build-up. He also offered Syria monitoring stations within Israel for their protection. The Syrians agreed but Begin balked.

The point is that in 2011, as in 1976, the size of your land mass is not important when you can monitor troop movements of your neighbors. And today you do not even need early electronic monitoring stations since you have the use of spy drones and satellite surveillance.

Point two: Before Congress Netanyahu declared that Jerusalem must be solely under Israeli control. This essentially kills a peace agreement. It denies Muslim attachments to that city which are as emotionally valid as Jewish emotional ties to Jerusalem. The Quran reports that Mohammed ascended to heaven from the Temple Mount. It is as impossible for a Muslim to give up sovereignty over portions of Jerusalem as it would be for Jews to give up sovereignty over the Western Wall. It is unthinkable for either side, thus Netanyahu's position is a basis for continued war and strife, not peace.

Point three: Netanyahu rejects any return of Palestinian refugees to Israel proper. Of course, Israel cannot accept Palestinian refugees en masse since it would destroy the Jewish majority in the country. But serious Palestinians are thinking in terms of 50,000 returnees to reunite families. This is not a deal-breaker, but Netanyahu's position shows no empathy for the humanity of the "enemy."

Point four: Netanyahu will not deal with Hamas. I have covered this in previous columns. He has long stated that he cannot deal with the Palestinian Authority because you cannot make peace with half a nation. Now with the formation of a Palestinian Unity Government that includes Hamas, Netanyahu will not bargain because Hamas is a terrorist organization. The bottom line is that he will find a reason not to negotiate. The PLO was a terrorist organization and it was illegal for an Israeli to even speak with Yasser

Arafat. Now it is a responsible bargaining partner—the result of negotiations. Terrorism is a tool, not an end in itself. It evaporates with serious negotiations and a peace accord.

Point Five: Palestinians must recognize Israel as a Jewish state. The Palestinian Authority recognizes Israel as a legitimate state. Whether it is a Jewish state or a democratic state with a Jewish majority is an internal domestic issue revolving around the status of Israeli Arabs and is not an issue for international negotiations.

As Netanyahu presented these points our members of Congress stood and applauded. It was testimony to the power of the Jewish lobby, AIPAC in particular, and the Evangelical lobby. For Netanyahu it was a brilliant act of duplicity, as he preached peace in the process of killing it. As to our members of Congress, it was a display of ignorance and political posturing. It was a sad sight.

Settlements, Arab Rejection and Preconditions
8/19/09

Earlier this month the Anti-Defamation League joined the chorus of right-wing Jewish organizations calling upon President Obama "to stop pressuring (Israel) our vital friend and ally." In a full page advertisement in the *New York Times* (reprinted in various Jewish newspapers including the *Jewish Journal*) the ADL declared in blaring headlines: "THE PROBLEM ISN'T SETTLEMENTS, IT'S ARAB REJECTION."

The ad continued: "The obstacle to peace is not Israel. The settlements are not the impediment. The issue is simple: the Arab and Palestinian rejection of Israel's right to exist . . . With recognition, Israel has said again and again that everything is on the table without preconditions."

It is these three points that I will discuss in this column: settlements, Arab rejection of Israel and Israeli preconditions.

Settlements: The Palestinians are not blind. They see the settlers gobbling up the West Bank day by day under the guise of "natural growth." According to a new IDF (Israel Defense Force) report as of June 30 West Bank settlements have 304, 569 residents with a population increase in the first six months of 2009 of 2.3 percent. The fastest growing settlements were small sites deep inside the West Bank, the very settlements that are meant to permanently kill the concept of an independent Palestinian state. The IDF report did not include settlers living in East Jerusalem whose intent is to preclude East Jerusalem from becoming the capital of a future Palestinian state.

President Obama's call for Israel to freeze settlement activity is not a new American policy. The 1993 Oslo Accords provided for a settlement freeze that was ignored by Israel. The Road Map of 2003 agreed to by Israel and the United States called for a settlement freeze. Even Foreign Minister Avigdor Lieberman acknowledged that in his maiden address before the Knesset. Yet Israel has increased the settlements by almost a third over the past six years.

What is new is that our president is attempting to implement our agreement with Israel rather than wink at Israeli actions as did George Bush. *Haaretz* columnist Zvi Bar'el agrees with that. He notes that America has changed "its diplomatic behavior, and its tone." Bar'el continues, "But it is truly difficult to complain about someone no longer willing to stand for the verbal contortions and the lies that Israel has been feeding Washington."

I repeat: The Palestinians are not blind. In late July they witnessed several thousand West Bank settlers establish 11 new settler outposts in one day as a personal rebuke to President Obama. A leading settler rabbi declared that all of the West Bank is Jewish land. The *Times* reported: "The message to President Obama, he said, is that this is Jewish land. He did not use the president's name, but an insulting Hebrew slang for a black man and the phrase 'that Arab they call a president.'"

Let's talk about Arab rejection of Israel. First, it is not universal. Jordan, Egypt and the Palestinian Authority accept Israel as a reality. So do Saudi Arabia, Morocco and other moderate Arab countries, even if they don't have diplomatic relations with Israel. It's not 1948 and they are not waging war against Israel. Yes, Hamas does not recognize Israel's right to exist in its charter. But neither did the PLO before the Oslo Accords. Neither did Jordan or Egypt accept Israel until after a peace agreement. The point is that recognition comes after negotiations, not before.

If I were a Hamas leader I would not cheerfully accede to the legitimacy of Israel without something in return. In order to weaken Hamas' rule in Gaza, Israel is applying a cruel food embargo on all Gaza citizens. *Haaretz* reports that Israel refuses "to allow such innocuous-seeming foods as pasta or beans to cross the border." The report continues: "In the eyes of many observers, Israel's policy of limiting foods that enter the Strip is almost tantamount to starvation."

The *Haaretz* writer asks, "Can the experts please explain: Why does the Health Ministry recommendation for the diet of Israeli infants and toddlers—'soft fruit such as bananas and avocado, cooked chicken and beef, and cheese cubes'—not apply to Palestinian children? These particular items are all strictly forbidden from entering Gaza, while rice and a limited selection of meat and produce are the only food items in fact allowed to enter."

If you lived under this regime, would you rush to recognize the legitimacy of the state that seals your borders and controls your life down to your child's diet? We should not expect love, respect or recognition. All of that comes after a negotiated peace agreement. To demand otherwise is to consciously put roadblocks in the way of meaningful negotiations, which, sad to say, Israel is now doing

Finally, the ADL ad tells us that Israel is willing to negotiate "without preconditions." Yet Netanyahu has repeatedly said that he will not negotiate with Hamas because Hamas does not recognize Israel's right to exist. Patently this is a precondition. Netanyahu has also repeatedly said that Jerusalem will never be divided and this is not a subject for negotiation. This too is a precondition, especially since the Palestinians want to negotiate East Jerusalem as the capital of their future state. From the Palestinian perspective, why negotiate with someone who already tells you he won't negotiate?

The ADL ad is an attempt to undercut the Obama administration's quest for a peace settlement. It is an attempt to bolster a right-wing Israeli coalition that is committed to a Greater Israel from the Mediterranean to the Jordan River, no matter its public statements to the contrary. Most American Jews realize that this is ultimately bad for Israel and for American interests in the Middle East. That's why they overwhelmingly support Obama's pressure on Israel. I doubt whether the ADL will change that fact.

A Critique of Elie Wiesel on Jerusalem
5/19/10

Nobel Prize-winning author and Holocaust survivor Elie Wiesel recently wrote an open letter to President Obama that he published in the *New York Times*, *Wall Street Journal*, *Washington Post* and other media. I missed it in the *Times*, but, no worry, it is floating around the internet at the speed of light. It is being circulated by right-wing American Jews as the ultimate word of the arbiter of morality and the keeper of Jewish ethics.

Up front, let me say that I deeply respect Wiesel as an outstanding writer who has, more than any other Jew, conveyed the reality of the Holocaust to the general public. His memoir, "Night," seared the Holocaust into my conscience when I was a young man. I will be forever indebted to him.

By his demeanor as well as his writing, by the aura that has built up around him, he has come closest to being the Jewish counterpart to the Dalai Lama. When he speaks people flock by the thousands to hear his words of wisdom. And mostly they have been well rewarded. Unlike other writers, he has led an exemplary life and has tried to improve the lot of Jews and humanity as a whole.

But there has been one exception that has saddened me over the years. Wiesel has never criticized the government of Israel in any way in relation to its interaction with the Palestinians. I am told that he has commented that he cannot bring himself to criticize his own people after their trauma of the Holocaust. For whatever reason, this exception leaves him far short of prophet status. The prophets were canonized into the bible precisely because they had the insight and honesty to chastise their own people. This Wiesel has never done. It leaves him an outstanding novelist, but short of sainthood.

This brings us to the text of his advertisement. In his recitation of the usual talking points of the conservative Israel lobby, he commits four errors.

First, he writes: "(Jerusalem) is mentioned more than six hundred times in Scripture—and not a single time in the Koran." This is a mantra of the right to show that Jerusalem is not important to Muslims. But it is incorrect. The Arabic name for Jerusalem is Al-Quds (the Holy Place) and the Koran tells of Muhammad ascending to heaven from the top of the Temple Mount in Jerusalem. The Koran reports that Muhammad instructed that Muslims should make a pilgrimage to only three mosques, each located in Mecca, Medinah and Jerusalem (the Al-Aqsa mosque on top of the Temple Mount).

Textual correction aside, it is the height of arrogance for Jews to determine what is or is not spiritually important to adherents of other religions, whether it be Islam or Christianity. Yet we do this with impunity to strengthen our exclusive land title to Jerusalem. Wiesel wrote that "the anguish over Jerusalem is not about real estate but about memory." He is correct, but who are we that we have a right to define or diminish Muslim memory? Do we believe that we are the only people who live within an historical context??

Error number two: Wiesel writes: "Contrary to certain media reports, Jews, Christians and Muslims ARE allowed to build their homes anywhere in the City." This is his variation on the mantra that Arabs can build and live anywhere in Jerusalem, so Jews must be allowed to build and live anywhere, including East Jerusalem. Not True.

Daniel Seidermann, a Jerusalemite attorney and expert on the legalities of land ownership in Israel writes: "Most of West Jerusalem is off limits to Palestinian residents of Jerusalem in terms of their ability to purchase property. This is because most of West Jerusalem, like most of Israel, is 'State Land' (in all, 93% of land in Israel is 'State Land'). Under Israeli law, to qualify to purchase property that is 'State Land' the purchaser must either be a citizen of Israel (Palestinian Jerusalemites are legal residents of the city, not citizens of Israel) or legally entitled to citizenship under the law of return (i.e. Jewish)."

Seidermann continues: "In addition, it should be emphasized that the ban on purchase of property of 'State Land' by Palestinian residents of Jerusalem extends to East Jerusalem. Not only are Palestinian Jerusalemites barred from purchasing property in most of West Jerusalem, but they are also barred from purchasing property in the 35% of East Jerusalem that Israel has expropriated as 'State Land' since 1967, and on which Israel's East Jerusalem settlements have been built. This means that in more than 1/3 of East Jerusalem, Israelis and Jews from anywhere in the world have a right to buy property, but not Palestinian residents of Jerusalem, including the very residents whose land was expropriated to build these settlements."

I might add that a Palestinian wishing to build on the 65% of non-state land in East Jerusalem will have to wait until hell freezes over before he receives a building permit from the local Israeli authorities.

Error number three: Wiesel writes that "Pressure will not produce a solution." This flies in the face of history. President Jimmy Carter spent 12 excruciatingly difficult days at Camp David pressuring both Begin and Sadat into a peace agreement. The only significant peace agreement between Israel and its enemies was the direct result of American pressure—and it was very beneficial for Israel.

Error number four: Concerning Jerusalem, Wiesel writes: "Why tackle the most complex and sensitive problem prematurely? Why not take first steps which will allow Israeli and Palestinian communities to find ways to live together in an atmosphere of security? Why not leave the most difficult, the most sensitive issue, for such a time?"

This sounds reasonable, except that it also ignores history. This was precisely the road travelled under the Oslo Accords in 1993 and we found that both the Israelis and the Palestinians cheated like mad. Both sides ignored their confidence building obligations. Oslo called for a cessation of terrorism on one side and a settlement freeze on the other. Settlements proliferated like new-born rabbits and terrorism increased simultaneously.

Today, anyone serious about reaching a peace agreement believes that only a final settlement, including the most difficult issues, can actually work. Putting off the Jerusalem question means putting off the peace.

Wiesel concluded his full-page statement citing the Hasidic master Rebbe Nahman of Bratslav: "Everything in this world has a heart; the heart itself has its own heart." And Wiesel concludes: "Jerusalem is the heart of our heart, the soul of our soul." I agree. But I also know that the Palestinians have hearts and souls, and we cannot feed our own hearts by breaking theirs.

It's time to move beyond the poetry and mysticism and enter into the realm of reason and rationality. Repeating right-wing talking points will not lead us to peace and will not serve the long-range security and viability of

Israel. Compromise and respect for the "other" will accomplish that end. That's where our hearts and souls should be.

The Ambassador Tells the Truth
1/11/12

This past month U.S. Ambassador to Belgium Howard Gutman caused what one report characterized as a "firestorm" by his remarks made at the European Jewish Union Conference. He made a distinction between traditional anti-Semitism and Muslim hatred stemming from the Israeli-Palestinian conflict. Further, he said that an Israeli-Palestinian peace treaty will "significantly diminish Muslim anti-Semitism."

To understand his statement one must understand two historical truths. First, ancient texts do not define modern expressions of faith. There are horribly wicked portions of the Jewish bible, the New testament and the Quran and there are beautifully uplifting passages that call upon the better nature of humankind.

Jewish settlers and their supporters who are committed to a Greater Israel from the Mediterranean to the Jordan specialize in quoting the anti-Semitic passages in the Quran in proof that you can never make a peace treaty with the Palestinians. Such passages also exist in the New Testament, so should Jews be at war with our Christian neighbors? (Lest we are too critical of other people's basic literature, let us remember that there is a passage in our Torah that calls for total genocide against our enemies—the slaughter of men, women, children and all their cattle.)

This leads us to the second truth: Putting aside the basic texts, anti-Semitism has not been a significant part of the history between Jews and Muslims, as it has been with Christianity. Some years ago I shared a podium with Dr. Ahrar Ahmad at a Truman Symposium. I presented a paper on Truman and the Jews and Dr. Ahmad spoke on peace in the Middle East as it relates to Islamic thought. Six years ago I quoted him, but it warrants repeating here.

"In the Muslim world we do not see the kind of vicious anti-Semitism that we see elsewhere. The Muslims did not destroy any Jewish or Christian places of worship when they captured Jerusalem in 638, in fact the Muslim Caliph ordered the Wailing Wall area to be cleaned up. It was not the Muslims that drove out the Jews from Jerusalem in 1099 when the city went under Crusader control; in fact Salah al din invited them back after he recaptured it in 1187. The Muslims did not expel the Jews from Spain in 1492 (indeed in Spain they lived in particularly harmonious amity), it was the Muslims who welcomed the expelled Jews into the Ottoman Empire (where they were allowed legal autonomy and spiritual jurisdiction over themselves). In fact by the 17th century almost 30% of the population of Istanbul was Jewish, who were there by choice not conquest or coercion."

Now we can get back to Ambassador Gutman's statement. Understanding history, he made the distinction between traditional western anti-Semitism and anti-Israeli sentiments that can morph into anti-Semitism. Since this hatred is based on a political battle (the carving out of two nations focused on one piece of land) and not an endemic religious hatred it was his correct conclusion that with a peace settlement it would cease. Gutman did not endorse anti-Israeli or anti-Semitic behavior; he merely put it in context. It's reasonable to me. I remember the intense hatred of Japan during World War II. I also remember how quickly it dissipated after the end of the war.

Also, Gutman did not blame Israel for the conflict or exonerate the Palestinians. He merely stated that there is a direct contributory causation between the existence of the conflict and Muslim hatred of Israel and even anti-Semitism.

So now we can look at the reaction. Here come the usual suspects. The Anti-Defamation League's Abe Foxman jumped in to protest that Gutman's statement "undermine(d) the important effort to combat the resurgence of anti-Semitism in Europe." The local executive director of the Zionist Organization of America (a group that denies a two-state solution and argues for a Greater Israel from the Mediterranean to the Jordan) proclaimed that Gutman's opinions were "a shameful attempt to rationalize the anti-Jewish bigotry" found within Islamic doctrine.

David Harris, the executive director of the American Jewish Committee who has dragged that organization further to the right over the last few years, wrote that, "We were appalled by his comments. Muslim anti-Semitism, he should know, has a long painful history of its own that has absolutely nothing to do with Israel."

Harris is best answered by Dr. Ahmad, who made this totally honest statement immediately after the quote that I cited earlier: "This does not mean that Jews and Christians in Islamic rule lived absolutely in peace and justice, and that they sat around campfires roasting marshmallows and singing Kumbaya. Surely there were bitter misunderstandings and savage encounters between Muslims and others. But, and this is my point, these incidents were episodic and determined by circumstance, neither systemic nor governed by doctrine."

What is disturbing is the use of this made-up brouhaha to attack the Obama Administration. The Harris quote along with a quote from the *Jerusalem Post* (a conservative Israeli newspaper) and another from Elliott Abrams (the neocon from both the Reagan and George W. Bush administrations) appeared in a full page ad in the *New York Times* proclaiming that the Obama Administration treats Israel like a punching bag. Its punch line was, "It's time for the Obama Administration to stop blaming Israel first." As if Ambassador Gutman's statement was doing that.

The ad was paid for by the Emergency Committee for Israel, a front organization founded by William Kristol, publisher and editor of the *Weekly Standard* and a frequent talking head on Fox News and Gary Bauer, an evangelical activist who once ran for president in the Republican primary and an avid supporter of George W. Bush.

My complaint is not that the usual suspects are conservatives. I think that they are wrong, but I do not demonize them for their conservative theology. My complaint is that in their mistaken belief that they are helping Israel they distort history and denigrate 1.3 billion Muslims and their religion. What they are really doing is turning a political battle into a religious war. Fourteen million Jews do not have to do battle with 1.3 billion Muslims. It's a stupid move and worse yet, it's very un-Jewish. It's a defiling of Jewish ethics.

A Call for Peace. Will We Answer?
6/19/13

Who would have thought that the Obama administration at this time would put a full-court press on both the Israelis and the Palestinians to resume serious peace negotiations? Secretary of State John Kerry has been to Israel every month since assuming his position in February. Who would have thought that with crucial legislation pending, such as immigration reform, that President Obama would face up to domestic critics who confuse pressure on Israel with anti-Israel or anti-Semitic animus (ignoring the fact that there is equal pressure on the Palestinians)? Yet that is what is happening, although it was little noticed until a pivotal speech by Kerry two weeks ago.

At the American Jewish Committee Global Forum Kerry spoke *tachlis* (straight forward, no bull-throwing, hard facts) to the assembled Jewish leaders. Beginning with the usual pleasantries, he reminded them that his brother Cam converted to Judaism 30 years ago, and he recently discovered his own Jewish roots and that members of his extended family perished in the Holocaust. Having settled the fact that he is both philo-Semitic and pro-Israel, he proceeded to tell it like it is and then to challenge the American Jewish community to action.

Kerry stressed the need for Israeli security. He then asked, "But what does that security look like? Certainly it's more than the absence of war . . .

lasting security for Israel requires regional stability and open markets that will let Israelis concentrate on building up their businesses and not just their defenses. You and I both know that the place where all this happens best is a strong, secure Israel that lives peacefully alongside a viable Palestinian state. I will tell you here today, examine every possibility, all of the parameters of this frozen conflict, and I will tell you a realistic one-state solution simply does not exist for either side."

Kerry debunked two arguments against a peace treaty at this time. The messy aftermath of the Arab Spring does not prohibit an Israeli-Palestinian peace accord, rather "now is exactly the kind of time to recast Israel's relationships" with the new emerging voices in the Arab world. He also refuted those who argue that Israel's unilateral withdrawal from Lebanon and Gaza merely resulted in more rockets aimed at them. Kerry made the important distinction between a unilateral withdrawal and a negotiated peace. He cited the success of both peace agreements with Jordan and Egypt.

For me the heart of the speech was Kerry's warning that we are running out of time: "If we do not succeed now, we may not get another chance . . . We will find ourselves in a negative spiral of response and counter-responses that could literally slam the door on a two-state solution." Kerry continued, "The status quo is not sustainable . . . and the insidious campaign to de-legitimize Israel will only gain steam." Although he said, "Yes, the United States of America will always have Israel's back," he warned that this may not be always adequate.

Finally, Kerry called for the American Jewish community to start a campaign in support of peace: "No one has a stronger voice in this than the American Jewish community. You can play a critical part in ensuring Israel's long-term security . . . I ask you today, send this message that you are behind this hopeful vision of what can be. Let your leaders and your neighbors alike know that you understand that this will be a tough process with tough decisions, but that you're ready to back the leaders who make them. For your children, do this; for your grandchildren, do this; for Israeli children and Palestinian children and for Israel, let them know that you stand behind negotiations that will lead to two states for two peoples living side-by-side in peace and security, and that you are part of the great constituency for peace."

The liberal pro-Israel, pro-peace American lobby, J Street, was the first to respond. J Street's President Jeremy Ben-Ami declared, "Secretary Kerry's speech encapsulated everything that J Street believes in and has been working for . . . He laid out a challenge to American Jews to vocalize our support for the two-state solution . . . It is up to our community, our leaders, activists and members to respond to this challenge and fulfill our historic responsibility by joining Kerry's great constituency for peace."

Americans for Peace Now (APN), the American support group for *Shalom Achshav*, the Israeli peace movement, echoed this plea to support Kerry's diplomatic thrust. But as of this writing (June 12), I have heard nothing but silence from the rest of the Jewish community. Where are the rabbis, federations, and community relations councils? As a local Jewish professional privately lamented to me, "We're all ready to galvanize our support when Israel's at war, but when it comes to supporting Israel's quest for peace, we are stunningly silent."

Why? I believe that most American Jewish leaders, especially rabbis and federation directors, are afraid of being attacked by the minority of right-wing Jews who would brand them as being pro-Palestinian or self-hating Jews. I've been there; I know. I have *rachmonus* for them. Their jobs are on the line.

Yet this flies in the face of a recent poll before the last presidential election that reports that 82 percent of Jewish voters support a two-state solution; that 79 percent support a two-state solution even if it means that East Jerusalem becomes the capital of a Palestinian state; and that 76 percent of Jews would support the United States putting forth its own plan for peace.

It's time that the majority of the American Jewish community sets its own agenda, that we heed the call of Secretary Kerry in support of a secure Israel, that we urge our rabbis and communal leaders to stand up to the vocal minority of right-wing Jewish activists. It's time that we tell our elected representatives to support this new initiative of the Obama administration because it's in the best interests of America and crucial for the long-term security of Israel.

Sorting Through the Lies of Jewish Emails
11/23/11

Right wing ideologues in the Jewish community insist upon bombarding us with emails that attempt to create their own truths by the sheer weight of their insistence on repeating their talking points.

One such email that is now popular and seems to be ubiquitous is a series of statements in support of the unstated premise of a Greater Israel from the Mediterranean to the Jordan River. I want to review its assertions in this column, point by point, followed by my comments.

"Israel became a nation in 1312, Two thousand years before the rise of Islam."
TRUE
The whole thrust of this argument is that we had the land first, therefore it's ours. Based on this theory the Indians own America. One would assume that the land is at least partially owned by those who have lived on it for the last couple hundred years, some for a thousand.

"Jerusalem is mentioned over 700 times in Tanach, the Jewish Holy scriptures. Jerusalem is not mentioned once in the Koran."
FALSE
The Arabic name for Jerusalem is Al Quds, meaning the Holy Place, and it is mentioned often in the Koran. The implication in the misleading quote is that Jerusalem is not important to Muslims, while it is our holy Jewish city. This leads us to the next statement in the email.

"King David founded the city of Jerusalem. Mohammed never came to Jerusalem."
TRUE AND FALSE
King David did found the city circa 1000 BCE. But the Koran tells us that Mohammed came to Jerusalem and ascended to heaven from the rock on top of the Temple Mount. The Al Aqsa mosque on the Temple Mount is the third most holy Muslim site in the world. The point is that Jerusalem has as much emotional attachment to Muslims as it does to us Jews. It takes a lot of chutzpah or ignorance to deny another people's emotional attachments.

"In 1948 the Arab refugees were encouraged to leave Israel by Arab leaders promising to purge the land of Jews. Sixty-eight percent left without ever seeing an Israeli soldier."
FALSE
This is in the realm of an urban legend, except it's a Jewish legend that we have been repeating for over 60 years. In a recent column I reported that based on Israeli government documents recently declassified, Israeli historians are showing that both the Arabs and the Jews in Palestine in the time leading up to the November, 1947 partition and afterwards were attempting to ethnic-cleanse each other. It is undeniable that Jewish massacres of Arab villages caused wholesale fleeing by Arabs. The Arabs, in turn, committed atrocities on the Jews. Both sides used despicable tactics. The point is that the vast majority of Arab refugees did not voluntarily leave the land to us Jews. We kicked them out. (Had they won, they would have done the same to us.)

"The Jewish refugees were forced to flee from Arab lands due to Arab brutality, persecution and pogroms."
TRUE
We hear this often as if to justify the Israeli expulsion of the Palestinians. It's a "you did it to us so we have the right to do it to you" argument. The only problem is that the Palestinians didn't do it to us. We would not think of equating a Catholic from Spain with a Catholic from Ireland. They are two different peoples. So it is with Arabs. The fact that Jews were expelled by Iraqis or Libyans from their countries does not reflect on Palestinians. This leads us to the next quote.

"Arab refugees were intentionally not absorbed or integrated into Arab lands to which they fled, despite the vast Arab territory."
TRUE
This merely proves the point that the Palestinian peoplehood is distinct from other Arab peoples. They were cynically mistreated by the Egyptians, Jordanians, Syrians and Lebanese who used them as pawns in their power games. They were not integrated into their communities because they were not looked upon as part of a single peoplehood. This also negates the idea that there is no legitimate Palestinian nation, a comment once made by Golda Meir.

"The PLO's Charter still calls for the destruction of the State of Israel."
FALSE
This is about as intelligent a statement as President Obama was born in Kenya, yet one third of Fox News viewers believe this as do 48 percent of South Carolina Republicans. The point is that if you hate deeply enough you will believe any lie that feeds that hate. The Charter was changed twice, not once, to assure people that the PLO and Fatah accept the existence of the State of Israel. They do not recognize Israel as a "Jewish State," rather a state with a majority Jewish population. It's not up to the PLO or any other country to categorize what kind of a state Israel is. It is an internal political question to be decided by its own citizens, including its 22 percent minority non-Jewish citizens. Before leaving this point, you can find "academic" studies to show that the PLO pulled the wool over everyone's eyes and really did not recognize Israel. I can also show you impressive studies that prove that the Holocaust never happened.

This particular email goes on to lambast the United Nations for being anti-Israel. This point, right or wrong, is irrelevant to the question of whether the

Palestinians are due a portion of the land, whether a two-state solution is the moral as well as the correct political thing to do.

There are powerful American Jewish organizations that do not believe in the two-state solution, including the Zionist Organization of America as well as a sizable portion of the Orthodox community. I believe they are morally wrong and in the long-run endanger the very existence of Israel. Putting aside those arguments, I wish that these firebrands would cease to inundate me with their ridiculous emails.

P.S. All of this hate is distributed as part of their Judaism. The emails ask that I send them along to 18 (chai) other people and even wish me a healthy and happy New Year.

What We Can Learn from Shin Bet Chiefs
3/6/13

"The Gatekeepers", a riveting 1 hour 37 minute Israeli documentary will open in South Florida in two days (March 8). I saw this movie the day that it opened in New York City on February 1st and intend to see it again. It received the Best Documentary Award from the Los Angeles critics and was a finalist at the Academy Awards. The director, Dror Moreh, interviewed the six ex-chiefs of the Shin Bet (the internal Israeli equivalent of the FBI, whose job it is to protect Israel from terrorism) from 1980 to 2011.

For the record the interviewees are: Avraham Shalom (1980-86), Yaacov Peri (86-94), Carmi Gillon (94-96), Ami Ayalon (96-2000), Avi Dichter (2000-05), and Yuval Diskin (05-11). On the whole they are a hard-bitten lot reflecting, as A.O. Scott in the *New York Times* wrote, "their shared professional ethos of ruthless, unsentimental pragmatism." They discuss targeted assassinations and torture (which they refer to as "moderate physical pressure") clinically, with no emotional overtones.

There is no way that one could characterize them as bleeding hearts or liberals, with the possible exception of Ami Ayalon. Yet they surprise us with their clear understanding of the negative consequences of the prolonged Israeli-Palestinian conflict.

Shalom is the oldest and probably the most hard-line, but it is he who comments that fighting the Arabs for 65 years has made Israeli society "cruel." I have written four columns over the past years, some with the title "The Soul of Israel is at Stake", about this very point. I have quoted the Israeli novelist A.B. Yehoshua arguing that, "A light finger on the trigger in Hebron or Gaza also leads to a light finger on the trigger for the crime organizations in Israel." Former Israeli Minister of Education, Yossi Sarid, wrote, "Israel is insufferably violent and that there is no longer anything to be proud of; only to be ashamed." It is one thing for these liberals to admit this, but entirely more believable when the hard-bitten ex-head of the Shin Bet says so.

In recent years this violence has intensified against Arab citizens of Israel. A most egregious example: A 17-year-old Israeli Arab youth, Jamal Juliani, was walking with his friends in Zion Square in Jerusalem when a gang of Jewish teenagers, ages 13 to 19, attacked them. His cousin reported that they suddenly found themselves being chased by a group of youths shouting "Arabs, death to Arabs." Jamal was pummeled to the ground and left unconscious. When the paramedics found him he was unresponsive and with no pulse. After using CPR and defibrillators for more than 10 minutes his pulse returned and he eventually recuperated in Hadassah Hospital. Here was the reaction of one of the attackers: "For my part he can die, he's an Arab." An Israeli newspaper columnist asked. "Where on earth does a bar-mitzvah-age child find so much evil in himself?" Shin Bet Chief Shalom can answer his question.

In a surprising statement, Shin Bet Chief Diskin said, "One man's terrorist is another man's freedom fighter." This underscores the reality that there is validity in the Palestinian narrative as well as the Israeli. It brings to mind former Israeli Prime Minister Yitzhak Shamir's statement that, "Neither Jewish ethics nor Jewish tradition can disqualify terrorism as a means of combat. Rather, terrorism had a great part to play in our war against the occupier."

Knowing that Israel used terrorism against both the British and the Palestinians during the early years of its formation, this is a good segue to the current Israeli and American position of not talking to Hamas because they are "terrorists," or are they "freedom fighters"—choose your own nomenclature. Shin Bet Chief Shalom derides this position. Talk to Hamas, he advises. In a subsequent interview with Y-Net Magazine, Yuval Diskin said, "After all these years of fighting terror and seeing so much death and killing in battle fields, on Israeli streets, in refugees camps and in villages in the West Bank, the Gaza Strip and Lebanon—there comes a time when you realize you must do everything, everything, to find some other way to talk and compromise . . ." When an American Reform rabbi says that Israel and the U.S. should talk to Hamas some people sneer. Will they feel comfortable sneering at these Shin Bet chiefs?

In reflecting on his tough approach toward Palestinian terrorists, Ami Ayalon said, "We wanted security and got more terrorism." In retrospect, after every targeted assassination a new leader arose to take the place of the fallen martyr, one with even more hatred, bred of hatred, a continuation of a deadly cycle. More Israeli detentions only bred more terrorists who then spoke fluent Hebrew learned in Israeli prisons.

In an interview with CNN's Christiane Amonpour, the director, Dror Moreh, said that this is "the most pro-Israel film" he could have created. "When you see the Titanic heading toward the iceberg, what would you do?" He continued: "They are all pragmatists. These are the six heads of the secret service of Israel saying in one and clear voice enough of the occupation—you cannot argue with that." Moreh said that none of the former chiefs has come to him with any problems with the final product and all of them told him they stand behind the film.

I urge every Jew, especially American Jewish leaders, to see this movie. It is more than just talking heads. There is ample amount of historical footage including the Rabin assassination by a Jewish terrorist. The *New York Times* reviewer effused: "It is hard to imagine a movie about the Middle East that could be more timely, more painfully urgent, more challenging to conventional wisdom on all sides of the conflict."

For me, this movie provides an exclamation point to Albert Einstein's statement: "Should we be unable to find a way to honest cooperation and honest pacts with the Arabs, then we have learned absolutely nothing during our two thousand years of suffering and deserve all that will come to us."

Israel on the Road to Pariah State
12/19/12

Tom Friedman began a column last year by stating that, "Friends don't let friends drive drunk and Israel is driving drunk." Friedman is not exactly a radical and for him to acknowledge this highlights the need for criticism. Unfortunately that criticism is lacking from Jewish communal leaders. Put bluntly, rabbis and other Jewish community workers fear for their jobs if they do not parrot the official Israeli talking points. Being retired I don't have to worry about being fired. Friends don't let friends drive drunk, and I'm a friend of Israel. I am free to tell the truth as I see it.

Now on to the meat of this column, the recent United Nations vote to accept Palestine as a member state. Israeli Foreign Minister Avigdor Lieberman, referring to the president of the Palestinian Authority, stated: "Abbas's appeal to the UN is pure political terror." Following the official Israeli line, my (thank God lame-duck) Congressman Allen West declared, in a press release that was widely disseminated by Jewish sources, that "The vote is yet another step towards delegitimizing Israel's right to exist as a Jewish state."

This hysteria ignores the fact that the UN resolution twice, not once but twice, affirmed "the vision of two States, an independent, sovereign, democratic, contiguous and viable State of Palestine, living side by side in peace and security with Israel, on the basis of the pre-1967 borders." While affirming their own statehood the Palestinians through the UN resolution are also affirming the legitimacy of Israel. This was a move for peace, not war, not terrorism.

Liberals in Israel understand this. There was a rally in Tel Aviv in support of the UN resolution. Dr. Alon Liel, former Director-General of Israel's Foreign Ministry, stated that the UN vote was no "diplomatic gimmick." He continued, "It is the culmination of a consistent and long-term policy by Palestinian President Mahmud Abbas designed to realize historical justice though political means, without bloodshed."

The world understands this. The UN resolution passed by a vote of 138 to 9. The United States was joined in opposition by the likes of Micronesia, Naura, Palau and the Marshall Islands. All of Western Europe supported the Palestinians with the exceptions of the UK, Netherlands and Germany which abstained. All other major world powers, including Russia and China favored upgrading the Palestinian Authority to that of a State. The jig is up. The world is telling Israel that it must commit itself to a two-state solution.

The Israeli response was belligerence. In retaliation, Netanyahu announced that Israel would build 3,000 more units in East Jerusalem and would build an Israeli neighborhood in the crucial E-1 corridor between Jerusalem and the West Bank settlement of Ma'aleh Adumim. For years Israel has had approved plans that call for 3,900 housing units, 2,192 hotel rooms and an industrial park as well as the existing police station in the E-1 corridor. It never implemented these plans under American and European pressure.

The problem is that Israeli building in the E-1 corridor bisects the West Bank and cuts off Ramallah and the north from Bethlehem and the south, as well as cutting off the entire West Bank from East Jerusalem, which would be the capital of the State of Palestine. It would destroy the contiguity and viability of a Palestinian state. In short, it would kill the two-state solution and ensure a Greater Israel from the Mediterranean Sea to the River Jordan. Dani Seidemann, a Jerusalem lawyer and peace activist, called it the "doomsday weapon."

A little history is needed here. After the last Israeli election Tzipi Livni, then head of the Kadima Party, offered to join a coalition headed by Netanyahu. With the Kadima, Labor and Likud parties in the coalition Netanyahu could have pieced together a centrist coalition. Livni had one crucial request of Netanyahu—that he accept the concept of a two-state solution as the basis of bargaining with the Palestinians. He refused to do that and he created the rightwing government that he currently heads.

Under pressure from the United States Netanyahu finally committed himself to the concept of a two-state solution in a speech at Bar-Ilan University in 2009. After his announcement concerning the E-1 corridor the Israeli newspaper *Haaretz* editorialized: "The government's decision is the last nail in the coffin of Prime Minister Benjamin Netanyahu's Bar-Ilan University speech in 2009. It is proof positive that this speech, in which he ostensibly accepted the principle of two states, was merely a deception." Duh? Did anyone really believe him?

I've written this before, but it is the logical conclusion of this discussion and warrants repeating. Israel is headed toward a one-state conclusion, ruling over five million Palestinians in a Jewish state from the Mediterranean to the Jordan.

Only three options are then on the table: First, to remain a democracy it will have to give the Palestinians voting rights. It will not do that because the Arab population will soon outnumber the Jews and the Jewish nature of the state would disappear. Outcome: the loss of the oft-quoted "only democratic state in the Middle East."

Second, it could rule over the Palestinians in this Greater Israel state but reserve voting for Jews only. There is a word for that—apartheid. The world will not accept it.

Third, Israel could ethnic cleanse all non-Jews from the state. I need to remind the reader that ethnic cleansing is considered a crime against humanity under international conventions. One of these three alternatives is the inexorable outcome of a one-state solution. One must live in a bubble to deny this reality

The logical outcome of the current decisions of the Israeli government is that Israel will become a pariah nation. That's the reason that we American Jews had better stop blindly supporting the policies of this Netanyahu coalition and start applying tough love. After all, friends don't let friends drive drunk.

Peace or Apartheid—Approaching the Point of No Return
8/7/13

I write this column in anticipation of the imminent peace negotiations between Israel and the Palestinians, thanks to the valiant efforts of Secretary of State Kerry and President Obama.

Anyone who reads my columns knows that I am very pessimistic concerning the ability or the will of the current Israeli government to make peace. In Netanyahu's coalition many key players are on record against a two-state solution. Naftali Bennett, Chairman of the key Knesset Finance Committee, has called for the annexation of Area C of the West Bank. Minister of Housing, Uri Ariel, wants to annex the entire West Bank, and Interior Minister, Gideon Saar, has made it clear that Likud's election platform does not include "two states for two people." Netanyahu has supported the concept of the formation of a Palestinian state only after extreme pressure from Washington. So, is there hope?

Deeply buried within my pessimistic soul is a flickering optimism, a fleck of hope, borne of Jewish longing, or as Edmund Fleg wrote in his famous poem, "I am a Jew because every time when despair cries out, the Jew hopes."

If there is to be a two-state solution it has to be now. In his seminal speech in June before the American Jewish Committee Kerry stressed that, "If we do not succeed now, we may not get another chance." It's one thing for an American diplomat to say that, but it is even more convincing when Yuval Diskin, the immediate past head of the Shin Bet (Israel's internal security service, comparable to the FBI) comes to the same conclusion. It's even more compelling when you realize that Diskin, as head of the Shin Bet, directed the targeted killings of Hamas leaders. He is not a bleeding heart liberal by any stretch of the imagination.

Diskin is a hard-headed pragmatist who has called for peace with the Palestinians. In a recent column in the *Jerusalem Post* he opined: "We are approaching a point of no return regarding the Israeli-Palestinian conflict. In fact, it may be that we have already crossed it . . . the number of settlers or 'inhabitants' in the West Bank, outside the main settlement blocs, is growing to (if they have not already arrived at) dimensions that no Israeli government will be able to dismantle in an orderly fashion . . ." He lamented that Netanyahu has lulled the Israeli public into focusing on Iran rather than on the crucial question of peace with the Palestinians.

If in fact we have gone beyond the point of no return, Diskin points to the obvious conclusion that either Israel will become a democratic bi-national state with an Arab majority with the right to vote, or—and his language here is crucial—Israel will be an "ostracized apartheid state." Yes, he uses the A-word. Remember when President Carter correctly used that word (in reference to the current situation in the West Bank, not Israel proper) he was pilloried by the conservative Jewish establishment as an anti-Semite.

Diskin maintains that "everyone knows what the parameters of settlement will inevitably entail"—A demilitarized Palestinian state based on the 1967 lines with territorial swaps, dismantling of the settlements, a political partition of Jerusalem and "a creative solution regarding sovereignty over the holy sites in the Old City." Everyone knows, except Netanyahu. At this point he publicly refuses to start negotiations based on the 1967 borders. Let us see if this changes in Washington when negotiations really begin.

Writing for JTA (the Jewish version of the Associated Press) Ephraim Sneh, twice Israel's Deputy Minister of Defense, and Robert Lifton, a prominent American Jew who is currently Co-Chair of the Middle East Project of the Council on Foreign Relations, also are cautiously optimistic concerning the upcoming negotiations. (Their column was published in the *Jewish Journal* two weeks ago.) They stressed the added security for Israel that peace with the Palestinians would bring: "The U.S. can build a new regional axis to confront Iran and the radical Islamists. It should be based on the Gulf States—Bahrain, Kuwait, Oman, Saudi Arabia and the United Arab Emirates—plus Jordan, Israel and Palestine." Lifton wrote that Saudi officials in 2008 and Jordan's King Abdullah in 2011 both assured him that with the end of the Palestinian conflict their countries would welcome the opportunity to join with Israel against Iran.

Both Diskin and Sneh-Lifton presented challenges to the participants in Washington. Sneh and Lifton challenged the Obama administration not to believe that it is a political risk to pressure Israel. They maintain, as do I, that the majority of American Jews would support an American government that was proactive in presenting solutions, rather than passively watching the Israelis and Palestinians talk their way into oblivion. Sneh and Lifton propose that Kerry should present both sides "with a made in America 'take it or leave it' offer."

Writing in Israel, Diskin challenges: "This is Netanyahu's moment of truth. He can prove to all of his most vociferous naysayers and critics (me among them) that he is not just a politician passing his—and our—time in the prime minister's office, but a leader who is capable of grasping the gravity of the situation; a leader who is capable of freeing himself of his trepidations, fears and secret advisors . . . I have huge doubts as to whether Netanyahu is such a leader, but I will be the first one to praise him if he proves otherwise."

I have huge doubts as to whether the Obama administration or Netanyahu can meet these challenges. Yet I cling to my flickering optimism. I pray that this speck of hope can gestate into a body of peace that will redound to the benefit of both the Palestinians and the Israelis.

Applying the Lessons of the Yom Kippur War to Iran
10/9/13

This past Sunday we marked the 40th anniversary of the Yom Kippur War. For a committed Jew October 6, 1973 is one of those days that one never forgets, very much like where one was on the day that President Kennedy was assassinated. For me it had a double meaning—it was both Yom Kippur and my son Michael's third birthday. Like most Diaspora Jews I was traumatized awaiting the outcome of those first horrifying days of the conflict.

It was only in later years that we could analyze the political decisions that led to that war. In 2004 I wrote an extensive column based on the Israeli historian Avi Shlaim's book "The Iron Wall." Relying on the declassified minutes of the Israeli Cabinet meetings during that period, he came to the conclusion that the war could have been avoided had Golda Meir been more open to diplomacy rather than having succumbed to the arrogance that followed Israel's decisive victory in the 1967 Six Day War. The complete analysis in my 2004 column can be found reprinted in my book of collected columns, "Provocative Columns," (available through Amazon).

Here let me briefly summarize his conclusions. In the period from December 1969 and ending in March 1972 the Israeli Cabinet, under the leadership of Golda Meir, rebuffed seven legitimate peace offers as relates to Egypt:

First, U.S. Secretary of State William Rogers proposed a return to the 1967 Egyptian-Israeli borders. Meir answered by deep bombings into Egypt (3,300 sorties, dropping 8,000 tons of ordinance) in an attempt to topple Nasser.

Second, Egypt answered this military might by inviting 15,000 Soviet soldiers and 200 pilots to Egypt. Buttressed by this defense, Nasser made a second attempt to discuss peace. He invited Dr. Nahum Goldmann, President of the World Jewish Congress, to Egypt. Golda refused to allow Goldmann to travel there.

Third, After Nasser died in September 1970, his successor Anwar Sadat in February 1971 proposed returning to the 1967 borders offering in return, for the first time, a total peace between the two countries. Israel rejected the offer.

Fourth, In March 1971 Israel rebuffed an American initiative that would require Israeli troop withdrawal 40 Kilometers from the Suez Canal, thereby allowing it to reopen. Israel would have had the right of passage through the newly reopened canal.

Fifth, In May 1971 the U.S. proposed an Israeli withdrawal to the Gidi and Mitla Passes, which even the hawk Moshe Dayan supported, in an attempt to start peace negotiations. Golda nixed it. In frustration, the United States suspended the supply of phantom jets to Israel.

Sixth, In October 1971 Secretary of State Rogers suggested "proximity talks" in New York City between Egypt and Israel. Once again the Cabinet, following Golda's leadership, rejected this peace initiative.

Finally, in March 1972 King Hussein of Jordan offered a Federal Plan that would unite the West Bank with Jordan, coupled with a peace treaty with Israel. It was immediately rejected by Israel. Arafat told his biographer that the plan would have put the PLO out of business. He commented, "Sometimes I think we are lucky to have the Israelis as our enemies. They have saved us many times."

Lessons to be learned from the above: Beware of leaders who think in black and white, who have burning convictions that they are always right, who rely on military strength rather than diplomacy and who do not see the enemy in human terms, but rather demonize them. Had Golda Meir and her Cabinet responded positively to any of these proposals there is a strong possibility that the Yom Kippur War death toll could have been avoided (2,838 Israelis and 8,528 Egyptians).

Let's apply the lessons learned from the above narrative to the current Israeli-Iranian situation. The Netanyahu government is convinced that a nuclear Iran is an existential threat to Israel and believes that diplomacy is useless, relying only on a military strike against its nuclear installations.

Iran's newly elected president, Hassan Rouhani, is making conciliatory gestures toward Israel and Jews, obviously in an attempt to initiate diplomatic contact. He and his foreign minister recently wished Jews worldwide and the free 25,000-strong Jewish community in Iran a Happy New Year. In a CNN interview, in contrast to his predecessor Mahmoud Ahmadinejad who was a Holocaust denier, he not only acknowledged the Holocaust as a "crime the Nazi created towards the Jews," but called it "reprehensible and condemnable."

At the United Nations Rouhani declared that Iran is prepared to engage in nuclear talks and proclaimed: "Nuclear weapons and other weapons of mass destruction have no place in Iran's security and defense doctrine, and contradict our fundamental religious and ethical convictions."

Two questions immediately surface: First, is this for real? Certainly we do not accept all diplomatic or political statements at face value. But neither should countries make the same mistakes that Golda Meir made and reject them out of hand. Secondly, can Rouhani deliver a nuclear agreement since the ultimate decision is made by Iran's supreme leader Ayatollah Ali Khamenei? As of now, it appears that he can.

As one Iranian insider commented, Rouhani would not be reaching out at this moment without the support of the Ayatollah. This is confirmed by the *New York Times* report that the Iranian hard line institutions that oppose Rouhani—the Revolutionary Guards, the Prayer venues, the judiciary and the state broadcasters—have all been ordered by Ayatollah Khamenei not to sabotage Rouhani's efforts with criticism or controversial remarks.

This brings us back to the history leading up to the Yom Kippur War. The question is: has Netanyahu learned anything from Golda Meir's blunders? It appears not. He rejects Rouhani as a wolf in sheep's clothing. He directed the Israeli U.N. delegation to boycott the Iranian president's speech declaring that Iran is only offering "cosmetic concessions." The Israeli delegation dramatically walked out of the chamber immediately before Rouhani began speaking without hearing his message.

What is very scary is that the *Times* reported, "After a year in which Jerusalem and Washington had been more aligned on Iran, some now worry that Mr Rouhani's diplomatic offensive and relative embrace it has received could revive the momentum for a unilateral Israeli strike."

It is apparent that Benjamin Netanyahu is no more flexible than was Golda Meir. He has learned nothing from the history of his own nation. He rejects diplomacy and relies on Israel's military might, which did not stop the outbreak of the Yom Kippur War.

In his U.N. speech President Obama said, "Iran's conciliatory words will have to be matched by action that is transparent and verifiable." That is a given, but such action is the outcome of diplomacy. Unlike Israel, our government did not boycott Rouhani's speech. Rather we are using it as a building block toward a peaceful resolution. Let us hope that the Obama administration can temper any military decisions by a recalcitrant Netanyahu.

A PALESTINIAN STATE

U.N. Recognition of Palestine—Good or Bad for Israel?
10/19/11

Let me make an analogy. Let us assume that two people are negotiating over how to split a pizza pie. As they carry on protracted discussion one of the two is ever more rapidly consuming the pie. The other person soon realizes that he can no longer participate in this charade of negotiations and that the intent of the other person is to consume the whole pie.

If his life depended on eating a portion of that pie, we would not expect him to walk away meekly. He may even turn to violence or some other tactic. Maybe he would call upon others to help him dissuade the pizza eater to control his voracious appetite. If his life depended on his receiving a portion of that pie, he would have to do something. We cannot expect less of him.

Certainly the future life of a Palestinian state depends on stopping the continual increase of Israeli settlers on the West Bank and in East Jerusalem, yet Israel continues the expansion of settlements. Now we can discuss the current Palestinian request for recognition as a state in the United Nations.

The Palestinians tried other tactics without much success. There were two intifadas with limited results (putting aside the ethical problem of the use of terrorism). They are initiating a BDS campaign against Israel—boycott, divestment and sanctions. The prospect of this working—of isolating Israel in the world community of nations—is fairly good over the long run, but it is a process that can take 10 to 20 years.

Meanwhile Israel is creating facts on the ground that are analogous to its consuming the entire pizza pie. If you doubt this last statement, Israel's answer to the Palestinian Authority's request for U.N. membership was to announce that it will construct 1,100 new Jewish housing units in East Jerusalem. It is spitting in the face of Palestinian aspirations.

Benjamin Netanyahu, in his speech before the joint session of Congress, proclaimed that the Palestinians "want a country, but not peace." He also said that Israel would not negotiate with the Palestinian Authority as long as it pursued a unity government with Hamas: "The Palestinian Authority must choose either peace with Israel or peace with Hamas." For many years Israel insisted that it was impossible to bargain a peace treaty with half a people (the West bank without Gaza). Now it objects to bargaining with a united Palestinian people, if, in fact, Fatah and Hamas can overcome their animosity and create a truly whole Palestine.

Netanyahu's official position is that his government will not bargain with a terrorist organization. Period. I am writing this column immediately after the announcement that Israel has agreed to swap over a thousand Palestinian prisoners for the release of Gilad Shalit. This deal was the result of extensive negotiations with Hamas over a two year period—the same two years that Netanyahu has been proclaiming that he refuses to negotiate peace with a terrorist organization.

But he had no problem talking to Hamas to rescue one Israeli soldier. Is the life of one soldier more important than a peace agreement that could save thousands of lives? The obvious reason that Netanyahu's government refused to confront the peace issue is that it wanted to consume more of the pizza pie—and there are parties in his coalition government that demand a Greater Israel that encompasses the whole of Palestine from the Mediterranean to the Jordan River, the whole pie.

Now the key question: Is Palestinian statehood, recognized by the United Nations, good or bad for Israel? If you believe AIPAC and its cohorts, it would be a disaster. I believe, along with influential Israeli experts (more on this later), that it would be very good for Israel. The main problem in the peace negotiations is the lack of equal bargaining power. Israel is a recognized state with a powerful army. Palestine is neither a recognized state, nor has it much military capability. It is this lack of symmetry that feeds Netanyahu's hubris (chutzpah).

In the long run, if there is not a breakthrough in the peace process, the likelihood of a third and more lethal intifada is great. This is patently bad for Israel, certainly worse than their fears concerning Palestinian statehood. U.N. recognition gives the Palestinians the dignity that they long for and need. Increased bargaining power and dignity for the Palestinians will produce a peace treaty that will give Israel the security that it needs—long term security with a peaceful neighbor, not the kind of tentative security based on military might that it currently has.

I mentioned that I am not alone in this analysis. Efraim Halevy, former head of the Mossad (Israel's CIA) believes that a Palestinian state with provisional borders should be recognized now. So does Shaul Mofaz, former chief of staff of the Israel Defense Forces (IDF) and currently head of the Knesset Defense Committee.

I am indebted to J.J. Goldberg of the *Forward* for his in-depth reporting of the positions of the former heads of the Israeli intelligence services concerning Palestinian statehood. He writes: "Here is a rough roll call: Of the six living IDF chiefs, all but (one) favors a Palestinian state within borders, either now or eventually, on the 1967 lines. Of the six living ex-Shin Bet (Israel's FBI) chiefs, all say likewise except Yuval Diskin, who retired this summer and hasn't yet spoken publicly. Of the seven living ex-Mossad chiefs, the three oldest haven't spoken out lately; all the others publicly support the positions described."

How different is the consensus in the American Jewish community. The problem is that we listen to the propaganda of the Netanyahu government without delving deeper into the Israeli dialogue. Palestinian statehood, approved by the U.N., can bring peace and stability to Israel. American Jewry should support it. Our government should be supporting it, not threatening to veto it.

A Palestinian Unity Government is Good for Israel
5/18/11

Three weeks ago Fatah and Hamas dramatically announced that they would form a Unity Government in a joint effort to attain an independent Palestinian state in the West Bank and Gaza. This détente was brokered by the new Egyptian regime.

Some observers believe that the marriage will not last, but most experts think that it will. Egypt will open the Rafah crossing into its country, thereby breaking the hermetic seal that Israel has placed around the Gaza Strip. This will dramatically alter life in Gaza. The price that Egypt requires is that Hamas must make a real commitment to the Unity Government.

For its part, in the past Fatah would never seriously attempt unity with Hamas for it would risk losing both monetary and diplomatic support from its protector, the United States. But recent developments convinced Mahmoud Abbas that in the end the U.S. will always be in the pocket of the Jewish and fundamentalist Christian lobbyists. The final breaking point was when this country vetoed a U.N. Security Council resolution calling on Israel to stop construction on the West Bank—a position that is official American policy. At that point we lost all leverage over Abbas. We destroyed our standing as an honest broker.

Israeli government reaction was to be expected. It gave Netanyahu and his right-wing coalition an ideal excuse to further refuse to negotiate a peace settlement and more time to expand the "facts on the ground" in its quest to create a Greater Israel from the Mediterranean to the Jordan River.

Netanyahu has always maintained that Fatah was not a reliable bargaining partner since he did not represent all of the Palestinians (how could one bargain with half a people?). Now he maintains that he won't bargain with the whole people because Hamas is a terrorist organization. His bottom line is he won't bargain. Period. He will participate in a charade for international consumption all the while his minions are gobbling up West Bank real estate.

Others in Israel see the Unity Government as "a strategic opportunity." *Haaretz* reports that Israeli Foreign Ministry professionals issued a confidential report that stated: "The Palestinian move is not only a security threat but also a strategic opportunity to create genuine change in the Palestinian context. Such change may serve the long-term interests of Israel."

The Israelis on the street have consistently supported speaking with Hamas. In 2008 64 percent of Israelis favored talking with Hamas. In June, 2010, after the traumatic flotilla event, that figure dropped to 49 percent, and in March of this year it has climbed again to 53 percent. The polls asked whether one would talk to Hamas separately. It is assumed that the percentage would rise dramatically if Hamas were part of a Unity Government with Fatah.

Prominent Israeli security figures have long supported negotiations with Hamas. Three years ago I reported that the group included former Shin Bet head Yaacov Peri, former National Security Advisor Giora Eiland and former IDF Chief of Staff Shaul Mofaz.

Efraim Halevy, a noted hawk, who served three prime ministers as chief of Mossad, called upon both the Bush administration and Israel to talk to Hamas. After the recent announcement of a proposed Palestinian Unity Government he reiterated his position: "There will be no serious progress in the Israeli-Palestinian conflict without some way of including Hamas in the process so as to transform them from being part of the problem to being part of the solution."

The major disappointment in the Obama administration is that it continues the bankrupt policies of the Bush era. It still adheres to the formula that it will not talk to Hamas until it renounces violence, recognizes Israel and agrees to follow previous obligations of the Palestinian Authority. This ignores the fact that the current moderate PLO and Fatah once had the same position that Hamas has today. These concessions come after negotiations, not before.

I believe that Obama understands this but has capitulated to AIPAC and the Evangelicals and Congress, which has been bought and paid for by the

Israeli lobby. I would like to know how much right-wing Jewish money has gone to Ileana Ros-Lehtinen, our Miami-Dade County congresswoman who is a champion of the Netanyahu government and is stridently against this Palestinian Unity Government.

The usual suspects in Congress are calling for the U.S. to cut off all aid to the Palestinian Authority unless it renounces its unity with Hamas. The only result of this move would be for the new Palestinian Unity Government to turn to Europe or Iran for funding. Abbas has rightly given up on us, and we have lost our ability to control events. Thank God, because we haven't done a very good job so far—thanks to our internal political pressures.

The nonagenarian ex-Knesset member Uri Avnery has written: "Hamas is part of Palestinian reality. Sure, it is extremist, but as the British have taught us many times, it is better to make peace with extremists than with moderates. Make peace with the moderates, and you must still deal with the extremists. Make peace with the extremists and the business is finished." Obama and the State Department should know this.

But Avnery continues: "Actually, Hamas is not quite as extreme as it likes to present itself. It has declared many times that it will accept a peace agreement based on the 1967 lines signed by Mahmoud Abbas if it is ratified by the people in a referendum or a vote in parliament."

With the new Unity Government on the horizon, with the potential that Hamas will actually be a part of the solution, in the words of the Israeli Foreign Ministry professionals, we are presented with "a strategic opportunity."

I don't expect Netanyahu and his reactionary coalition to accept this fact, but I hope that the U.S. State department will put domestic political considerations aside and seize the moment. But knowing politicians in general, even intelligent Democratic politicians, I won't bet the family farm on it.

Peace with a Palestinian Unity Government?
4/25/12

Once again Fatah and Hamas have announced the formation of a Palestinian Unity Government. Their accord was first signed last May and almost one year later they are still struggling to produce a formula that will bring it to fruition. It was recently announced that the Palestinian Authority President Mahmoud Abbas would head the new government. Although there is much skepticism that there actually will be a Unity Government, many experts believe that in the end it will have to come to pass—if for no other reason the Palestinian quest for statehood depends on it.

Israeli Prime Minister Benjamin Netanyahu responded to the latest developments with the comment he would not negotiate with a Unity Government because Hamas is "an Iranian-backed terror organization committed to Israel's destruction." For once, he is correct, but only technically; and he should deal with it because you bargain with enemies not friends.

But let's discuss Netanyahu's three points. First, Hamas certainly has used terrorism in its fight for Palestinian independence. However, all countries and liberation movements have utilized terrorism. The Stern Gang and the Irgun used terrorism against the British to drive them out of Palestine and against Arab villagers to ethnic cleanse them from what would become Israel. Yitzhak Shamir proclaimed: "Neither Jewish ethics nor Jewish tradition can disqualify terrorism as a means of combat. Rather, terrorism had a great part to play in our war against the occupier." And he subsequently became Prime Minister of Israel.

The precise definition of terrorism is the targeting of civilians in an effort to obtain a military end. My country, the United States, did this in 1945 when we fire-bombed 67 Japanese cities killing over a million old men, women and children in our effort to force the Japanese to surrender so that we would not have to lose what we expected would be over a million military lives in an invasion of their mainland.

So it's a little hypocritical for either Israel or the United States to declare that it would not bargain with a terrorist. People in glass houses should not throw stones. In fact, both countries have done it and will continue to do so. Netanyahu had no trouble bargaining with Hamas to secure the release of one Israeli soldier, Gilead Schalit, so why should he hesitate to bargain for a peace that could save many lives? Our State Department interacts with despotic governments that utilize terrorism every day, so why should we single out Hamas as the one exception, except to placate the domestic Israel lobby?

Hamas is Iranian backed and its Prime Minister, Ismail Haniyah, recently traveled to Iran and reiterated there its commitment to Israel's destruction. He sounded like an Iranian Mullah. This belies the real nature of Hamas. Of course, it takes money from where it could get it, and other than Iran the pickings have been lean. These outbursts are more a part of economic necessity than of theology.

This point is underscored by the recent statement of an influential Hamas leader that Hamas would not participate in a war between Israel and Iran if it were to come to pass. Obviously, Hamas is willing to embrace Iranian money but not its political or military designs.

Hamas is an Islamic movement, but quite different than the Iranian Mullahs or al Qaeda. I have personally heard two Israeli academic experts in this field declare that Hamas is a nationalist movement overlaid with religion rather than a religious movement overlaid with nationalism. Yes, they are religious, just as a good part of Netanyahu's government is comprised of Orthodox Jews. But, there is sensible religion and fanatic religion. The Hamas leadership is definitely of the former.

The Hamas leaders are not the products of some radical Islamic madrasa where they eschew secular knowledge and find all truth in the Quran. Khaled Meshal, the Chairman of Hamas' Political Bureau (the number one person in the movement), earned a Bachelor of Science degree in Physics from Kuwait University and he taught in the Kuwaiti school system for eight years. Ismail Haniyah, Hamas' Prime Minister, received a Bachelor degree in Islamic literature from the Islamic University of Gaza, where he later acted as Dean. This is a real university, not a madrasa. Don't let the name fool you—think of the Hebrew University in Jerusalem. It teaches more than Hebrew.

The bottom line is that, yes, Hamas accepts money from Iran, but it reflects a different kind of Islam (actually it is Sunni while Iran is Shiite), much more accommodating to reality and compromise. These are people whom you could talk to if you are really interested in peace and a two-state solution rather than a Greater Israel from the Mediterranean Sea to the Jordan River.

Hamas is a terrorist organization, backed by Iran, and now on to Netanyahu's third point: They are committed to the destruction of Israel; as proof just listen to Haniya's recent Teheran speech. It was this kind of thinking that led Israel to outlaw even speaking to any Palestinian Liberation Organization person during the 1980's. All you had to do was read the PLO Charter to realize that they would never make peace. But they did. The charter was changed and now President Abbas (who was Yassir Arafat's number two man!) is a moderate that Israel recognizes as a legitimate negotiator.

Meshal, the most militant of the Hamas leadership, has been telling the world that it should not pay attention to its charter but rather to its current actions. It has ceded the presidency of the incipient Unity Government to the more conservative Fatah leadership. It has clearly stated that Abbas should do the bargaining with Israel and if the outcome is fair and equitable to Palestinian national aspirations that it would support a peace settlement.

Netanyahu insists that Hamas recognize Israel before the negotiations begin rather than as a result of negotiations. Egypt and Jordan never recognized Israel's legitimacy before they made peace. Why should Hamas be held to a higher standard? The PLO recognized Israel and all it got for it has been protracted negotiations while the West bank is being colonized by Jewish religious fanatics. Hamas will not make that mistake again. Its position is eminently rational: Talk to us and then we can make peace after the definite outline of a Palestinian state is accepted by Israel.

The very fact that Meshal has relocated to Qatar from Damascus and that Qatar will be a moderating influence on the movement points to a new beginning if Netanyahu can bring himself to the table opposite a Unity Government. I am sorry to say that I believe this will not happen because his right-wing coalition is more interested in West bank land than peace. As a rabbi and Jew, this saddens me.

THE JEWISH LOBBY

The Power of AIPAC Continues
9/7/11

During the congressional recess this past month 81 members of the House of Representatives enjoyed a deluxe one week tour of Israel (first class accommodations and air travel) compliments of the American Israel Public Affairs Committee (AIPAC), a registered lobby for Israel.

Well, not exactly. It wasn't paid for by AIPAC, but rather by its affiliated not-for-profit charity, the American Israel Education Foundation. The AIEF is an amazing organization of which no one has ever heard. This past year it had income of $26 million and it coordinated three trips to Israel, one for 26 Democratic House members and two for 55 Republicans. Yet it has no paid employees.

AIPAC acknowledges that it contributed more than $3 million of employee salaries to cover the staff requirements of the AIEF. So what we have here is a tax-deductible not-for-profit front organization for a non-tax-deductible lobby. It means that these propaganda trips, so important to the Netanyahu government, are paid for in part by American taxpayers since a good portion of that $26 million ends up as tax deductions for American millionaires contributing to AIPAC, excuse me, contributing to its front organization, AIEF. It's amazing that someone hasn't filed suit to stop this charade.

Why am I so exercised over this? I certainly want people to visit Israel and be pro-Israel. But what is being pro-Israel? AIPAC's definition is to blindly support the Netanyahu government, which in turn supports the settler fanatics on the West Bank, which in turn precludes any peace settlement with the Palestinians, and finally, which in turn consigns Israel to another 100 years of strife and eventual isolation from the rest of the world. Is this what liberal Jews want for Israel?

Yet AIPAC is extremely effective. It has basically purchased the Congress, not only through trips to Israel but by the direct political contributions of the many political action committees (PACS) that are part of the AIPAC entourage. And that power is now increased exponentially since the Supreme Court in the *Citizens United* case has allowed anonymous contributions with no limits.

There is nothing nefarious about AIPAC. We Jews are very sensitive about being perceived as controlling our government as if it were vindication of the notorious Protocols of Zion tract. Abe Foxman of the ADL even wrote a book entitled, "The Deadliest Lies—The Israel Lobby and the Myth of Jewish Control." But there is nothing of which to be ashamed. Everyone buys our Congress. AIPAC is no more nefarious than the Wall Street lobby, the insurance lobby, the oil lobby (Exxon-Mobil pays no taxes) etc.

AIPAC's power extends to the presidency as well. Jennifer Rubin, a columnist for the *Washington Post* and a staunch supporter of Israel and Netanyahu, reported that AIPAC has been indirectly pressuring President Obama. There is no doubt that our president lives in fear of AIPAC during this crucial pre-election year. This was reflected in a *Haaretz* headline this past month concerning our new ambassador to Israel: "New U.S. envoy in Israel to clear obstacles for Obama's second term." The report continued, "Dan Shapiro was not sent here to promote peace between Israeli and Palestinian leaders, but between Obama and American Jewish leaders."

My only critique of *Haaretz* is that it mislabels "American Jewish Leaders" as the small, wealthy and conservative (at least as it relates to Israel) crowd that purports to speak for the generally liberal six million American Jews (after all, 78 percent of us voted Democratic in the last election). The peace process is on hold, thanks to AIPAC. This does not reflect the desires of the overwhelming percentage of American Jews.

All of the above has a deleterious effect on American Jewry and on the United States in general. Let's start with the Jews. AIPAC has convinced a portion of our community that it's OK to send a Michelle Bachman to Israel. (The 2009 trip. This year she was busy in Iowa.) It's OK for Jews to align themselves with the evangelical right. Alan Dershowitz just wrote an opinion piece proclaiming that it is wonderful that Glenn Beck plans to hold an event in Israel ("I certainly admire Beck's decision to go to Israel.") My God, this is the Glenn Beck that is so right-wing that he was thrown off Fox News. All sins are forgiven if one shows fealty to Israel.

I know the retort: We can work with them on Israel, but we don't have to agree with them on the other social issues that we hold so dear. It sounds good, but it doesn't work that way. In real life, you make a little concession here and there to placate your "friends," and after a time you no longer stand for what you once stood. Real politics get in the way. Support of Netanyahu trumps support of women's free choice or the separation of church and state. Forget the rhetoric; anyone involved in politics knows what happens in the back room.

It's also bad for America. AIPAC is very proud of its bipartisan support. Thus it funnels money (through friendly PACS) to a Michelle Bachman or a Tom Tancredo (the former congressman from Colorado who spewed anti-immigration and anti-Muslim hatred before mercifully being defeated a few years ago). Jewish money going to Tea Party fanatics because they are "pro-Israel," at least by AIPAC standards, makes our Jewish community complicit in the destruction of our social fabric, the intended elimination of Social Security, Medicare and Medicaid, Pell Grants for needy students, etc.

Why funnel money to these Neanderthals? Because AIPAC tells us it's good for Israel. To the contrary, it's bad for Israel. It's bad for Judaism. It's bad for America. There is something dysfunctional in our Jewish community that allows the power of AIPAC to continue. It's about time that the average Jew recognizes this reality.

President Carter's Al Het and What it Means
1/13/10

It is a reflection of the power of the Israel lobby and its ability to demonize anyone who dares to criticize Israel that President Jimmy Carter recently apologized to the Jewish community in a formal Al Het (a plea for forgiveness, the Jewish equivalent of Mea Culpa).

In a letter to JTA (the Jewish AP, formerly known as the Jewish Telegraphic Agency) Carter wrote: "We must recognize Israel's achievements under difficult circumstances, even as we strive in a positive way to help Israel continue to improve its relations with its Arab populations, but we must not permit criticisms for improvement to stigmatize Israel. As I would have noted at Rosh Hashanah and Yom Kippur, but which is appropriate at any time of the year, I offer an Al Het for any words or deeds of mine that may have done so."

How sad it is for me to see an ex-president of this nation capitulate to Jewish pressure, especially since he has no real reason to apologize. Very few Jews read his book "Palestine: Peace not Apartheid," yet most Jews that I know are convinced that he is anti-Israel, or worse yet, anti-Jewish. This reminds me of the mindless Christians who picketed Martin Scorcese's brilliant movie "The Last Temptation of Christ" having never seen it.

Self-appointed leaders like Alan Dershowitz rushed into the fray to literally defile a president who personally brought Menachem Begin and Anwar Sadat to the peace table to Israel's everlasting benefit. Anyone who read the book would know that Carter was describing the West Bank, not Israel proper. In fact, he went out of his way to praise Israel as the only democracy in the Middle East. Carter has nothing for which to apologize.

I have been in the West Bank often and it is an apartheid society. There are Jew-only roads on which West Bank Palestinians cannot drive. The movement of the local Arab population is restricted by approximately 500 checkpoints manned by Israeli soldiers, yet Jewish settlers in the West Bank have total freedom of movement. I don't know what you would call this, but I call it apartheid, as do many liberal Israeli politicians. One can argue over the security need for the checkpoints (a spurious argument in most cases) but one cannot argue over the outcome, which is apartheid.

Carter has also been demonized for statements on his book tour intimating that the pro-Israel lobby has inhibited an evenhanded U.S. policy concerning Israelis and Palestinians. Is there really any doubt about that? Just as the Cuban lobby has affected U.S. foreign policy with regard to Cuba, it is incontrovertible that the Israel lobby has affected American foreign policy. If we had no effect, what has AIPAC been doing all these years? Are we to believe that lobbies in general have no effect on Washington legislation or foreign policy? If you believe that you are not sharing the same planet as I inhabit. Yet Carter has been demonized for stating the obvious.

JTA reported that President Carter chose to apologize because his grandson, a 34-year-old Atlanta lawyer, may run for State Senator if the incumbent is confirmed as ambassador to Singapore. It is assumed that the younger Carter has political ambitions beyond this district and his grandfather fears that Jewish animus against him would be transferred to his grandson. It is understandable—what we won't do for our grandchildren!

JTA also reports that Carter had been personally hurt by the irrational avalanche of calumny against him by erstwhile Jewish friends. It is reported that longtime friends Stuart Eizenstat and Rabbi Alvin Sugarman urged him to approach the Jewish community. Carter wanted to give his Al Het in a synagogue or another Jewish setting but he was rebuffed, so he had to settle for a letter to the JTA. Isn't it amazing that Jews have so demonized this man that he could not find an invitation to a single synagogue or Jewish setting? Something is wrong in our community.

It was particularly sad for me to see Carter in the subsequent JTA interview attempt to curry favor with Jews and show impartiality by criticizing the

Palestinians for not accepting merely a partial halt to West Bank settlements before agreeing to peace talks. Carter knows that the Oslo Accords in 1993 demanded a complete halt to settlements by Jews and a complete halt to violence by Palestinians as a prerequisite to peace talks. Now Jews say that some new settlements should be allowed. If we show some slack to Jews I assume that we must logically allow the Palestinians a little room to kill a few Israelis along the way. After all, each side should have an equal amount of wiggle room.

Oh, but this conversation has gone much beyond the humbling of an ex-American president out of love for his grandchild. Getting back to the core of the column, this whole affair reflects the power of the American Jewish lobby and especially AIPAC. This scares me, because in their misguided love for Israel, American Jews inhibit genuine peace talks and consign Israel to continue as a garrison state, rather than a country at peace with its neighbors. In the long run, garrison states fail.

Not to end this column on such a dour note, I have hope that the new liberal pro-Israel, pro-peace lobby, J-Street, will begin to break AIPAC's hold on the Jewish community. Then we will not have the need to demonize anyone who dares to propose legitimate criticism of Israel or of the American Jewish community. We should all live to see that day.

Pressure Tactics of the Jewish Lobby
5/26/09

U.S.-Israeli relations are becoming more hopeful or are deteriorating, depending on your point of view. One thing is for sure—the Obama administration will not become a cheering squad for the Israeli government as was the Bush administration.

Chief of Staff Rahm Emanuel recently told an AIPAC donors' conference that, "Relations between Israel and the U.S. are unbreakable." But Israel's largest newspaper *Yediot Acharanot* reported that Emanuel told an American Jewish leader that, "In the next four years there will be a final agreement between Israel and the Palestinians, based on 'two states for two peoples,' and we couldn't care less who the prime minister is."

Haaretz, Israel's *New York Times*, published a classified document between General James Jones, national security advisor to President Obama, and a European foreign minister where he wrote, "The new administration will convince Israel to compromise on the Palestinian question. We will not push Israel under the wheels of a bus, but we will be more forceful toward Israel than we have been under Bush."

The clash begins with the Israeli policy decision that denies the validity of a Palestinian state. This position forms the basis for the new coalition government. Netanyahu could have formed a coalition with Kadima and the Labor party that would have recognized a two-state solution, but he didn't because he has no intention of allowing the Palestinians an independent state in the West Bank and Gaza.

Even if he were pliable under American pressure he would have to convince Foreign Minister Avigdor Lieberman and his Israel Our Home Party to accept American terms. Without Lieberman in the coalition his majority in the Knesset evaporates and his government falls. Lieberman is an acknowledged racist who has suggested nuking Hamas in Gaza and deporting Israeli Arab citizens from Israel. He once proposed bombing the Aswan dam. The chance of Netanyahu convincing Lieberman to support a two-state solution is equal to the possibility of converting the pope to Judaism.

The political scientist and former member of the Knesset Uri Avnery suggests that Netanyahu's survival will be based on the well-used Israeli tactic of deception. He writes: "Now the task is to present to the world, and especially the US and Europe, a false picture, pretending that our new government is yearning for peace, acting for peace, indeed turning every stone in search of peace—while doing the exact opposite. The world will be submerged by a deluge of declarations and promises accompanied by lots of meaningless gestures, conferences and meetings."

Avnery continues: "But deceiving, like dancing the tango, takes two: one who deceives and one who wants to be deceived. Netanyahu believes that Obama will want to be deceived. Why would he want to quarrel with Israel, confront the mighty pro-Israel lobby and the US Congress, when he can settle for soothing words from Netanyahu? Avnery then asks the question that every American liberal Jew wants answered: "Is Obama ready to play, like most of his predecessors, the role of the deceived lover?"

Jewish pressure will be immense on the administration. No doubt AIPAC will obtain its usual Congressional resolutions declaring the U.S. should not put Israel's security in danger, as if the feeble Palestinians could topple Israel, which most military experts believe to have the third most powerful army in the world.

More right wing Jewish groups, such as the Zionist Organization of America, will declare the Obama administration not only tactically wrong but downright anti-Semitic. I have already received an email diatribe that proclaims, "Make no mistake about it, his (Obama's) twenty years at the feet of Rev. Wright, Louis Farrakhan, Rashid Khalidi and his absorption of Saul Alinsky's writings have sunk in and created a dangerous president whose obvious goal is the extinction of the State of Israel." Of course, this nonsense ignores the fact that the Obama policy is being forged and implemented by traditional, observant Jews such as Rahm Emanuel and David Axelrod.

Expect the usual suspects to flood the talk shows. Alan Dershowitz will probably write another propaganda book defending 'poor little Israel." Some Jewish Federations will use American pressure on Israel as a talking point to raise more money because "only Jews really care about Jews." The Jewish victim mentality will flourish and for some Jews a new Holocaust will be lurking just around the corner.

But, hopefully, the majority of Jews in the United States, who are liberal (having voted 78 percent for Obama) and who are moderate in their religious practice (94 percent of American Jews are Reform, Conservative, Reconstructionist, Humanistic or unaffiliated Jews) will realize that the Obama administration's policy is pro-Israel and is the only long-run solution to Israel's security.

Recognition of a two-state formula was the official policy of all Israeli governments preceding the current Netanyahu coalition. Not to recognize the legitimate national aspirations of the Palestinians is a stance that will guarantee a continued 100-year war in the Middle East.

The question now is whether Obama is ready to play the role of the deceived lover, or will he stand up to the AIPAC crowd?

(Postscript: As of the beginning of 2014 this is still an open question. Secretary of State John Kerry is in the midst of a new American-instigated peace process, but as of this writing no one knows whether Obama will press Netanyahu into accepting a peace agreement that actually establishes a Palestinian state.)

ISRAEL-U.S. RELATIONS

Is Israel Still a Strategic Asset?
4/7/10

By now we are all acquainted with the recent "slap in the face" that Israeli Prime Minister Netanyahu delivered to Vice President Biden when he recently visited Jerusalem. Upon his arrival Netanyahu's government announced plans to build 1600 new Jewish housing units in East Jerusalem against the explicit wishes of our government. While Biden was still in Israel *Haaretz* reported that the Netanyahu government had plans to increase that number to 50,000. These moves obviously undermine chances for a bilateral peace agreement with the Palestinians who want to have East Jerusalem as the capital of their independent state.

In response to this affront to Israel's American partner in the peace process, Biden rushed to the telephone to confer with Washington. The result was that he kept Netanyahu waiting for an hour and one half before arriving for their private dinner.

The more appropriate outrage was expressed by the pro-Israel Jewish columnist Thomas Friedman in the *New York Times*: "The vice president missed a chance to send a powerful public signal: He should have snapped his notebook shut, gotten right back on Air Force Two, flown home and left the following scribbled note behind: 'Message from America to the Israeli government: Friends don't let friends drive drunk. And right now, you're driving drunk. You think you can embarrass your only true ally in the world, to satisfy some domestic political need, with no consequences? You have lost contact with reality. Call us when you're serious. We need to focus on building our country.'"

Of course, traditional Israeli enemies and anti-Semites love the intransigence of the current Israeli government. Pat Buchanan crowed: "We

126

got what grovelers deserve . . . Joe's performance before he got the wet mitten across the face only underscored the point: The mighty superpower is a poodle of Israel." The sad fact is that as vicious as Buchanan is, he may not be wrong. Even the Israeli commentator, Amir Oren, wrote in *Haaretz*: "The American dog is tired of being wagged by the Israeli tail. And the dog doesn't care if the tail in not its own master, or is also being wagged by the tip of the settlers' tail."

The Israeli newspaper *Yediot Ahronoth* reported that at their dinner Biden did tell Netanyahu that "This is starting to get dangerous for us. What you're doing here undermines the security of our troops who are fighting in Iraq, Afghanistan and Pakistan. That endangers us and it endangers regional peace."

Biden's comment did not represent a spur-of-the-moment comment. It reflected current re-evaluation of American policy. General David Petraeus recently testified before the Senate Armed Services Committee that the number one "root cause of instability" in the area under his command (the Middle East) is "insufficient progress toward a comprehensive Middle East peace."

General Petraeus is a student of international relations as well as the most respected general in America. He has a Ph.D. from Princeton and was a professor at West Point before becoming the hero of the Iraq war. Before the Senate committee he listed six reasons why the United States needs an Israeli-Palestinian peace agreement (exclusive of Israel's needs). I shall quote him directly but I will insert the numerals to clearly distinguish the points.

He testified: "The enduring hostilities between Israel and some of its neighbors present distinct challenges to our ability to advance our interests in the AOR (area of responsibility). Israeli-Palestinian tensions (1) often flair into violence and large-scale armed confrontations. (2) The conflict foments anti-American sentiment, due to a perception of U.S. favoritism for Israel. (3) Arab anger over the Palestinian question limits the strength and depth of U.S. partnerships with governments and people in the AOR and (4) weakens the legitimacy of moderate regimes in the Arab world. (5) Meanwhile, al-Qaeda and other militant groups exploit that anger to mobilize support. (6) The conflict also gives Iran influence in the Arab world through its clients, Lebanese Hisballah and Hamas."

General Petraeus sent his senior officers from CENTCOM (Central Command) to brief Joint Chiefs of Staff Chairman Adm. Michael Mullen and it is reported in *Foreign Policy* "that the 33-slide, 45-minute Power Point briefing stunned Mullen." Here we begin to see a realization, at least in the military, that Israeli and American interests do not always coincide. As much as American Jews wish it were not true, and as much as the Israeli lobby will insist that Israel and America always share the same foreign policy objectives, the fact is that we are two distinct nations with sometimes contradictory needs.

I hate to quote Pat Buchanan, a man I suspect of all kinds of ill feelings, but he is correct when he writes: "Israeli and U.S. interests often run parallel, but they are not the same. Israel is concerned with a neighborhood. We are concerned with a world of 300 million Arabs and a billion Muslims. Our policies cannot be the same. If they are, we will end up with all of Israel's enemies, who are legion, and only Israel's friends, who are few." I amend this statement to say that it reflects our relationship with the disastrous Netanyahu government, not to the nation as a whole. But there is no doubt that serious people in and out of government are looking at the concept, thanks to Netanyahu and his cohorts, that Israel is no longer a strategic asset to America.

How will American Jews react to this? Specifically, how will the Israel lobby react? Some believe that it will brand General Petraeus an anti-Semite, an old and true tactic. If so, the Israel lobby should beware. As Mark Perry in *Foreign Policy* pointed out, "There are important and powerful lobbies in America: the NRA, the American Medical Association, the lawyers—and the Israeli lobby. But no lobby is as important, or as powerful, as the U.S. military." I believe that it behooves us Jews not to take on the generals. I remember that it was when Joe McCarthy turned on the military that the establishment decided to cut his legs off.

The Israeli commentator and ex-Knesset Member Uri Avneri writes with approval: "Most American Jews are ready to do anything—just anything—for the government of Israel. With one exception: they will not do anything that appears to hurt the security of the United States. When the flag of security is hoisted, the Jews, like all Americans, snap to attention and salute."

I agree and as an American I'm proud of that. I am a committed Jew, but my nationality is American, not Israeli. I love Israel as much as I loathe its current government. But when Netanyahu puts Israeli above American interests, I know where I stand. And I believe that most American Jews agree with me. The Israel lobby should take heed. My advice: Embrace the generals and tell Israel to stop driving drunk.

Chuck Hagel is Good for America and Israel
2/20/13

I am writing on February 13th, approximately a week before you will be reading this and during the interregnum on Chuck Hagel's Senate confirmation hearings. As expected, he is being attacked by Republicans as a payback for his support of President Obama in the last election. That is of little interest to me. I want to focus on the Jewish opposition to his appointment as Secretary of Defense.

To begin, we find the usual outbursts from right-wing Jewish ideologues. Elliot Abrams, a national security advisor to George Bush and one of the architects of the Iraq war, labeled Hagel an anti-Semite. William Kristol's Emergency Committee for Israel opposes him because he has called for direct talks with groups like Hamas. Well, so have some ex-chiefs of Israel's Shin Bet (the Israeli FBI and the agency in charge of anti-terrorism—but that will be the topic of a future column). The sometime commentator and television personality Ben Stein has declared Hagel, "the most clearly anti-Israel, anti-Semitic member of the Senate." He concludes, "This means a vote to confirm Mr. Hagel is a vote that expresses no interest in whether Israel survives."

Putting aside these excesses, there are two statements by Hagel that have been scrutinized in the press as being either anti-Semitic or anti-Israel.

First, Hagel made reference to AIPAC as the "Jewish lobby." Jennifer Rubin, the *Washington Post's* resident Jewish conservative, considered this, "the worst expression of anti-Semitism, the accusation of disloyalty. There is no other meaning to Hagel's phrase, 'Jewish lobby'." But Rabbi Henry Siegman, the ex-head of both the Synagogue Council of America and the American Jewish Congress, one of the elder statesmen of the Jewish community, writing in the *New York Times*, reminded us that since the founding of AIPAC in 1951 everyone in the Jewish community has referred to AIPAC as "the Jewish lobby for Israel."

I find Hagel's reference to the Jewish lobby to be accurate. There are two primary conservative lobbies in Washington that support Israel, the Jewish lobby and the Evangelical lobby. Lobbying is as American as apple pie. Why should the Jewish community that is actively participating in the American political system try to hide its identity. Whether that lobby is conservative (AIPAC) or liberal (J-Street), its Jewish source is nothing of which to be ashamed.

Was Hagel inaccurate? The Israeli political pundit and former nine-year Knesset member, Uri Avnery writes: "Many years ago he (Hagel) called the pro-Israel lobby in Washington (would you believe it?) the 'Jewish lobby.' Until then, it was understood that AIPAC is mainly composed of Buddhists and financed by Arab billionaires like Abu Sheldon and Abel al-Adelson."

The second complaint against Hagel is that, probably in reaction to constant pressure from AIPAC, he complained that, "I am an American senator, not an Israeli senator."

This reminds me of the incident when lobbying on behalf of the soon-to-be State of Israel, Rabbi Abba Hillel Silver, the leading Zionist of his time and a man of no small ego, actually stormed President Harry Truman's office and pounded his fists on his desk. Abba Eban wrote that, "Truman regarded Silver with severe aversion . . . (who) came second only to the Soviet Union as a primary target of President Truman's distrust." Yet frustration with the Jewish lobby did not stop Truman from being one of the greatest friends that Israel has ever had. Contrary to the worried American neoconservative Jews, several Israeli generals have come to Hagel's defense.

The irrepressible Uri Avnery understands the meaning of Hagel's comment. He reports that a television advertisement in the recent Israeli elections shows the scene of Netanyahu addressing the US Congress. He writes: "The senators and congressmen are seen wildly applauding after every single sentence, jumping up and down like children in gymnastics class. The text of the clip says: 'When Netanyahu speaks, the world listens!'"

Avnery then tells it like it is, as only an Israeli with his credentials can tell it without being labeled as anti-Semitic or anti-Israel—so forgive me for the extensive quote that follows: "Somebody sent me a satirical piece saying that if Hagel's appointment is not cancelled by the US Senate, Israel will have to use its veto power to block it. In such a case, the senate would have to muster a 90% majority to overcome the veto. If this fails, President Obama would have to choose another Defense Secretary from a list of three names provided by Netanyahu."

Avnery continues: "Americans must be a race of angels—how else to explain the incredible patience with which they suffer the fact that in a vital sphere of US interests, American policy is dictated by a foreign country? . . . I have warned many times that this can't go on forever. Sooner or later real anti-Semites—a dangerous breed—will exploit this situation to gain legitimacy. The hubris of AIPAC bears poisonous fruit."

Finally, Avnery comments: "The saddest part of the story is that all these false 'friends of Israel' in the US Congress and media are not really embracing 'Israel.' They are embracing the Israeli right-wing, including the extreme and even fascist right-wing. They are, thereby, helping the right-wing to tighten their control over our country . . . Speaking for myself, I hope that his appointment will herald a new American policy—a policy of support for a sober, rational, liberal, secular, democratic Israel, striving for peace with the Palestinian people."

It is precisely for this reason that liberal pro-Israel and pro-peace Jewish organizations such as J-Street and Americans for Peace Now support the Hagel nomination. Ultimately American policy concerning the Israeli-Palestinian peace talks (or the non-existence thereof), Iran and other Middle East considerations will be determined by President Obama, not the Defense Secretary. But Hagel, who is not afraid to speak his mind, will bring to the table a fresh perspective that the president will have to consider. That will be good for the United States and for Israel.

The Iranian Negotiations—What is Best for America?
12/4/13

Due to newspaper deadlines I am writing this in advance of the publishing date of December 4th. By the time you read this there very well could be an agreement between the P-5+1 powers (U.S., United Kingdom, Russia, China, France and Germany) and Iran over a plan to stop Iran from developing a nuclear bomb; the negotiations could still be in progress or the talks could have failed. No matter the outcome in early December, commentary is desperately needed.

I do not intend to discuss the nitty-gritty of the proceedings. Pundits and politicians have declared their opinions with little or no expertise on nuclear technology. I rely on the opinions of experts from the bargaining powers that a deal would slow down Iranian development and allow time for a more complete agreement in the next six months. Benjamin Netanyahu has proclaimed this is not the case and that the Iranians would be able to cheat and come to nuclear fruition within a few weeks. But that has been his position for the last two years, and the Iranians are not there yet.

In this column I want to review the broader issues of what are at stake for Iran and the United States and to discuss the lobbying of Congress against either a potential or consummated agreement with Iran.

There is no doubt that the economic sanctions have crippled the Iranian economy. Inflation is rampant and unemployment is soaring. The lifting of these sanctions is reason enough for them to give up any aspirations for a nuclear military capability. But there is also a longer range incentive. With a population of over 70 million people to feed, Iran cannot continue solely to rely on the gas and oil industry. It needs to modernize its economy, and to do this, it needs foreign investment and technology to expand its manufacturing base. It realizes that it must become part of the international community. The time is right for these negotiations.

And there are great advantages for America in a peaceful relationship with a non-military-nuclear Iran. To begin, if there is no agreement it is most likely that the Obama administration will follow through on its promise to bomb Iranian nuclear sites. The law of unintentional consequences will come into play. The results can range from mild disruption of Iranian oil, thereby slowing the world economy and our climb out of the Great Recession, to severe economic consequences. One thing is for sure: after Iraq and Afghanistan we don't need another war and we can very easily be dragged into one. American lives are at stake.

Iran can also be a great ally in our fight against al-Qaeda and its offspring. Al Qaeda, a Sunni Muslim movement, hates the Shiite regime in Tehran more than it hates the West. The same day that I write this the Iranian embassy in Beirut was bombed by Sunni militants. America and Iran have a common enemy. This is the reason that immediately after 9/11 the Iranians provided important logistical information to us when we attacked al Qaeda in Afghanistan. A fair deal is good for America.

But Benjamin Netanyahu and his right-wing coalition say that it is bad for Israel. Many political scientists in Israel believe otherwise. But Netanyahu is trapped in a web that he has been spinning for years. He has used Iran as a bogyman to divert energy from a Palestinian peace agreement to this outside danger. If peace were made with Iran, Netanyahu would have to face the prospect of seriously bargaining a two-state solution, thereby destroying hope for a Greater Israel from the Mediterranean Sea to the Jordan River. Netanyahu's coalition and thus his political life depend on either a complete regime change in Tehran or the bombing of Iranian nuclear installations.

To this end he has unleashed the Israel Lobby to kill in Congress any deal that the six major powers would sign with Iran. No other foreign leader has ever inserted himself or herself into an American decision on war or peace affecting our country as has Netanyahu. He has appeared on Sunday talk shows and given interviews to other media. The *Forward* reports: "At a mass gathering of American Jewish leaders in Jerusalem on November 10, Netanyahu made clear his resolve to fight against the still pending interim agreement, and his expectation that American Jews would sign on. Invoking memories of the Holocaust, the Israeli leader stressed the urgent need to stop the deal." Needless to say that Netanyahu perceives the whole world through the lens of the Holocaust.

The usual suspects have taken up the cudgels. Alan Dershowitz likened Secretary Kerry to Neville Chamberlain. Ben Stein, the columnist and television personality, also invoked the Holocaust and the possible "annihilation" of Jews. He queried, "Have we learned absolutely nothing from Hitler?" Someone should tell Jewish conservatives that not every adversary is a Hitler. Jonathan S. Tobin, the neo-Conservative who is an editor of *Commentary Magazine*, claimed that Kerry stabbed Israel in the back.

AIPAC has begun a full-court press on congressmen and senators, many of whom have received large donations from AIPAC supporters. (Of course, money does not talk in American political decision making, especially when war or peace is involved. That's sarcasm, if you didn't pick it up.) Pressure within the organized Jewish community is increasing.

After President Obama conferred with Jewish leaders on October 29th, the ADL broke with AIPAC, the American Jewish Committee and the Simon Wiesenthal Center. Abe Foxman told JTA (the Associated Press of the Jewish world) he supported Obama's request that Jewish groups suspend lobbying for 60 days for new congressional legislation that would intensify sanctions immediately, which, of course, would kill any deal with Iran.

Jewish reaction was swift. One email I received from a right wing Jewish Republican branded Foxman "a cringing Jewish Quisling." He called for people to stop donating to the ADL. Miraculously, on November 10th, merely twelve days later, the *New York Times* reported that Foxman, having just returned from Israel, "is lobbying vigorously against the preliminary deal."

The truth is the vast majority of American Jews put American interests first and is not beholden to Netanyahu or any other Israeli politician. Unfortunately, the major Jewish organizations are controlled by wealthy Republican Jews who meld their Republican interests (anything Obama wants they oppose) with a fealty to a foreign nation, albeit a Jewish foreign nation, which doesn't make it right.

I have no doubt that the overwhelming majority of American Jews, the same people who voted for Obama twice, will ignore the professional lobbies that purport to represent us, and will judge this issue on what is best for America (which happens to be what is best for Israel, but that is beside the point.)

M.J. Rosenberg put it best in a recent column: "The supreme national interest—American lives—must come first. And the lobby and Netanyahu need to be told that they are, to put it gently, out of line. For the sake of world peace, of Israel and Iran, and, above all, of the United States, these negotiations must succeed."

THE SOUL OF ISRAEL

The Unspoken Effects of War
7/8/09

As the Netanyahu government avoids speaking peace with the Palestinians and the Obama administration continues to support the Bush policy of not talking to Hamas, as peace talks seem destined not to happen until many years in the future, American Jews have no understanding of what a lack of peace means to Israeli society.

One can live with tension, sublimated and even overt hatred of the enemy at your border, the enemy under your control, even at the "enemy within," those Arab citizens of your country that many of your compatriots believe are subversive—one can live with all of this and remain a contented or even balanced human being for just so long. It takes its toll, a burden of which gung-ho American Jewish supporters have not even an inkling.

Ponder these statistics: A poll in 2007 reported that merely 69 percent of Jewish Israelis indicated that they want to remain in Israel. That means that nearly one in three Israelis are not happy with their lives in their own country. More striking, the poll showed that one in four Israelis are actually considering leaving Israel, and worse, that figure rises to 50 percent among the young people. In actuality, most of these people will remain in Israel for sundry reasons, but many will act on these impulses. Over 100,000 Israelis have already received European passports.

And many do leave. There are 750,000 former Israelis living outside Israel, and this comprises over 13 percent of Israeli Jews. Sometimes it feels that all of them are living in South Florida. Actually, there are sizable Israeli communities in most large American cities, with a heavy concentration in Los Angeles and New York. Walk the streets of New York and it seems that every other person you hear is speaking Hebrew, if you exclude the Spanish

134

speakers. Ask these Israelis living in the United States and a good portion of them will tell you that some day they will return to Israel—but they won't. That's just Jewish guilt speaking. The truth is that they made *aliyah* to this country.

What would we say of American society if 50 percent of our youth contemplated leaving this country or if 25 percent of them were seriously considering making such a move? What would we say if over 13 percent of Americans, which equals 40 million people, chose to live outside the United States? We would say that we have a serious problem that we should confront immediately.

Imminent war takes its toll in many ways. Not only does it lead to anomie and a desire to get out of your surroundings, but it coarsens society. There was a recent flap in the Israeli press when a group of soldiers who served in the recent war in Gaza claimed that Israeli soldiers killed women and children in cold blood and destroyed property with abandon. The Israeli Army investigated these accusations by its own soldiers and responded that "the IDF is the most moral army in the world."

Writing in the Israeli newspaper *Haaretz,* Gideon Levy sharply contested the IDF's assertion: "The IDF knew very well what its soldiers did in Gaza. It has long ceased to be the most moral army in the world. Far from it—it will not seriously investigate anything . . . The soldiers' transgressions are an inevitable result of the orders given during this brutal operation, and they are the natural continuation of the last nine years, when soldiers killed nearly 5,000 Palestinians, at least half of them innocent civilians, nearly 1,000 of them children and teenagers." Levy concluded: "To do this without any unnecessary moral qualms we have trained our soldiers to think that the lives and property of Palestinians have no value whatsoever. It is part of a process of dehumanization that has endured for dozens of years, the fruits of the occupation."

The fruits of occupation have not only coarsened the soldier. It has affected Israeli society. When my wife, Lynne, and I lived in Israel in 1966 a Jew murdering another Jew was a cause of scandal. Today it is reported on the Israeli news the same way that inner-city crime is reported on American television. Wife-beating was something that a Jew just did not do. Today it is a social problem in Israel, along with alcoholism and drugs.

David Ben Gurion and the founders of the state wanted Israel to be a normal country like all other nations. Well, they got their wish and it isn't pretty. Israel is no longer the benign and innocent country of its youth. There are many factors that contribute to a change in society, but being at war and the dehumanization of another people spill over into your own society. You can't send an 18-year old soldier into the West Bank, teach him to distain other human beings, if not to brutalize them, and expect him to return home without changing his character.

Golda Meir has been famously quoted: "We can forgive the Arabs for killing our children. We cannot forgive them for forcing us to kill their children." She understood the dehumanizing effect on Israeli society. Since I have long argued for peace between Israel and the Palestinians I have been accused of loving Palestinians more than Jews. I respect Palestinians, but it is precisely because I love Jews and Israel that I believe we (America and Israel) must seek peace. I fear what the continued state of war is doing to the Jewish soul.

The Effects of War, Part II
10/7/09

Three months ago I wrote a column entitled "The Unspoken Effects of War" which discussed how Israel's 61-year war with its neighbors coarsened its society. My thesis was that you cannot teach a young soldier to rule over another people without his losing a part of his own humanity.

This insight is shared by many others. The noted Israeli novelist A. B. Yehoshua has written, "Ethical norms that become distorted with respect to the Palestinian population that is under our control disturb the norms and the rules in Israel itself. A light finger on the trigger in Hebron or Gaza also leads to a light finger on the trigger for the crime organizations in Israel as they chase one another through the streets and indiscriminately injure innocent bystanders. Brutal violence by settlers against the army and the police then legitimizes brutal violence by Haredim in the streets of Jerusalem against police officers and municipal workers."

This is not mere speculation. The on-line Jewish magazine the *Tablet* (tabletmag.com) recently ran a five-part investigative series entitled "Holy Land Gangland." Crime tycoons walk around with two bodyguards. Different factions now use female hit-men. The series concluded, "Israelis, divided over many crucial issues, largely agree that organized crime poses one of the gravest threats to their society, taxing the police, challenging the justice system, and terrorizing the streets. While rarely reported about outside of Israel, the new generation of criminals, young and ruthless, are emerging as the country's biggest home-grown menace. If they are not curbed—an effort that would require not only major funding but also a collective effort on behalf of the population—the country may increasingly find itself tearing not from without but from within."

Yehoshua mentioned the Haredim, the ultra-Orthodox community that carries much weight in the Israeli political arena. Professor Noah Efron of Bar Ilan University and a member of the Tel Aviv City Council, writing in *Foreign Policy*, relates a recent incident when an ultra-Orthodox woman had starved her three-year-old son down to 15 pounds. Social workers seized the child and placed him in Hadassah Hospital.

Efron writes: "And then all hell breaks loose. A rabbi declares the event a blood libel, comparing the police to Cossacks, young men in black robes and fur hats take to the streets, setting bus stops and dumpsters ablaze, pelting police with stones, and decrying the doctors of Hadassah as latter-day Josef Mengeles. Someone sets aflame the government welfare and social services building in the ultra-Orthodox neighborhood of Me'ah Shearim; others enter the building, smashing computer screens as they go. In the first three days after the toddler is taken for treatment, dozens more are sent to the hospital with wounds from stones and broken glass, and hundreds of thousands of dollars worth of city property are burned or smashed."

Efron's piece in *Foreign Policy* was brought to my attention by M. J. Rosenberg in his weekly opinion column for the IPF (Israel Policy Forum). His comment on this lawlessness echoes Yehoshua's: "Most of Israel's most pressing problems today come not from outside its borders but from within."

One final source is worth quoting. Reflecting on the increase of random thuggery and killings on the streets of Israel, Yossi Sarid, a former member of the Knesset and Minister of Education, writing in *Haaretz* bemoans, "You may have noticed something while you slept: This country has become hell, into which not only sinners—but also the innocent—may be cast at any moment . . . Israel is insufferably violent and that there is no longer anything to be proud of; only to be ashamed, if not to despair."

Sarid continues: "I still remember my days at New York University. How we would lord it over the 'locals'—in Israel that could not happen, we say to our hosts as we looked, pained, at the daily, blood-curdling manifestations of violence. In Israel, we told them, little children can go around alone and nothing bad will happen to them. Meanwhile, things have gone the other way: Tel Aviv today is more like New York of yesterday, and even like pathological, legendary Chicago."

These voices understand something that Jews in the United States do not, simply because to most Jews in this country Israel is akin to Disney World, especially for the majority of American Jews who have never visited there. It doesn't exist in real time; it is a reflection of Jewish pride and emotion, something like my son the doctor who can do no wrong.

But it's a real country with real problems. American Jews who counsel it to hang tough and continue another 61 years denying a Palestinian state do not realize that they are consigning our beloved Israel to continuing decline in moral fiber. A hundred years of war does not produce a caring society. For Israel's sake, we should be supporting a fair peace with Israel's neighbors rather than demonizing our president for putting pressure on Israel to do what is good for itself.

The Soul of Israel is at Stake
3/23/11

Let's assume that the Palestinians don't deserve their own state, that their nationalist claims do not trump our Jewish God-given right to a Greater Israel from the Mediterranean to the Jordan River (which of course I do not believe), then for Israel's sake I would still have to support a two-state solution—not for the Palestinians but for the sake of the very soul of Israeli society. Sixty-three years of conflict (with a prospect of creating a second Hundred Years War) has eaten away at the very core of Jewish ethics, the supposed foundation of the Zionist dream.

Six years ago I wrote a column also entitled "The Soul of Israel is at Stake" in which I observed that war brutalizes young soldiers who then return to civilian society. I quoted Armored Corps officer Lt. Ziv Maavar's comments in *Maariv* (Israel's second largest and most conservative newspaper): "We are an entire generation of discharged soldiers. We are here to say, 'look what happened to us.' You've ruined an entire generation of fighters, the best of Israeli society, the most ideological, those who were to be the spearhead of society. We all underwent moral corruption. When we went to the induction center to be discharged, we couldn't unload what we went through along with our uniforms. We took it with us, and this is what we've become, violent on the roads, apathetic, insensitive to society, this is who we are. We are not against the army; we are not saying the army is bad. We are talking about a situation. We are bad. An entire generation was sent on a mission, this is its moral price."

Again in 2009 I twice returned to this topic under the caption "The Effects of War" because it is so obvious, yet so disregarded in the American Jewish press. In those articles I tried to explain that serious thinkers in Israel understand that lack of peace with the Palestinians is eroding Israel's moral fiber.

This trend has not abated. Now in the second decade of the 21st century we are seeing a new wrinkle in the deterioration of Israeli society directly linked to the continuing Israeli-Palestinian problem. With the ascension of the political right in the Netanyahu government we have seen an increase in the brutalization of Israeli Arab citizens and the rejection of a two-state solution.

Leading Israeli rabbis have publicly urged Israelis not to rent or sell property to Israeli Arabs who are full citizens of Israel. Thirty rabbis' wives have publicly called upon Jewish girls not to work in places where there are Israeli Arab men. This brings to mind the bigots of the American South under Jim Crow where every black man was a potential despoiler of the virtue of white women. *Haaretz* recently quoted the Israeli Reform rabbi Gilad Kariv: "Israeli society is falling into a deep, dark pit of racism and xenophobia."

In this environment it is becoming problematic whether Israel will settle for anything short of a Greater Israel with the concomitant problem of how to rule over four million Arabs who would have lesser status than full citizenship (the forbidden word is "apartheid").

A few months ago the pro-Israel national correspondent for *The Atlantic*, Jeffrey Goldberg, wrote: "I've had a couple of conversations this week with people, in Jerusalem and out of Jerusalem, that suggest to me that democracy is something less than a religious value for wide swaths of Israeli society." He was referring to four groups: the Haredim (ultra-Orthodox Jews), working class religious Sephardim, the settlers, and the million or so recent Russian immigrants.

Goldberg continued: "I believe it is premature to talk about the end of Israel as a democratic state—mainly because the disposition of the West Bank is still undecided—but I can't say that the thought hasn't crossed my mind that one day Israelis will make the conscious, active decision to preserve the state's Jewish character instead of its democratic character (I use the word 'Jewish' in the demographic sense, not the moral sense, obviously)." The specter of this eventuality haunts me as well.

Look, you don't have to give a damn for Palestinians to want Israel to stop building settlements on the West Bank and to seriously come to terms with the existence of an independent Palestinian state in the West Bank and Gaza. All you have to do is love Israel for what it could be, not for what it is becoming. Continuing war and strife destroys the moral fiber of any society. Israel is not exempt from this law of nature.

The Occupation and the soul of Israel
8/15/12

This past June marked the 45th year of Israeli occupation of the West Bank. In the early years the Israelis claimed that it was a "benevolent occupation," as if such a state of existence could exist. But time has taught us that an occupation hardens the hearts of the occupiers even more than those who have to live under their rule.

I have discussed this phenomenon in earlier columns under the heading "The soul of Israel is at stake." I return to it now because I just received the Annual Report of B'Tselem, the Israeli civil rights organization. B'Tselem, highly respected in Israel, is little known in this country; however, Americans may recognize some members of its board: the writers David Grossman, Amos Oz and A.B. Yehoshua, and Ruth Dayan, the widow of the legendry Israeli general, Moshe Dayan.

In its report entitled "Human Rights in the Occupied Territories" B'Tselem chronicles the widespread abuse of Palestinians by settlers with the complicit acceptance of both the military and the police on the West Bank. In many cases the abuse is directly perpetrated by both the military and the police. Between September of 2000 and the end of 2011 B'Tselem reported 485 cases, 241 involving soldiers and 244 involving police and Border Police officers.

But statistics are dry and do not tell the whole story. Here's one example (page 16 of the 63-page report): A shepherd, Nayaf Abayat, was grazing his family's flock on March 4, 2011 when three military jeeps pulled up. The Annual Report continues: "One of the soldiers asked him what he was doing there and kicked him before he could answer. The blow knocked Abayat to the ground, injuring his elbow, which began to bleed. The other soldiers searched him, cuffed his hands, and blindfolded him. Then they threw him onto the floor of the jeep. They drove for about two hours, during which the soldiers insulted and swore at him. The jeep came to the Etzion army base, where the soldiers left him waiting in the yard for a few hours, still blindfolded and cuffed. He was released several hours later."

The same day that the B'Tselem report reached my snail mail postal box I also received an email that included a video showing an Israeli border policeman in Hebron in early July ambushing a 9-year-old Palestinian boy. It is truly a disturbing sight. The policeman grabs the child, who curls up on the ground crying, and holds him there. Another policeman wanders over and kicks the child, then casually walks away after which the first policeman lets the child go.

This was caught on camera by a bystander who is part of B'Tselem's Camera Project in which small cameras are distributed to West Bank Palestinians to record possible violence against them. This video received almost 350,000 hits in just the first few days.

Shai Golden, writing in *Maariv* (Israel's second largest paid newspaper) reported many of the reactions to the video on the Facebook page of Israel's Channel 2 News, which included the following: Only kicked him, that's a shame; Right on! Border Police all the way; A string of filthy curses followed by, I'd have murdered him; That's what needs to be done to all the kids there; What a retarded soldier. Kill him, what are you waiting for; Truth—I'd have fired like five bullets into his head."

Golden commented: "We've turned into a nation that shoots at nine-year-old children, that kicks them with a military boot and which doesn't understand what the problem is. On the contrary: it believes that kicking a nine-year-old boy is just the precursor of what truly ought to be done to him."

That's what an occupation does to the soul of a country. If you don't want to accept a fair partition of the land (a two-state solution) because you don't care for the legitimate rights of the Palestinians, I suggest you do it to preserve an Israel that is free from hate and venom. This is not the Israel that was contemplated by Ben Gurion or by its American Zionist supporters at the time of its birth. But this is what 45 years of occupation has wrought.

Turning to American Jewish reaction, Lara Friedman, writing in *The Daily Beast* (dailybeast.com) asks the question, "Where's the Shame?" She writes: "Throughout all of this, American Jews remain shockingly silent. Shockingly, because most people would assume that ignoring and defending the abuse of children would be a bridge too far, even for the staunchest partisan of the 'Israel, right or wrong' approach."

Friedman points out that American Jews are quick to feel shame concerning a Bernie Madoff, Anthony Weiner, Elliot Spitzer or Jack Abramoff. In fact, we are so sensitive to Jewish shame that immediately after the Trayvon Martin shooting there were 2.8 million hits on Google with the question "is George Zimmerman Jewish?" I'm the first to admit a sense of relief when I found out he wasn't.

Why can we not transfer that sense of shame to Israeli actions when they warrant it? Why does American Jewry instinctively react in an apologetic mood? The test of a true moral compass is when it can be turned onto one's self. It's easy to criticize the "other," but it takes moral courage to examine one's own actions.

I am often asked why I constantly write about Israel's shortcomings. The answer is simple: because I love Israel enough to care about its soul; because I want it to truly be a light unto the nations; because I am sophisticated enough to know that it, like any other country, will never be perfect, but that is no excuse for standing silent in the face of the iron boot kicking a 9-year-old, just for the fun of it.

I implore my fellow Jews: love Israel and criticize it out of love. Help save its Jewish soul. And the first step in that process is to support a two-state solution. This requires pulling in the settlers and creating peace with the Palestinians and peace within its own soul.

HISTORY—PAST AND FUTURE

Understanding History as a Key to Peace
7/20/11

Each year on May 15 the Palestinians commemorate the nakba (the catastrophe) by which the Palestinians refer to the founding of the State of Israel. This year Mahmoud Abbas, the president of the Palestinian Authority, wrote an opinion piece in *The New York Times* in which he wrote: "Shortly thereafter (the UN partition plan of November 1947), Zionist forces expelled Palestinian Arabs to ensure a decisive Jewish majority in the future state of Israel, and Arab armies intervened."

Jewish reaction was swift. Surely, all Jews know that the War of Independence was started when seven Arab nations invaded Israel. David Harris of the American Jewish Committee declared that Abbas was "rewriting history," He continued: "Among the astonishing elements in his op-ed, Abbas ignores the war unleashed by Arab armies in 1948 to obliterate the new State of Israel." These two separate readings of history deserve our scrutiny.

In February of 1947 the British announced its intention of leaving Palestine. In response the U.N. established a Special Committee on Palestine, UNSCOP, whose job it was to devise a partition plan. The Palestinians believed that the U.N. had no authority to allot any portion of their land to "colonializers," and refused to cooperate with UNSCOP. This was a major mistake on their part, as I will discuss in a moment.

First, some key demographic information: In November of 1947 approximately 30 percent of the population of Palestine was Jewish and most of these Jews lived in the cities. Only 5.8 percent of the land of Palestine was Jewish owned. We Jews think of those kibbutzim as being pervasive, but, in truth, they were isolated fortified enclaves in an otherwise Arab country.

Based on population alone UNSCOP could have allotted maybe 90 percent to the Arabs.

But there were no Arab voices at the U.N., a result of their self-destructive boycott of the process. We Jews took advantage of their mistake and the pro-Jewish sympathy in the wake of the Holocaust. This enabled us to lobby for as great a percentage of the land as possible in the partition plan. Thus, the U.N. allotted 42 percent of the land to the Palestinians, comprising 818,000 Palestinians and 10,000 Jews, giving 56 percent of the land to us Jews, comprising 499,000 Jews and 438,000 Palestinians. The partition plan internationalized Jerusalem where the population of 200,000 was evenly divided between Jews and Arabs.

Obviously this would not have been a "Jewish state," since Jews barely outnumbered Palestinians in the 56 percent allotted to them. Zionist leaders, including David Ben-Gurion, long before 1947, understood this reality. As early as June,1938 Ben-Gurion announced to the Jewish Agency Executive, "I am for compulsory transfer; I do not see anything immoral in it."

To be fair, compulsory transfer, or ethnic cleansing as we call it today, was not a crime against humanity at that time. Today it would put Ben-Gurion before the International Criminal Court in The Hague. Let me be clear— the public understanding of the term ethnic cleansing conjures up images of mass graves of genocidal proportion. This is not what we are talking about here. Ethnic cleansing is simply the mass deportation of a population, not the killing of them. However, it robs them of their home and country and makes them refugees. That is the reason it is now considered a crime against humanity.

As early as the late 1930's the Jewish National Fund (JNF) had created a detailed registry of all Arab villages in Palestine, including the names of their leaders, the topography, the age of individual men from 16 to 50, and their relative strength as measured by their participation in the 1936 Arab revolt against the British rulers. As the Israeli historian Ilan Pappe commented; "This was not a mere academic exercise in geography." He quotes a recollection of Moshe Pasternak, a participant in accumulating this data: "We had to study the basic structure of the Arab village. This means the structure and how best to attack it. In the military schools, I had been taught to attack a modern European city, not a primitive village in the Near East." Mind you this was done in the late 1930's, in preparation for what they knew would be the eventual partition of the land.

Between November, 1947 and the day that the British withdrew its army on May 14, 1948 (and Ben-Gurion declared Israeli independence) there was open warfare between Arabs and Jews. The war did not start on May 15 with the invasion of the Arab armies; it started at the precise moment of U.N.

Resolution 181 in November, 1947. The British did nothing to stop this. They used their 100,000 troops only to protect their own safety.

The aim of the Arab militia was to ethnic cleanse the Jews from Palestine, but it was weak and poorly trained, having been decimated in the 1936 revolt against the British. There were a few volunteers from Iraq, but Ben-Gurion knew that they were not the equal of the Haganah whose members had fought with the British against Germany. For the Jewish leaders this was the moment of truth.

On March 10, 1948 the Jewish Agency (the effective Jewish government, headed by Ben-Gurion) adopted Plan Dalet (Plan D) which was a detailed plan to ethnic cleanse the entire Arab population from what is now Israel. It included the directive to dynamite each entire village to prevent anyone from returning in the future. It also had directions on which Arab leaders to eliminate.

Between November 1947 and May 15, 1948 we Jews had uprooted 250,000 Arabs and committed several massacres, the most famous being Deir Yassin on April 9th, where approximately 100 civilians, including women and children, were slaughtered. The massacres were a tool of war. (This is an atrocious crime distinct from ethnic cleansing and is a blot upon Judaism and Israel.) The news spread quickly and Arabs in neighboring villages fled in panic, thus hastening ethnic cleansing. It was not until after Deir Yassin, in late April, that the Arab League voted to invade Israel. The final tally for the entire war was the ethnic cleansing of 531 villages and 11 urban neighborhoods involving up to 800,000 people.

So, let's go back to Abbas's statement. As a 13-year-old boy he had to flee Safed to Syria. He personally experienced this history. For him to write that the invasion of seven Arab nations was the result of Jewish aggression is a plausible narrative, and does not rewrite history.

Recognizing that the war began in November, 1947, not May 15, 1948, there is a plausible Jewish narrative as well. Certainly Jewish settlements were attacked by Arab militias with the intent to ethnic cleanse Jews. Further, although the Arab League did not decide to intervene until late April, there is an argument that it was only because of bureaucratic fumbling and it was their intention irrespective of Jewish ethnic cleansing.

The point here is that naïve Jewish statements that paint a black-white picture of us Jews being the innocent recipients of Arab aggression do not stand the scrutiny of the historical record. Sure, as the Arabs were planning to wipe us into the sea (let us take that as a given, although there are Arab scholars who would disagree), we Jews were plotting the same toward them, except not into the sea, only north to Syria and Lebanon, east to Jordan and South to Egypt. There are no innocents involved here.

I am sure that many readers will challenge the facts that I have just discussed. I urge them to read Israeli historians. I recommend "The Iron Wall" by Avi Shlaim, an Israeli teaching at Oxford University; the many books by Benny Morris; and in particular a very readable and profound book entitled "The Ethnic Cleansing of Palestine" by Ilan Pappe, who was in the history department at Haifa University when he wrote the book and now teaches at the University of Exeter in the UK.

The best comment on all of this was made in a letter to the editor of *The New York Times* by David Schwartz from the Center for Jewish-Arab Economic Development in Raanana, Israel: "Arguing over (history) only perpetuates mistrust and bad feelings between Arabs and Jews. The sense of victimhood on all sides is our biggest obstacle to progress. After 63 years, it no longer matters who is to blame for our predicament . . . What we all need is reconciliation, trust and cooperation."

For that blessed end we need a viable peace process which respects the legitimate claims of both sides. Unfortunately the American Jewish community still believes in the simplistic stories fed to us in our youth and propagated by the Israel Lobby, primarily AIPAC, the American Jewish Committee and the plethora of right wing fanatics who do not believe in a two-state solution (ZOA etc.).

If we really love Israel, as I do, it is time for us to pressure our government to act as a neutral party to facilitate real peace, so that we don't have to contemplate our mutual ugly histories forever.

Re-Writing History in Israel and America
10/5/11

This is a column about the need for every nation to review its historical narrative, an exercise in examining the "truths" handed down to us by previous generations. I want to focus on the United States and Israel, but the process applies to all countries.

One example of this process: When I was young I learned that after the Civil War the Radical Republicans trampled the newly defeated southern states by installing carpetbagger governments which, with the aid of local whites sympathetic to the Union (Scalawags), oppressed the defeated southern whites.

As late as 1988 my handy Third College Edition of Webster's New World Dictionary defined the word carpetbagger as, "any of the Northern politicians or adventurers who went south to take advantage of unsettled conditions after the Civil War." The same dictionary defined scalawag first as a "scamp or rascal," and secondarily as "a Southern white who supported the Republicans during the Reconstruction."

Given enough time for reflection, 21st century historians have revised this historical "truth." In particular I recommend the work of Eric Foner, a history professor at Columbia University. In his book "A Short History of Reconstruction" he reviews the southern white reaction after the civil war.

The carpetbagger governments in the south were installed by the Federal authorities in reaction to the Black Codes which were attempts by the newly constituted southern state governments to impose slavery in a new guise. Foner writes: "Mississippi required all blacks to possess, each January, written evidence of employment for the coming year. Laborers leaving their jobs before the contract expired would forfeit wages already earned, and, as under slavery, be subject to arrest by any white citizen . . . South Carolina's Code required blacks to pay an annual tax from $10 to $100 if they wished to follow any occupation other than farmer or servant.

Foner continues: "Although blacks protested all these measures, their most bitter complaints centered on apprenticeship laws that obliged black minors to work without pay for planters. These laws allowed judges to bind to white employers black orphans and those whose parents were deemed unable to support them . . . the consent of parents was not required." (Stay with me, I'll get to Israel)

Along with the Black Codes the Ku Klux Klan inaugurated a wave of violence against the newly freed blacks. In Texas there were 1,000 murders of blacks by whites between 1865 and 1868. The Texas Bureau recorded the "reasons" for these murders. One victim "did not remove his hat"; another "wouldn't give up his whiskey flask"; a white man "wanted to thin out the niggers a little."

In South Carolina in October of 1870, in the Piedmont cotton belt, there was a "negro chase' in which bands of whites drove 150 freedmen from their homes and committed 13 murders. Here in Florida, Foner quotes a black clergyman describing the panhandle county of Jackson as "where Satan has his seat," and where 150 persons were killed including a Jewish merchant, Samuel Fleischman, because he dealt fairly with black customers.

It was in reaction to the dictionary's "unsettled conditions" that the Federal government installed the so-called "northern adventurers," the men who went south, with the help of local liberal whites (the "rascals" of the Webster's Dictionary) to eliminate de facto slavery and create civilized governance. Yet for over 100 years historians had it wrong. The carpetbaggers and the scalawags were the good guys and the "oppressed" southern whites were the bad guys. Only after time for research and reflection has the real truth emerged.

Now let's apply this process to Israel. New resources are now available. Israel has declassified the minutes of the early cabinet meetings and other government documents as well. A new generation of historians is able to look at Israeli history with the detachment that over 60 years allows. What they found is that the simplistic stories that were required during the stress of nation building are no longer true or needed. (This is analogous to the American labeling of Native Americans, Indians, as the consummate bad guys and the white settlers as innocent good guys.)

In July I wrote a column entitled "Understanding History as a Key to Peace" that reviewed the work of the Israeli historian Ilan Pappe, where he shows that there were no good or bad guys during the Israel War of Independence; that both the Jews and the Arabs were intending to ethnic cleanse one another. We just did a better job at it. The Arabs committed atrocities on Jews and Jews did likewise to them, not merely out of self-defense, but with pre-determined strategy.

The point of that column was that we Jews must realize that there is a legitimate Palestinian narrative as well as a legitimate Israeli one. With this realization each side can stop demonizing the other and begin recognizing the humanity of the adversary. This is a required step before peace can be reached.

These new, younger Israeli historians who are rewriting Israeli history have been attacked by the right wing Israeli political establishment and their American Jewish supporters as left wing propagandists. Before you believe that, I urge the reader to actually read their scholarly books. They are in the mainstream of modern historians who analyze the "truths" of a previous generation, given the help of new resources and calm historical perspective.

It's a process that works in all countries. It took American historians over 100 years to be able to reflect on the narratives produced in the early years of our nation. I applaud the Israeli historians who are doing it in little over 60 years. The lessons that they teach us are important to the pursuit of peace. Unfortunately the current leaders of Israel and their American Jewish supporters aren't listening.

A Short History of Israel
11/24/10

2010

The peace talks that were initiated by the Obama Administration collapsed with a thud. Netanyahu recognized that Obama was weakened by the midterm elections and essentially challenged him when pressed to make concessions. AIPAC accused the White House of not being sensitive to the security needs of Israel. The Republicans went a bit farther and accused the president of anti-Semitism because of his hidden Islamic beliefs. As West Bank settlements proliferated and Israel continued to build more Jewish units in East Jerusalem, the Palestinian leadership declared an independent Palestinian state and appealed to the United Nations for recognition.

2015

It took five years of political maneuvering and a slowly shifting world consensus until the United Nations' General Assembly finally recognized the legitimacy of a Palestinian state in the West Bank and Gaza and formally declared that Israeli settlements in the West Bank and East Jerusalem were illegal. Israel refused to recognize the decision of the General Assembly and demanded a vote by the Security Council where it could rely on a veto by the United States. This was refused since Israel's very legitimacy was declared only by the General Assembly in 1947.

Since the U.N. declared the West Bank and East Jerusalem to be legally part of Palestine, the new Palestinian government approved physical attacks on the settlements. Israel described these attacks as terrorism while Palestine maintained that they were the tactic of last resort since these illegals would not voluntarily remove themselves to their own country. The world, with the exception of the United States, sided with the Palestinians.

2020

In reaction to these events the Israeli populous turned more to the right and elected Avigdor Lieberman as Prime Minister. He declared that the United Nations and the European counties were anti-Semitic and were no better than the Nazis. Lieberman's rhetoric, for which he was both famous and loved by the Israelis since they believed that the whole world was against them, ignited a world-wide backlash. Israel was stripped of its special trading relationship with the European Union. Other countries simply boycotted Israel.

2025

The Arab Israeli citizens were increasingly critical of the Lieberman government. The Israeli Jewish population began to look upon them as a fifth column and they were stripped of their voting rights. Liberal Israeli Jews who sided with the Arab minority were also denied the right to vote. It was in this year the Israeli brain drain began in earnest. It started with academics and quickly spread to the technology sector. Most of these people migrated to the United States where they received top positions in American universities and technology companies.

2030

The split in the American Jewish community had widened to the point where no one remembered the old Jewish Federation slogan "We are One." There were definitely two Jewish communities in the Diaspora—a small Orthodox and nationalistic pro-Israel contingent and a larger liberal Jewish community that was highly critical of Israel. The pity was that it was no longer critical out of love, but rather out of animus. Rabbis were declaring that Israel was destroying Jewish religious values. Sadly, by this time the majority of Jews walked away from the issue and totally disassociated themselves from organized Judaism.

2040

In 1995 there were 250,000 Jews in the West Bank and East Jerusalem. In 2010, the year of the last attempt at peace talks, there were 500,000. By 2040 there were now 1.5 million Jews living in the West Bank and East Jerusalem. The Likud party that was headed by Lieberman was superseded by a new, more radical party called the "Never Again party." It was headed by adherents to the blessed memory of its spiritual inspiration, Rabbi Meir Kahane. The two most visited gravesites in Israel were that of Kahane and his disciple Baruch Goldstein, who courageously killed 29 Muslims while they prayed at a mosque in Hebron in 1994.

2045

The Israeli government coalition, headed by the Never Again Party and a group of ultra-Orthodox parties that entered the government on the condition that the fledgling Conservative and Reform movements be banned, agreed that it had to decide the crucial question that everyone had put off for the previous 30 years—what to do with the Palestinians, both internally to Israel and those living in the West Bank, who still considered themselves an independent country. They faced three choices: First they could formally declare them a part of Greater Israel and give them an equal vote. This was not seriously contemplated.

That left two other difficult choices. They could continue to rule over them as a colonial power and forget that the world labeled this as apartheid. With this choice they would have to continue to live as a pariah nation in the eyes of much of the world.

The third choice was to solve the problem once and for all and ethnic cleanse Greater Israel (the land from the Mediterranean to the Jordan River) of all Arabs. With this completed they reasoned that the whole problem finally would be over and in time the world would accept the new facts on the ground. The feeling was that time heals everything. The electorate voted overwhelmingly for this choice. The small pro-Israel contingent in the United States defended this action since it was the result of a democratic election.

2048

The cleansing began, but it went terribly. Jordan refused to accept any refugees and Egypt did likewise. Lebanon, which was now ruled by a Hezbollah majority, responded by lobbing missiles into the very center of Tel Aviv. As Arabs and liberal Jewish sympathizers were rounded up into detention camps, there was no nation that would accept them. Chaos reigned for over two years.

2050

The inevitable happened. Although Iran never did get a nuclear bomb, Pakistan still maintained its nuclear arsenal. After that country fell into political chaos over the Pashtun uprising in its northwestern territory, a large portion of its nuclear warheads went missing. The world referred to them as the "missing Muslim threat." One of these warheads landed on Tel Aviv on Israel Independence Day of 2050 killing 1.5 million Jews. The Israeli government immediately retaliated by dropping three mini nuclear bombs on Gaza, Ramallah and Nablus, killing an equal number of Palestinians. The head of the Never Again Party quoted Deuteronomy, Chapter 19, verse 21, "an eye for an eye."

That is when the United Nations, Europe, Russia and the United States jointly invaded Israel. After a short-lived resistance, Israel surrendered. For the sake of world security, the United Nations then placed the entire region under a new international mandate that would last for 100 years until the Jews and Arabs could figure a way to divide territory. This marked the end of both Palestinian and Israeli control of the land. The state of Israel ceased to exist 102 years after its founding in 1948.

2051

At a conference at New York University a panel of political scientists discussed what went wrong. They agreed that the turning point was in 2010 when the Obama administration could not muster the political will to force both the Jews and Arabs to accept an equitable peace agreement. It was the last chance that failed. The academics also criticized the American Jewish community, especially AIPAC, and the born-again lobby for making it impossible for the administration to pressure both sides. Politics trumped peace.

At this point I awakened from my nightmare in a cold sweat. Initially I was afraid to mention this to anyone for fear that I would be branded a self-hating Jew or worse. Instead, I opened a prayer book and prayed for the peace of Jerusalem.

ISRAEL AND GAZA

Who Started This War?
1/13/09

I write this on January 5th as Israel is still in the process of decimating the Gaza Strip while the world looks on passively and American Jews are supporting the Israeli invasion with the same enthusiasm that is reserved for the hometown football team. What I am about to write will disturb many, but I ask you to analyze the facts and leave emotions aside. Daniel Patrick Moynihan once commented that everyone has a right to an opinion, but there can be only one set of facts. It is these facts that I want to present.

Fact: Hamas offered a ceasefire to Israel in December of 2007, but Israel refused to accept it because it would not deal with "terrorists." Only after another 200 or so dead and Egyptian intervention did Israel reluctantly agree to a six-month ceasefire beginning on June 19, 2008 with an end date of December 19. The agreement was that Israel would significantly loosen the blockade of Gaza and Hamas would cease lobbing rockets into Israel.

Some background is needed at this point. Although Ariel Sharon pulled the Jewish settlements and the Israeli military out of Gaza in 2005, it was not with the intent of making peace with the Palestinians. Dov Weisglass, Sharon's senior advisor, summed it up succinctly: "The disengagement (from Gaza) is actually formaldehyde. It supplies the amount of formaldehyde that is necessary so that there will not be a political process with the Palestinians . . . this whole package that is called the Palestinian state has been removed from our agenda indefinitely."

After withdrawal the Israelis immediately hermetically sealed Gaza. The lone airport strip was bombed so that there could be no contact with the outside world by plane. The crossing points between Gaza and Israel and Egypt were shut tight, thereby destroying the ability of the Palestinians to export any agricultural or manufactured products. These crossing points were open only for a trickle of food and medical supplies. The Gaza seacoast was patrolled by Israeli gunboats to assure that there would be no entry or exit by the sea. Gaza was under the complete control of Israel. In essence, Israel never returned Gaza to the Palestinians. As a reaction to this, Hamas won a democratic election in 2007. After this victory Israel tightened the screws on Gaza even more. Weisglass quipped that the Gazans were being "put on a diet."

Then the ceasefire was agreed upon on June 19, 2008. Fact: During the entire six months of the ceasefire not one Israeli was killed by a Hamas rocket, although an occasional rocket was fired. In May of 2008 more than 300 rockets were fired into Israel. By September, under the ceasefire, the number was reduced to 5 to 10, depending on who was counting. There is an explanation for these 5 or 10. Israel never ceased targeted assassinations of Hamas leaders both in Gaza and the West Bank during the ceasefire. Whenever Israel killed a Hamas leader, they symbolically fired rockets in return. The fact that there were so few rocket attacks and no deaths indicate that it was a political response. Hamas wanted and needed the ceasefire.

Fact: Israel broke the ceasefire, not Hamas. Little noted in the western press, on November 5, 2008, six weeks before the scheduled end of the ceasefire, Israel made a major military incursion inside the Gaza Strip on a scale that could only mean that it had ended its adherence to the ceasefire. Simultaneously Israel cut off food supplies that were trucked through the checkpoints. UNRWA (the UN relief agency) feeds approximately 750,000 people in Gaza given the economic situation as a result of the blockade. There is 50 percent unemployment there. Beginning on November 5, the day of the Israeli military attack on Gaza, to the end of the month Israel allowed only 23 UNRWA trucks to enter, rather than the 375 trucks that were required to feed the Gazans. The people were reduced from Weisglass' diet to near starvation.

A British journalist, writing in *The Independent*, reported, "When I was last in besieged Gaza . . . I met hungry children stumbling around the streets scavenging for food." During this same period in November, before the end of the ceasefire, Israel stopped the supply of industrial diesel fuel into Gaza forcing Gaza's only power station to suspend operations, shutting down its turbines. Hamas' reaction was to increase the amount of rockets into Israel, but still not one Israeli was killed by this response.

Fact: In December of 2008 Hamas offered to renew the ceasefire. The Israeli press reported that Yuval Diskin, the head of the Shin Bet, "told the Israeli cabinet that Hamas is interested in continuing the truce, but wants to improve the terms." Hamas wanted an end to the blockade and an end to

Israeli assassinations of Hamas people on the West Bank. The cabinet chose to ignore this request for negotiations, turning instead to military force. Ephraim Halevy, former head of the Mossad, commented, "Israel, for reasons of its own, did not want to turn the ceasefire into the start of a diplomatic process with Hamas."

Next week I will discuss these reasons. (This column is printed immediately below) As of now, let us at least recognize that Hamas rocket fire into Israel was not the precipitating cause of this ugly war. Israel chose for its own reasons to flex its military might. As a rabbi I believe that this is a *shanda* (a disgrace, for our gentile readers).

Going to War for the Wrong Reasons
1/20/09

Last week I discussed the fact that Israel chose to break the existing ceasefire notwithstanding Hamas' request for a continuance. (And remember that not one Israeli was killed by Hamas rocket fire during the six-month ceasefire.) I quoted Ephraim Halevy, former head of the Mossad: "Israel, for reasons of its own, did not want to turn the ceasefire into the start of a diplomatic process with Hamas." Today I will discuss the two main reasons that Israel chose to decimate Gaza.

These reasons are not arcane and are known to any reader of the Israeli press, or for that matter, the *New York Times*. First and foremost, it was a political decision by Defense Minister Ehud Barak and supported by Foreign Minister Tzipi Livni. In the beginning of November, immediately before November 5, when Israel effectively broke the ceasefire (read last week's column), Ehud Barak's political standing was the lowest in Labor Party history. He was leading a party that was projected to win only 10 seats in the Knesset (an alternative poll had it at 8 seats), down from its current paltry 19 seats, while Benjamin Netanyahu was grabbing 34 seats and Livni was amassing 28 seats.

The former Knesset member and political commentator Uri Avnery commented: "Ehud Barak is a walking disaster. But he cannot be removed from the leadership of Labor before the elections. The party is crawling towards its rout with eyes wide shut." It is an open secret that Barak did what many other politicians have done in the same circumstance. He started a war. Remember when Ronald Reagan's poll numbers diminished in the wake of the Iran Contra scandal, he invaded Grenada. It was not important that there were no communists taking possession of that Caribbean island. The

American people responded with their usual patriotic fervor and Reagan's poll numbers rose.

Barak is no different than any other egocentric politician. As defense minister he led his country against Hamas, an easy target since it is an acknowledged enemy of Israel. In his words, "The time has come to fight." That's the Israeli equivalent of Bush's "bring 'em on." (And as of January 6th, the date of this writing, Labor Party seats in the Knesset increased to 16. The Gaza incursion is still in progress and if it turns out poorly Barak's numbers may plummet before the February 10 election—but so far the usual political ploy has worked.)

Tzipi Livni had a different kind of political problem. Going into December she was trailing Netanyahu but not badly, however she was politically vulnerable due to her lack of charisma and the fact that she is a woman. She had, and still has, the same burden that Hillary Clinton had—can a woman be tough enough at a time of war? Will she be ready when the call comes in the middle of the night? Likud had attacked her with billboards picturing her tired and overwhelmed with the slogan, "Out of her league." Showing strength against a hated enemy was what the doctor ordered for her malady.

The second reason for Israel's eagerness to attack Gaza and to destroy Hamas also had nothing to do with rocket attacks although that is the propaganda that is accepted by western media. The *New York Times* reported it openly. Under the headline "With Strikes, Israel Reminds Foes It Has Teeth," Ethan Bronner, in a news analysis, stated the Israeli position that it attacked Hamas in order to stop rocket attacks. He then continued: "But it has another goal as well: to expunge the ghost of its flawed 2006 war against Hezbollah in Lebanon and re-establish Israeli deterrence . . . it worries that its enemies are less afraid of it than they once were, or should be. Israeli leaders are calculating that a display of power in Gaza could fix that."

Mark Heller, a senior researcher at the Institute for National Security Studies at Tel Aviv University, comments: "There has been a nagging sense of uncertainty in the last couple years of whether anyone is really afraid of Israel anymore. The concern is that in the past—perhaps a mythical past—people didn't mess with Israel because they were afraid of the consequences. Now the region is filled with provocative rhetoric about Israel the paper tiger. This operation is an attempt to re-establish the perception that if you provoke or attack you are going to pay a disproportionate price."

Of course, to wipe out the memory of the Lebanon debacle benefited the lame duck Prime Minister Ehud Olmert. Thus you had the triumvirate leadership of Israel ready and eager for war. This all makes political and maybe even military sense, but it does not make sense to the almost 700 dead

Palestinians, including well over a hundred women and children or the ten dead Israelis or the over 2000 injured Palestinians, many minus limbs and eyesight and other serious injuries, as of the date of my writing (January 7).

Sensitive people and hopefully committed Jews should have learned from Bush's Iraq folly that war should never be used as a diplomatic option. It should always be a last resort when diplomacy fails. It grieves me as a rabbi that a Jewish country that should reflect Jewish ethics would rush to war for political gain and a show of strength. Yes, indeed Israel does have teeth. But does it have a heart and a soul?

Did Israel Intentionally Target Civilians in Gaza?
5/4/11

On April 1 Richard Goldstone, the South African Jewish jurist and lead person on the U.N. Report on Israel's 2009 invasion into Gaza (Operation Cast Lead), cast a bombshell into the Middle East dialogue when he wrote an opinion piece in the *Washington Post*. In it he recanted one of the major conclusions of the Report, namely that Israel intentionally targeted Palestinian civilians during the three week offensive that claimed the lives of 1400 Palestinians, (including 758 civilians, 318 of them children—figures provided by B'Tselem, the respected Israeli civil rights organization.)

He based his recantation on the fact that when his original report was written Israel refused to cooperate with the U.N., but subsequent internal Israeli investigations show that the killing of civilians was not intentional. Goldstone's reversal was limited to the one point covering intentionality of killing civilians.

The 575 page report covered much more ground. It accused Israel of intentionally destroying civilian infrastructure in Gaza—a flour mill, sewage plant, chicken coops, water wells, a cement plant and about 4,000 homes.

The report also said that Israel waged "a deliberately disproportionate attack designed to punish, humiliate and terrorize a civilian population, radically diminish its local economic capacity both to work and to provide for itself, and to force upon it an ever increasing sense of dependency and vulnerability." Goldstone never repudiated these portions of his report.

Israeli and American Jewish reaction was swift. Prime Minister Benjamin Netanyahu crowed: "The fact that Goldstone backtracked must lead to the shelving of this report once and for all." Ronald Lauder, president of the World Jewish Congress, in light of Goldstone's *Washington Post* column, called the entire report "blatantly dishonest and biased."

David Harris, the executive director of the American Jewish Committee, which has been veering to the right on Israel under his leadership, indignantly proclaimed, "Judge Goldstone should apologize to the State of Israel . . . He should present his updated conclusions to the U.N. Human Rights Council, as well as to the General Assembly, which endorsed the skewed report, and press for its rejection."

In a statement issued on April 14, the other three members of the U.N. investigative committee that was headed by Goldstone had their say: "We concur in our view that there is no justification for any demand or expectation for reconsideration of the report as nothing of substance has appeared that would in any way change the context, findings or conclusions of that report . . . We firmly stand by these conclusions."

As for the internal Israeli reviews that Goldstone relied upon, they cited a subsequent U.N. committee of independent experts headed by New York Judge Mary McGowan Davis. In March of 2011, before Goldstone's bombshell, she reported that Israel used military personnel from the same command structure as those under investigation to review the alleged wrongdoing. Of some 400 investigations, only three have been submitted for prosecution with two convictions, one for theft of a credit card and another for using a Palestinian child as a human shield, which resulted in a suspended sentence of three months.

Thirty members of the Israel Defense Forces who fought in Operation Cast Lead issued a report entitled "Breaking the Silence" which complained about the loose rules of engagement issued by their commanders, which explains why so little care was taken to avoid civilian casualties. Is this proof of a direct intention to kill civilians, or just careless disregard for the humanity of Palestinians? Even if the latter were the case, it does not reflect well on Israel. Neither does it give one much faith in their internal investigations when one realizes that the Israeli government rejected calls for an independent Israeli review board rather than a military board, which has every reason to whitewash itself.

Even if this issue were murky one would think that it would not be a basis for Goldstone's recantation. Which brings us to the question, why did he do it? Since no one can get into his head, we are left to speculate. One thing is for sure—subsequent to his report, this esteemed international jurist, committed Jew and Zionist (his daughter lived in Israel and he had close ties to the country) was basically put in *cherem* (formal excommunication from the Jewish community).

The leaders of the South African Jewish community threatened to picket his grandson's bar mitzvah if he attended. It was called off after delicate negotiations, and he did attend. The *Forward* reports that Goldstone was confronted by the leaders of the South African Jewish community and told that his findings that Israeli soldiers had committed war crimes had made it impossible for young South African Jewish émigrés who served in the Israeli army to return home for visits.

The *Forward* article asked, "Did all of this add up to an emotional punch that would cause Goldstone's turnaround? It may be too simplistic to reduce the process to that. But several friends cited what they viewed as the cumulative toll of a stream of calumny hurled at the famously unemotional jurist." Goldstone's friend, Letty Cottin Pogrebin, said, "It has been like watching an innocent man whipped at the stake."

My main complaint about Operation Cast Lead does not involve any of the issues raised in the Goldstone report, albeit their importance is without doubt. During the first three weeks of 2009 I wrote three columns decrying the fact Israel had no reason to invade Gaza; that it broke the ceasefire with Hamas for internal political purposes and external military considerations that had nothing to do with rockets being lobbed into Israel. During the cease fire, there were practically no rockets launched and not a single Israeli lost his or her life from them.

The final conclusion about Operation Cast Lead has nothing to do with the U.N. report. It is the fact that Israel's action in the first three weeks of 2009 was the turning point in world opinion against Israel. It may very well culminate in the United Nations recognition of an independent Palestinian state in September of this year. The lesson to be learned is that brute force will not help Israel. Only serious peace negotiations will.

(Postscript: Indeed, later that year Palestine was accepted as a member state in the United Nations.)

Operation Pillar of Cloud
12/5/12

This past month we witnessed a near war with Hamas when Israel initiated Operation Pillar of Defense, its anticipated invasion into Gaza. In Hebrew it was called Pillar of Cloud in reference to the biblical story when God led the Jews through the desert using a pillar of cloud. No doubt this reference was for the benefit of the religious parties in the coalition who assumed that the Israeli military was doing God's work. For ignorant American Jews it was mistranslated into Pillar of Defense to stress the defense against Hamas rockets and probably to hide the theological implications.

It is true that the amount of rockets coming from Gaza has increased over the three years since Operation Cast Lead in late 2008 and early 2009 (which killed 1400 Palestinians, mostly civilians) from 200 per year to 700. Israelis as well as the American media and the Obama administration constantly stress Israel's right to defend itself against these rockets, which, of course, it has. But no one dares to see this conflict from the Palestinian point of view. No one asks the question whether these attacks are caused by the Israeli siege, or blockade if you will, of Gaza.

A little history can help. Ariel Sharon never really pulled Israel out of Gaza. From the beginning, the residents in Gaza were trapped in an open air jail. They could not use their perfectly good port because it was blockaded by Israel. Their airport could be made operational in a few months, but Israel will not allow them to use it. Their access into and out of the Strip is controlled by Israel (and for many years by Mubarak's Egypt in cooperation with Israel). Yet the American conservative columnist Charles Krauthammer wrote with a straight face, "What occupation? Seven years ago, in front of the world, Israel pulled out of Gaza."

After fair elections in 2006 Hamas assumed control. Unhappy with the outcome Israel and the United States planned a coup that would have unseated Hamas. In response to this Hamas preempted them and evicted Fatah from the Strip. In turn, Israel decided to turn the screws of occupation even tighter. Dov Weisglass, an advisor to then Prime Minister Ehud Olmert, said, "The idea is to put the Palestinians on a diet, but not to make them die of hunger."

Gisha, an Israeli human rights organization, obtained a court order that forced the Israeli government to release its records detailing the plans for the "diet." Jonathon Cook, an English columnist based in Nazareth, summarized these plans: "Health officials provided calculations of the minimum number of calories needed by Gaza's 1.5 million inhabitants to avoid malnutrition. Those figures were then translated into truckloads of food Israel was supposed to allow in each day . . . An average of only 67 trucks—much less than half of the minimum requirement—entered Gaza daily. This compared to more than 400 trucks before the blockade began."

Juan Cole, a Middle East scholar at the University of Michigan, observed the fruit of this "diet." He wrote: "About 10 percent of Palestinian children in Gaza under the age of 5 have had their growth stunted by malnutrition . . . In addition, anemia is widespread, affecting over two-thirds of infants, 58.6 percent of schoolchildren, and over a third of pregnant women."

It pays to read sources other than the Jewish press. Al-Hewar, The Center for Arab Culture and Dialogue, recently published a picture of an elderly grey-bearded Gaza resident holding a scrawled sign that read: "YOU take my water, burn my olive trees, destroy my house, take my job, steal my land, imprison my father, kill my mother, bomb my country, starve us all, humiliate us all, BUT I am to blame: I shot a rocket back."

Al-Hewar then commented: "**To the American Media: It's the Occupation, Stupid.** It is not a war between two countries. It is not a war against terrorism like the US is fighting. It is decades of struggle of an occupied people to be free from the grinding, inhuman oppression of their occupiers and to have their own independent state."

Yes, sending rockets into Israel is an unacceptable terrorist act. Holding 1.5 million Gaza residents under an inhuman siege is also an act of terrorism that no one seems to talk about. And killing over 100 Palestinians in the recently aborted Operation Pillar of Cloud (May *Hashem* continue to guide us) is also an act that many sane and impartial observers would classify as an act of terrorism.

True, something over100 dead is better than 1,400 dead as in Operation Cast Lead in 2008-09. But tell that to Jamal Dalu, a Gaza shop owner, "when an Israeli blast wiped out nearly his entire family: His sister, wife, two daughters, daughter-in-law and four grandchildren ages 2 to 6 all perished under the rubble, along with two neighbors, an 18-year-old and his grandmother," as reported by the *New York Times*. Tell that to the BBC journalist in Gaza who lost his 11-month-old baby and who wailed, "What did my son do to die like this?"

Yes, Hamas does not recognize the legitimacy of Israel. Neither did the PLO, but Israel spoke with them and they are now a moderate bargaining partner. Speaking to your friends is of little value. Speaking to your enemies can produce peace. Israel bargained with Hamas to obtain the release of one solitary Israeli soldier. Then why will they not bargain with them to obtain peace? Unless they really do not want a peace agreement.

A peace agreement would create two independent states and would preclude further settlement of the West Bank and the possibility of a Greater Israel. Instead, the metaphor that the Israeli government uses is "cutting the grass," meaning that a military operation will be required every so many years to keep the Palestinians subservient. Meanwhile West Bank Jewish settlers will continue to gobble up land that will forever preclude an independent Palestinian state.

Cutting the Grass is relatively easy to do if you have the second or third most powerful military in the world. Maybe in a couple of years, when the grass has to be cut again, it will be called Operation God's Will. I'm sure that it will be translated for us American Jewish cheerleaders as "Operation Defense of Poor Little Israel."

It's the Occupation, Stupid, not the rockets.

ADDITIONAL TOPICS

The Ultra-Orthodox Problem in Israel
6/5/13

At the founding of the State of Israel David Ben Gurion made a crucial mistake. He needed the religious party in his coalition and he willingly made some major concessions to include them. He acceded to the existence of a separate religious school system, paid for by the state, so that Orthodox students do not have to study or interact with more secular children. He agreed to a series of subsidies including paying for men to study the Talmud at state expense, thereby relieving them of the need to work for a living, and he exempted them from Army service (although some do voluntarily serve).

In retrospect, one could ask why he would have made such sweeping concessions to a small party and a small segment of the population. The answer is that he and most political and social observers of the time assumed that the Orthodox, and certainly the Ultra-Orthodox, would soon die out as liberal religion and modern social thought swept post-WWII society. As Ethan Bronner and Isabel Kershner in the *New York Times*, wrote, "He thought he was providing the group with a dignified funeral." Ben Gurion was not alone in not anticipating the rise of fundamentalism in all religions in the latter half of the 20th century.

And so we are now confronted with a million Orthodox, comprising approximately 20 percent of the Jewish population in Israel, and many of them are Ultra-Orthodox who practice a Judaism that most American Jews do not even recognize as Jewish. As their numbers and political clout increase they are making demands on Israeli society that pose a greater threat to the existence of a democratic Israel than outside military considerations. The Ultra-Orthodox are attempting to control public space and discourse, especially as it relates to women.

Here are a couple of examples: The Ultra-Orthodox convinced the Egged Bus Company to require women to sit in the back of busses, segregated from males, on routes that service their neighborhoods. This was eventually declared illegal by the Israeli Supreme Court, but Israel is notorious for not implementing Court decisions. Women have also won lawsuits against segregated sidewalks in Ultra-Orthodox neighborhoods. This, too, does not mean that they do not exist today. As one commentator wrote, "Woe to the girl or woman who refuses to move to the back of the bus."

The Haredim, as the Ultra-Orthodox are called in Israel, believe that a woman's voice or any part of her body exposed, including her face, is a sexual temptation to men and should be banned in public. Please note that this is precisely the position of the Taliban, Al Qaeda, and other distorters of Islam. The only difference is that daily we read about crazy Muslims, but not about crazy Jews.

To this end, women in Israel are prohibited from delivering eulogies because there are no non-Orthodox burials for Jews. Conservative and Reform rabbis are also prohibited from performing burials (and weddings) by law and Orthodox burial societies have a government enforced monopoly. The director-general of the Ministry of Religious Services issued a directive to allow women to speak. However, the legal department of the Ministry stated that it had no authority to enforce his directive.

The power of a woman's voice: Rabbis have demanded that religious soldiers may leave any military ceremony where female soldiers are allowed to sing, proclaiming, "A woman's voice is her sexual part." A prominent rabbi proclaimed that a soldier should rather face a firing squad than listen to a woman singing. The Chief Rabbi of the Air Force actually resigned his post because the Army refused to excuse Ultra-Orthodox soldiers from attending these events.

This fear of women's sexuality affects varied settings. A prominent female medical professor was awarded a prize by the Health Ministry for her book on hereditary diseases common to Jews, but was not allowed on the podium to accept her honor by the acting Health Minister because he was Ultra-Orthodox. An Ultra-Orthodox radio station licensed by the government, which controls all airwaves as in America, refused to allow a woman's voice on air—no female call-ins, no female broadcasters, studio guests or interviewees. Under government pressure, it now allows five hours, out of 144 hours of programming, for phone-in during which women may talk.

Last month Israel's Attorney General issued a non-binding advisory that discrimination against women, from busses to burials and air waves, is illegal and should end immediately. The operative word here is "non-binding." Absent serious legislative action, this will have no effect on current practices.

This is so un-Jewish! Don't believe me; believe Orthodox Rabbi Dov Linzer, the Dean of Yeshivat Chovevei Torah Rabbinical School (founded by Rabbi Avi Weiss who writes the Dvar Torah that is carried weekly in the *Jewish Journal*). Rabbi Linzer writes: "What is behind these deeply disturbing events? We are told that they arise from a religious concern about modesty, that women must be covered and sequestered so that men do not have improper sexual thoughts. It seems, then, that a religious tenet that begins with men's sexual thoughts ends with men controlling women's bodies."

Rabbi Linzer continues: "At heart we are talking about a blame-the-victim mentality. It shifts the responsibility of managing a man's sexual urges from himself to every woman he may or may not encounter. It is a cousin to the mentality behind the claim, 'She was asking for it.' . . . All of this is done in the name of Torah and Jewish law. But it's actually a complete perversion . . . (the Talmud) does not tell women that men's sexual urges are their responsibility . . . The Talmud tells the religious man, in effect: If you have a problem, you deal with it. It is the male gaze—the way men look at women—that needs to be desexualized, not women in public."

What is fearful is that the Ultra-Orthodox segment of Israeli society is growing much faster than more liberal Jews. The average Haredi family has eight to ten children. An Ultra-Orthodox rabbi was quoted in the *Times* making reference to his 38 grandchildren. And that's not so unusual. It is expected in the not-too-distant future that fully 50 percent of all incoming first grade students in Israeli schools will be Orthodox. These children will not be taught the concept of democracy in their separate Orthodox school system. In fact they will be taught very few secular subjects.

According to a recent study by the Israel Democracy Institute at Tel Aviv University, when Israelis were asked if Halacha (Jewish Law, the counterpart of Islamic Shariah Law) contradicts democratic principles, "should democracy always take precedence?" only 44 percent said yes. 56 percent had doubts (20 percent said no, and the other 36 percent would decide on a case by case basis). It is findings like this that move Israeli commentators to worry about a trend toward theocracy and a diminution of democratic principles.

Whatever will happen will be through small incremental steps. The end result will not be seen immediately, but it is a serious problem that cannot be ignored. As Shelly Yacimovich, a Member of the Knesset and the head of the Labor Party, commented, "The Haredi issue is a force flowing underground, like lava, and it could explode."

Israel, the Bomb and Iran—What to Do?
3/7/12

No one wants Iran to have a nuclear weapons capacity, that's a given. The question is how to stop it, and if that's impossible, how to live with it. Here is where opinions vary greatly. The United States and Europe are relying on severe sanctions that appear to be working. Both Prime Minister Benjamin Netanyahu and Defense Minister Ehud Barak seem to be heading toward an Israeli preemptive attack on Iran's nuclear installations.

Within Israel there is much opposition to this outcome by people who should know what they are talking about. Meir Dagan, the past head of the Mossad (Israel's CIA) has declared that an Israeli attack would be of little value: "It is possible to cause a delay, but even that would be for a limited period of time." Rafi Eitan, a seasoned Mossad operative (more widely known in the U.S. as Jonathan Pollard's manager) goes even further: "Not even three months . . . You'll manage to hit the entrances (to the underground caverns), and they'll have them rebuilt in three months." Former Israeli Chief of Staff Gabi Ashkenazi, as well as most of the former Shin Bet (Israel's FBI) and military intelligence chiefs, agree that it would be a colossal mistake.

Therefore, from whence comes the motivation? The answer to that is two-fold. For Netanyahu it is delusional. He equates Iranian leadership with Hitler and the Nazis. This ignores the existence of 25,000 Jews who voluntarily live in Iran as free citizens unmolested by the government. The Iranian dictatorship is cruel, as all dictatorships are, and is relatively dangerous, but it is not an "existential danger" to Israel, as was explicitly stated by the current chief of the Mossad this past December. This is also the opinion of the majority of security experts in Israel and the United States.

Ehud Barak is a different story. There are two kinds of generals. Dwight Eisenhower typified the first kind, one who has seen war and therefore prefers diplomacy. General Curtis LeMay typified the second kind who shoots first and asks questions later. He actually advocated nuking Cuba during the Cuban crisis. Barak's history, especially during Operation Cast Lead's invasion of Gaza, places him in the second category along with LeMay and George Patton. He believes that military might solves all problems.

The dangers resulting from an Israeli attack on Iran are many, for Israel and for the incipient democratic opposition in Iran.

Israel—There is no doubt that Iran would vigorously retaliate. Barak has declared that it would be a five day war with minimum Israeli casualties. David Ignatius reports in the *Washington Post* that Israeli sources tell him that there could be 500 Israeli civilian casualties. Last month Israel's current military intelligence chief estimated that there are 200,000 missiles and rockets in Gaza, Lebanon and Syria. Hezbolah alone has over 50,000 missiles that could reach Tel Aviv and other civilian centers. Iran has Shabab missiles that have a range of 1500 miles, capable of doing great damage in Israel.

Meir Dagan believes that it is very possible that a regional war could erupt, dragging Syria and Lebanon into the fray, in which case Israel could be looking at thousands of military casualties and untold civilian losses. Who is correct, Barak or these other military experts? Who knows, but does one want to roll the dice?

The democratic movement in Iran—Netanyahu has actually stated that an Israeli attack would be welcomed by current dissidents in Iran. Most astute observers believe that if Iran were invaded by any foreign country it would consolidate the current regime and essentially kill the rising democratic opposition. It is as elemental as the "rally around the flag" syndrome.

Finally, would the world come to an end if Iran eventually were to go nuclear? Let's learn from history. In the late 1940's and early 50's there was great anxiety in this country at the prospect of the Soviet Union obtaining nuclear capacity. Many people advocated a preemptory attack to forestall this. President Eisenhower kept his cool. He replied: "A preventive war, to my mind, is an impossibility today. How could you have one, if one of its features would be several cities lying in ruins, where many, many thousands of people would be dead and injured and mangled? . . . That isn't preventive war; that is war."

The United States chose the MAD concept—Mutually Assured Destruction. Both the Soviet Union and the U.S. learned to live with the knowledge that the use of a nuclear device by either side would mean the destruction of both sides. And it worked. Today we are at peace with Russia. In fact our companies are falling over each other running to invest in that country.

Ah, but one argues that Iran is not rational and you cannot rely on the mutually assured destruction concept. Wrong. Iran is a united country culturally (unlike Pakistan that is a conglomerate of disparate tribes that was pieced together by the British at the end of its colonial period—and it has a bomb!), and Iran has a level of sophistication that derives from its Persian history tracing back almost three thousand years.

Fareed Zakaria put it well in his CNN blog: "Over the past decade, there have been thousands of suicide bombings by Saudis, Egyptians, Lebanese, Palestinians and Pakistanis, but not a single suicide attack by an Iranian. Is the Iranian regime—even if it got one crude device in a few years—likely to launch the first?"

Since I'm writing in a Jewish newspaper, I will finish with a warning to my fellow Jews: Do not be caught up in Netanyahu's delusions or Barak's militarism out of a feeling that you are supporting Israel. Listen to the Israeli intelligence experts and support the United States administration that is trying to save Israel from its own possible mistakes, as well as protect our economy and prosperity, and possibly even American lives.

The Month of Jewish Crazies
7/7/10

It is always dangerous to label a political opponent or a philosophical adversary as being crazy. It's the first step to delegitimizing him. The right wing does this frequently, and I'm very often the object of such attacks. I also acknowledge that there are crazies on the left as well as the right who use these tactics, albeit less frequently.

Having said the above, this past May some Jewish right wing crazies were so busy spreading their venom that it deserves special attention. It started with a beauty contest, of all things. One wonders how an ideologue could turn a beauty pageant into an attack on Jewish interests. Well, here's the story.

The Miss USA contest crowned Rima Fakih, a striking Lebanese-American immigrant from Michigan. The runner-up was Miss Oklahoma, a blond all-American specimen of conventional beauty contest standards.

One would think that this Semitic looking beauty would be welcomed by the Jewish community, since she validates the beauty of Jewish women. Thinking of this takes me back to my high school years in the 1950s when most Jewish teenage males longed for the Shiksa Goddess, a blond, snub-nosed white skinned creature that just stepped out of the movie "The Last Picture Show." These days Jewish women don't have to get nose jobs and color their hair to be considered desirable. Witness our Lebanese cousin, Rima Fakih, who one blogger described as "smok'n hot."

That's not how the Jewish crazies see the world. The right wing Jewish activist Daniel Pipes, noting Fakih's Muslim Arab background and other beauty contests where Muslims have been successful, "makes me suspect an odd form of affirmative action." The Jewish radio talk host, Debbie Schlussel, is more agitated. She declares that Fakih's relatives in Lebanon had ties to a terrorist organization and that Fakih's "bid for the pageant was financed by an Islamic terrorist." She suggested that the contest was "rigged" and a reflection of a "politically correct, Islamo-pandering climate."

It would be easy to write her off as just another crazy, except that she has written for the *New York Post*, the *Wall Street Journal*, the *Jerusalem Post* and other "mainstream" conservative media. It is a reflection of how far right we have turned. Aaron Goldstein writes for *The American Spectator*, a conservative journal. One comment on his blog noted that "this chick is well connected with the jihadi community. She is serving their purposes. I learned this from debbieschlussel.com" And thus one crazy feeds the next until it is accepted as gospel (or in this case, Talmudic) truth.

As I said, last month was surfeited with crazies. Leaving beauty contests and turning our attention to President Obama's relationship to Israel, we find even more egregious behavior. It is perfectly respectable to doubt that the administration's policy is good for Israel. I think it is; you may think not. That's legitimate political dialogue.

But the Jewish crazies live in another universe. David Horowitz heads an organization called The David Horowitz Freedom Center. His recent letter to "fellow defenders of Israel" asks for money to distribute a pamphlet entitled "Barack Obama's War Against the Jews." One can doubt the wisdom of our president, but a war against the Jews? In Horowitz's twisted mind, by attempting to implement a peace plan in the Middle East he is not merely in a war against Israel but against all Jews. Would this include observant Jews in the White House such as Rahm Emanuel (who was a civilian volunteer in the Israeli army and whose father is Israeli) or David Axelrod?

Daniel Greenberg is a New York-based freelancer and blogger who writes that Obama wants to "bring Israel to its knees and destroy it," and that Obama "believes that Israel was a mistake." Further he writes that "Obama shares no common history with Americans, and his Jewish associates do not share one with the Jewish people." It's good to know that our president is not a real American and that Emanuel, Axelrod, and I guess people who agree with them, such as me, are not real Jews. I did have a brit, a bar mitzvah and ordination, but I have no common history with the Jewish people?

Maybe the most ludicrous Jewish crazy of the month was Buddy Korn, the editor of the Jewish Federation of Philadelphia's newspaper, the *Jewish Exponent*. He is disturbed by the administration's pressure on Israel and as a response he has established an organization entitled "Jews for Palin," with a website JewsforSarah.com, despite the fact that Palin has referred to the United States as a "Christian nation" and does not support the separation of church and state. In an interview in the *Forward* he said, "I was captivated—not by her looks, for goodness sake—but by her charisma, her brilliance, her grasp not just of the issues, but of the moment."

Her brilliance? Her grasp of the issues? Run that by me again. I'm tempted to write a letter to the editor of the *Forward* to confirm that he wasn't misquoted. But knowing his politics, I think not. What's even more disturbing is that supposedly sane Jewish conservatives as William Kristol, Norman Podhoretz and Seth Lipsky think highly of her. Lipsky welcomes

Korn's group and feels that Palin is "staking out a terrific set of positions." Again, what universe do these people live in?

From beauty pageants to Jews for Palin (I guess it's better than Jews for Jesus) it's been an interesting month. I just hope that the crazies will climb back into their caves and let the rest of us have a civilized dialogue.

PART THREE—UNITED STATES POLITICAL PARTIES AND THE ELECTORAL PROCESS

Another Look at the Electoral College
11/7/12

This column is being published one day after the presidential elections and due to newspaper deadlines I am writing this before I know the results. As you either exult or mourn the returns, I want to turn your attention to a little discussed part of the whole process—the dysfunctional role that the existence of the Electoral College has played in this election, played in past elections and will play in future elections, unless we change the system.

My major frustration during this recent campaign was that it was not directed at 330 million Americans. Four or five swing states decided who was to be president. The rest of Americans were essentially onlookers. This does not augur well for the future of a democracy.

Every four years I write about this and until recently nothing seems to change, but there is hope. More on that later, but now let's review why we have the present system and its defects.

The Electoral College is not sacrosanct. It was a compromise at the Constitutional Convention in 1787. One faction wanted the president to be elected by the state senates while another wanted the president to be chosen by direct popular vote. The Electoral College emerged as the compromise. It is a peculiar institution that is found nowhere in any other democracy. To the rest of the world it is a perplexing phenomenon since they cannot fathom the possibility of a person being elected president without winning the popular vote, as was the case with George W. Bush in 2000 when he received more than half a million votes less than Al Gore.

The existence of the Electoral College negates the concept that every vote counts. If you live in a heavily Democratic state, your Republican vote does not count, and vice-versa. What motivation is there for a Republican in Massachusetts or a Democrat in Mississippi to vote, knowing that he or she cannot really change the outcome of the electoral votes from those states?

The Electoral College also distorts the true vote by favoring small states. Each state gets three automatic electors (one for each senator and a House member). Based purely on population there are small states that would receive only one or two electoral votes. We have to live with this inequity in the Senate where Rhode Island has the same representation as New York, but there is no reason to compound the inequity through the Electoral College.

Here's a scary thought: Once the electors are chosen they are not legally required to vote for the person to whom they are pledged. That means that in a close election one person in the Electoral College can change his or her mind and change the outcome, in spite of approximately 120 million combined votes or 538 electoral votes. There could come a time when we are jolted into this reality, and, depending on who sits on the Supreme Court, the final changed vote will be upheld (strict constitutional construction).

There is also the real possibility of a 269-269 tie in the Electoral College which would throw the election into the House of Representatives where each state has one vote, which could also produce a 25-25 tie. The constitutional questions then become mind boggling. Will the Supreme Court once again choose our president, and at what point do we have rebellion in the streets?

The only answer is to change the system to allow the president to be elected by the popular vote tally. This could be done in one of two ways. First, amend the Constitution. This is a long, drawn out process that will not happen. Fortunately some very creative people have devised another solution called the National Popular Vote Bill.

It works this way: Each state enacts a law that guarantees that its Electoral College votes go to the candidate who receives the most popular votes in all 50 states plus the District of Columbia. The bill would take effect only when enacted, in identical form, by states possessing a majority of the electoral votes (270 of 538). Thus the total popular vote automatically has a majority of the electoral votes. The Electoral College would still exist, but it would have no value, like an appendix in a human being.

When I last wrote about the Electoral College in 2008 only four states passed such a law and they possessed merely 50 electoral votes, only 19 percent of the 270 necessary to bring the law into effect. Here's the good news. As of today the law has been passed by nine states possessing 132 electoral votes—49 percent of the 270 needed to legalize the popular vote.

Here's more good news. In nine other states the National Popular Vote Law has passed one of their houses, either the Senate or the House. These states possess an additional 92 electoral votes. If the law were passed there, the count would rise to 224 votes—83 percent of the needed 270.

Here's something to ponder: if merely five states (Texas, Florida, Pennsylvania, New York and Ohio) were to pass such a law the total would reach 266 votes. Then any small state could push it over the top.

This is not a partisan issue. It is supported by prominent Republicans such as former President George H.W. Bush and the likes of former Congressman Tom Tancredo of the "expel 12 million illegals" fame. Never in my life did I believe that I would agree with him on any issue. Former Republican Senator and presidential candidate Fred Thompson is the co-chair of the National Popular Vote Law campaign.

In Florida a bill was introduced in both the Senate and the House in 2009 by two African American Democrats. It never reached a floor vote, having been killed by the Republican controlled leadership. But there is no reason to think in partisan terms. In Tennessee both former chairs of the Democratic and Republican parties issued a joint statement of support. In that polarized state it's probably the only thing the two parties could agree upon.

Nationally 72 percent of the people support the National Popular Vote Law. In Florida it's 78 percent. National newspapers have endorsed it, including the *New York Times, Los Angeles Times, Chicago Sun-Times, Miami Herald*, and the *Philadelphia Inquirer*. It has also been endorsed by the League of Women Voters.

So the conclusion is that there is hope. If we work at it we could have an election in 2016 that is decided by the popular vote. Then the president would be elected by all 50 states and not just a few swing states. And we will never again have to face the situation when a candidate with half a million votes less than his opponent becomes president.

You can keep abreast of this issue by going to nationalpopularvote.com on the Internet.

The future of the Republican Party
11/21/12

Republicans are beginning to reflect on their recent loss to President Obama, as well they should, given the unprecedented victory by an incumbent in an economy that has an unemployment rate hovering at eight percent. They also have to ponder the fact that their party has lost the popular vote in five of the last six presidential elections.

Many conservative pundits are blaming Hurricane Sandy for interrupting Romney's supposed surge in popularity. Others are focusing on the weakness of their candidate (Romney's Bain Capital baggage, etc.). The *New York Times* resident conservative intellectual columnist, David Brooks, to his credit, ignores these factors as a side show of political spin and focuses on the core philosophy of the Republican Party—a philosophy that the American people just won't buy.

In a nutshell, it goes back to Ronald Reagan's famous proclamation that "government is the problem, not the solution." Brooks writes: "During the 2012 campaign, Republicans kept circling back to the spot where government expansion threatens personal initiative; you didn't build that; makers versus takers; the supposed dependency of the 47 percent. Again and again, Republicans argued that the vital essence of the country is threatened by overweening government."

Brooks traces this stance back to the rugged individuality of frontier America and decides that "this is not an Ayn Randian, radically individualistic belief system." Here is where I disagree with him. With the rise of the Tea Party that has captured the devotion of the Republican masses and with the choice of Paul Ryan as the vice presidential candidate, Ayn Rand became the intellectual icon, the Moses or Jesus figure of the Republican Party.

During the recent campaign Paul Ryan said, "The reason I got involved in public service, by and large, if I had to credit one thinker, one person, it would be Ayn Rand." Early in his congressional career he would distribute copies of Ayn Rand's book "Atlas Shrugged" as Christmas presents.

Rand was a political thinker and novelist who developed a cult following fifty years ago. She opposed all forms of welfare, unemployment insurance, support for the poor or middle class, any regulation of industry, and government expenditures for roads or other infrastructure. For her the only roles for government were law enforcement, defense and a court system.

Most important, Rand viewed the world as divided into two groups, the "moochers" and the "producers," i.e. the poor and the rich. This stark philosophy was transformed into the simple idea espoused in the last campaign by Republicans that government expansion threatens personal initiative.

Again to Brook's credit, he debunks this premise, a major concession from a conservative thinker. He points out that the Pew Research Center found that Asian-Americans and Hispanics have, in Brook's words, "an awesome commitment to work. By most measures, members of these groups value industriousness more than whites." But unlike Tea Party members and Ayn Randians, they believe that government programs can incite hard work and enhance opportunity, rather than undermining the work ethic and crushing opportunity.

No wonder that the Asian community voted for Obama by 3 to 1 and the Hispanics were not far behind. But it is surprising to me that Brooks, who is Jewish, ignored the Jewish vote. Exit polls are murky regarding the Jewish vote because of the small samples, but it appears that nationally 70 percent of Jews voted for Obama. Even though a little smaller margin than in 2008, it's not a shabby outcome.

For the record: Jews have an awesome commitment to work and we probably value industriousness more than whites (for purposes of polling, we Jews are not whites). You can attribute our commitment to the Democratic Party as a genetic thing handed down from generation to generation, or, having been outcasts for long periods in our history we naturally side with the downtrodden and dispossessed, the supposed 47 percent that Romney so abruptly dismissed.

But there is a deeper reason. Our religious values which have been instilled in most Jews, even those who do not consider themselves "religious," stress communal responsibility over rugged individuality. Empirically, this does not diminish our awesome commitment to work or our personal achievements. Judaism eschews the Me Generation—"me first," "looking out for number one."

We are noted for our charitable contributions. But we do not give charity. We give tzedakah, which is incorrectly translated as charity.

The word charity comes from the Latin caritas, meaning "from the heart," or "heartfelt." It is a voluntary act. If your heart is not moved, there is no requirement to give. The root of tzedakah is tzedek, meaning "justice." We are commanded to give tzedakah. There is no personal choice. Justice requires that the unfortunate are cared for by the fortunate. This is a direct repudiation of the world as seen divided into the "Moochers" and the "producers."

We Jews gravitate to the Democratic Party because we see government as the extension of this communal obligation. We also see it as a help, not a hindrance, to our entrepreneurial spirit and our committed work ethic. According to the Pew Research Center it appears that Hispanics and Asians feel the same. Obviously, many plain old whites believe this as well.

If the Republican Party does not want to lose the popular vote in the next five out of six presidential elections, it had better shed the Tea Party crowd and the Ayn Randians, including Paul Ryan and Rand Paul and their cohorts in the House and Senate. I don't see that happening, which is really a shame since we need two vigorous and sane political parties for the stability of our democracy.

Philosophically, Which Side Are You On?
6/8/11

This past month the House passed a federal budget bill prepared by Representative Paul Ryan in which Medicare is privatized, and Pell Grants, food stamps and other aid to the poor are slashed. At the same time the Bush tax cuts for the upper one-percent are maintained and the top tax rates for individuals and corporations are reduced from 35 percent to 25 percent.

This is supposed to reduce deficits on the theory that feeding the rich will cause economic stimulation that will increase government income (the trickle down theory). It didn't work for Herbert Hoover and it won't work today. As was expected, this legislation was defeated in the Senate.

But since every Democrat in Congress voted against it and all Republicans in the House voted for it, with the exception of five dissenters, and 42 of the 47 Republicans in the Senate voted for it, this legislation highlights the difference in political philosophy between the two parties.

Jonathon Chait, in *Newsweek*, points out the basis for both Ryan's and the Tea Party's commitment to smaller government. The Tea Party was founded after a rant by CNBC commentator Rick Santelli. In it he talked of his abhorrence of government. He concluded the rant saying "At the end of the day I'm an Ayn Rander."

He was making reference to the novelist-philosopher Ayn Rand, 1905-1982, (*The Fountainhead, Atlas Shrugged*) in which she distained the poor and idealized the rich. Chait describes her philosophy as, "Marxism flipped upside down. Rand viewed the capitalists, not the workers, as the producers of all wealth, and the workers, not the capitalists, as useless parasites." Chait quotes the protagonist in *Atlas Shrugged*: "The man at the bottom who, left to himself, would starve in his hopeless ineptitude, contributes nothing to those above him, but receives the bonus of all their brains."

Paul Ryan, who voted for the Bush tax cuts and two wars and Plan D Medicare, all unfunded, now in the guise of fiscal responsibility proposes his draconian budget. But what is his real intention? It turns out that Ryan is also a devotee of Ayn Rand. Appearing at an event to honor her philosophy, he said: "The reason I got involved in public service, by and large, if I had to credit one thinker, one person, it would be Ayn Rand." Ryan requires his staffers to digest what Chait calls "her creepy tracts."

Rand's philosophy became the bedrock of the Libertarian Party and, with the help of the Tea Party and Republicans like Ryan, it has become the operating premise of the Republican Party, with a little help from Ronald Reagan ("Government is the problem, not the answer").

Essentially, libertarianism says that in this Darwinian world it is the survival of the fittest and there is no role for government to help those who can't help themselves. The rich owe nothing to the poor except that which trickles down to them in the capitalist's quest for even more riches. In essence, all people are self made, and if you can't do it yourself, you deserve your lot.

Let me become personal. I am the product of a middle class family, but during my teenage years my father's business was failing. Not having the resources to go away to school, I commuted to Wilkes College in Wilkes-Barre, Pennsylvania (and received a great education) and worked from 30 to 40 hours per week while attending undergraduate school. I then attended Yale University where I received a law degree and a Masters in economics. I washed dishes at lunchtime in the cafeteria in return for three meals a day. I also worked as a waiter in a local restaurant in the evenings. Still I would not have been able to afford graduate school had Yale not given me extensive scholarship money.

If I were arrogant (I have many defects, arrogance not being one of them) I could claim to be a self-made person. I would be lying. I am the recipient of both private charity and government subsidy, although both were faceless to me. The very existence of Wilkes College was based on community leaders who decided that poor kids needed a local college if they were going to have a chance to get ahead in life. Yale was able to provide me with a scholarship because it received money from the government and private donors to assure that needy students could attend.

The bottom line is that there is no such thing as a self-made person. We are all the products of a communal responsibility which is shared by private charities and government support. But given the needs of mankind there is no way that private sources can meet the demand alone.

Without government care for the needy, not just in education or health care, but in all aspects of society, we are left with the frightful spectacle of millionaires and billionaires building their McMansions in South Florida while people in America literally starve. You think that's an exaggeration? Today 45 million Americans, most of them working, cannot feed their families without the help of food stamps. One in five children in this country depends on food stamps to eat.

Paul Ryan and the Republicans would reduce the food stamp program significantly, and probably abolish it if they could, understanding that it is against their philosophy of government. Surely, Ayn Rand would not approve of it.

If nothing else, the Tea Party and leaders like Ryan have clearly delineated the philosophical difference between what the Republican Party has become—a libertarian front—and the Democratic Party. There's a famous union song written in 1931 during a miner's strike in West Virginia entitled, "Which Side Are You On?" and each of us has to look ourselves in the mirror and answer that question.

SENATE FILIBUSTER

The Filibuster Creates a Non-Functioning Government
12/7/11

I have been discussing the filibuster in these columns for the last six years and I thought that I would never have to return to this subject. I was wrong. What moved me to write this column was the Republican filibuster in the Senate of Obama's jobs bill, even though it had no chance to pass the Republican controlled House. Now the filibuster is being used not merely to block legislation but to stifle a debate on any topic that the minority does not want to address. It is now a tool to close down the democratic process. The end result is that our government is non-operative.

There are many reasons that government has ceased operating, including the increased influence of uncontrolled money contributions (thanks to the *Citizens United* decision by the Supreme Court) and the general lack of civility in politics promulgated in the 1990's by Newt Gingrich and intensified by others over the last 25 years.

But I believe that the most potent reason for government paralysis is the existence of the filibuster. Once a rarely used Senate rule, it has become the major impediment to good government. Even during the first two years of the Obama administration when the Democrats controlled both the House and the Senate, the minority party was able to essentially close down the legislative process through the use of the filibuster.

It is no longer a rare, desperate phenomenon used in the course of democratic dialogue. It is now a blunt hammer to be used for partisan reasons. Senators have filibustered more since 2006 than they had in the 60 years between 1920 and 1980. Put another way, in the single year of 2009 the filibuster was used more than in the 20 year period from 1950 to 1970.

To run an efficient business or government decisions have to be made and cannot be constantly foiled by a minority. Yes, the minority must be heard and respected, but there comes a time when the majority must rule. The filibuster has been defended based on the fear that minority interests would be trampled if it were not for checks and balances, including the filibuster. I guess that I am a Hamiltonian in that a little spark within my soul fears mob rule and respects checks and balances.

Our Constitution has provided these checks and balances. First we have two legislative bodies—the House, with two-year terms, to reflect the immediate mood of the electorate, and the Senate, with six-year terms to reflect more long range principles. Then the president has the check on the legislative branch through the veto. In turn the Congress can overrule the president with a two-thirds vote. Note they constantly check one another. Finally the Supreme Court can check both the President and Congress by declaring a law unconstitutional. That's a lot of checks and balances. We do not need a rule of the Senate to add another one.

This is not a partisan problem. When the Republicans are in power, the Democrats believe in the filibuster and vice-versa. There are one hundred senators and almost all of them do not want to give up power, and there is great power in the use of the filibuster. There is a famous quote from then Senator Obama defending the filibuster in 2005 when the Republicans threatened to eliminate it in the furor over judicial nominations. Even greater power is wielded in the ability of just one senator to "put on hold" a piece of legislation, a companion rule of the filibuster that also should be eliminated.

In late 2010 there was a feeble attempt to either dilute the power of the filibuster or to entirely eliminate it. Democratic Senators Merkley, Harkin and Udall introduced a bill that went nowhere. Fellow Democrats Dodd and Majority Leader Reid dismissed the idea. At that time the Religious Action Center of Reform Judaism and the Central Conference of American Rabbis issued a call for filibuster reform. Again to no avail.

I am aware that there is the possibility of Republican control of the White House and both houses of Congress after the 2012 elections. I shudder to think of the legislation that would be forthcoming. I am sure that conservatives also shudder at the thought of Democratic control of both branches of government without the filibuster. But this is the price that the left and the right will have to pay to repair a broken system, to allow government to function within the checks and balances that the Constitution provides, minus the added power that the Senate imposed on itself through its own rule-making.

I am surprised that someone has not instituted a law suit to declare the filibuster unconstitutional. Article I, Section 5, of the Constitution does say that "Each house may determine the rules of its proceedings." But a reading of the full Constitution makes it clear that our democracy works on the premise of a simple majority (50 percent plus one vote).

This premise is reinforced by the fact that whenever a vote of more than a majority is required it is specifically stated as an exception, as when two-thirds is needed in the following instances: to convict a president who has been impeached; to overrule a presidential veto; to ratify a treaty; and to propose amendments to the Constitution. The argument for the unconstitutionality of the filibuster is that although the Senate can determine its own rules, it cannot overrule the basic premise of the Constitution, anymore than it can pass a law violating any of the rights protected by that document.

The basis of our Constitution and democracy is majority rule within the stated checks and balances of our governing document. We don't need the Senate to change a majority into 60 votes to enhance the power of each individual senator or a political party. We must get our government working again, and except for a constitutional challenge I see little hope for removing the filibuster.

Living or Dying With the Filibuster Rule
12/9/09

I plead guilty. Some years ago I wrote a column defending the existence of the filibuster in the Senate based on my appreciation for the concept of checks and balances in government. I have come to the conclusion that the filibuster is detrimental to the democratic process, not because it is being used as a weapon in the current debate over health care. My concern is really non-partisan. I now realize that the coming together of disproportional representation and checks and balances in the Constitution coupled with the filibuster renders government nearly inoperative.

Let's start with the checks and balances that are written into the Constitution. They were meant to make the legislative process difficult. James Madison understood the tyranny of the majority. In his native Virginia he fought the suppression of the Baptists by the ruling Presbyterian hierarchy. As a young man he realized that government could be used for evil as well as good.

Alexander Hamilton was born in Nevus and reared in St. Croix. As a teenager he experienced the tyranny of mob rule on those islands. He feared the possible instability created by the masses if they were given suffrage. At the Constitutional Convention he proposed a presidency and Senate that would serve for life. He went so far as to use the phrase "elected monarch" for the president.

Together Madison and Hamilton spearheaded the system of checks and balances that we have today. The Senate sits for six years to insulate it from the passions of the day that affect members of the House who must stand for election every two years. The Supreme Court has the authority to negate a law if it considers it unconstitutional. The president has the veto power over both houses and he can be overruled only by a two-thirds vote. The Constitutional Convention debated whether it should require three-fourths vote to overrule a veto, but decided that would place too much power in the president. With all of these checks and balances, it is amazing that anything gets done. But they have served us well.

Added to these checks and balances, we have a disproportional representation problem built into the Constitution. Madison believed that membership in the Senate should be based on a state's population, not on the current system of two senators per state. He presented that before the Convention but the smaller states balked. In fact, William Patterson of New Jersey threatened that his state would refuse to join the new government unless the smaller states had equal numerical representation in the Senate. The current system (The Great Compromise) was accepted only after three separate votes over a six week period and passed by the thin majority of 5 o 4.

What's the outcome of the above? It means that our smallest state, Wyoming, with a population of 532,000, has two votes in the Senate as does our largest state, California, which has 37 million residents. Thus Wyoming with a population of a little less than one and a half percent of California's population has the same power in the Senate. Put another way, a majority of 52 senators come from the smallest 26 states with a combined population of 53 million, just 18 percent of the nation's 300 million citizens. This means that the majority of the Senate represent rural and small town America and can dictate the future of the vast majority of Americans who live in sophisticated urban settings. It represents a skewed outlook on pressing problems that affect the other 247 million Americans who expect our democracy to work on their behalf. Coupled with the entire system of checks and balances that is also wisely incorporated into the Constitution, we have the reality that almost nothing can get done, and what does get done often does not reflect the opinions of the majority who live in major metropolitan areas.

Now let's see how the filibuster adds to the problem. It takes merely 41 senators to stop legislation under a filibuster. That means that the smallest 21 states with a combined population of only 34 million, representing merely 11 percent of the country's population, can stop all legislation. This is not what one expects from the democratic process. What is worse, we know that the

Constitution should not be changed as regards checks and balances and can not be changed as regards disproportional representation, although it would be good for the country—but the filibuster is merely a procedural rule of the Senate. It is not written in cement. In 1975 the filibuster rule was changed from a required 67 votes to the current 60. There is a movement abroad to change it to 55. I believe that it should be abandoned. Majority rule should be 50 percent plus one, the same way these senators are elected.

Last month the *New York Times* columnist Tom Friedman wrote a fine column concerning American leadership in the world. He refuses to acknowledge that China will own the 21st century. He argues that the future belongs to the country that has both imagination and good governance. Imagination we have. He frets that for a combination of reason including money in politics our government is non-operative. He writes: "These six factors are pushing our system, which was designed to have divided powers and to force compromise, into the realm of paralysis. To get anything done now, we have to generate so many compromises—couched in 1,000-plus-page bills—with so many interest groups that the solutions are totally suboptimal. We just get the sum of all the interest groups."

Friedman concludes: "China's leaders, using authoritarian means, still can. They don't have to always settle for suboptimal." He then asks, "What can we do?" I will answer that question. For starters, we can get rid of the filibuster rule or at least weaken it to 55 votes. It is the final straw that breaks the back of American democracy. It incapacitates the democratic process.

CHURCH AND STATE

Beware Military in the Service of God
11/10/10

Four years ago Mikey Weinstein, the founder of the Military Religious Freedom Foundation, led the fight to cleanse the Air Force Academy of Christian proselytizing. At that time cadets were pressured by faculty members and chaplains in command to accept Jesus. The football coach displayed a banner proclaiming "Team Jesus Christ." Pressure was put upon cadets to view Mel Gibson's movie, "The Passion of Christ."

When a Lutheran Air Force chaplain complained that the cadets were being abused by "systematic and pervasive" proselytizing she was immediately transferred to Asia. Finally the superintendant of the Academy acknowledged the problem and predicted that it will take years to rid the campus of religious intolerance: "If everything goes well, it's probably going to take six years to fix it."

Apparently everything is not going well. This month Weinstein is preparing legal action against the Academy in light of new evidence that Cadets for Christ, an organization that many consider a cult, including Evangelicals like Pat Robertson, is actively proselytizing on campus with the help of officers and some faculty.

When confronted with evidence of this activity by the Military Religious Freedom Foundation the Academy Superintendant Lt. Gen. Michael Gould answered through a press release that, "To date, the allegation is not substantiated." But at the same time Gen. Gould has not released the annual Climate Survey for the first time in the history of the Academy. The obvious question is what does he know that he doesn't want us to know?

Veterans Today published a first-hand report by Darryl Wimberley, a former Air Force Academy professor, who wrote: "The cadets don't harass other cadets under religious pretext on their own; they take their cues from officers, junior and senior, a core of whom believe, or at least behave as if, the USAFA is the seminary of God's Air Force." He continues, "One of the officers speaking with Gen. Gould, at the meeting where I was present, spoke of how his own son had been punished for not attending a 'voluntary' prayer service." He also reported that the wife of an officer was told that her husband would never be promoted unless he started to attend Sunday school.

Mikey Weinstein has allegations from 51 cadets who have corroborated that Cadets for Christ is actively influencing cadets on the academy grounds. One of those cadets writes: "Mr. Weinstein, USAFA is literally overrun with Christian conservative fanatics . . . I keep 'Christian" books and 'Christian CD's in my room so others will be fooled and leave me alone."

Why does this cadet feel pressured? He explains: "We all need those discretionary academic instructor points. We all need our AOCs and Wing and Group and Squadron staff to want to support us. We all want more playing time with our athletic teams. We all need help from 'the system' in an infinite number of ways, but we will never get that help if we do not appear to be extreme conservative evangelistic Christians in every way."

This past month has not been a good time for the separation of church and state, the bedrock of religious freedom as guaranteed by the First Amendment. The *Army Times* reported that 80 soldiers at Fort Eustis, Virginia were confined to their barracks and put in "lockdown" because they refused to attend a Christian rock concert. Pvt. Anthony Smith, one of those soldiers said, "Anybody in the military will tell you that lockdown is a form of punishment. When we don't want to go to this concert and we're not allowed to use our laptops or our cell phones or music, we're not allowed to be sitting in our beds—that's a form of punishment."

What is truly scary is that this concert was part of the "Commanding General's Spiritual Fitness Concert Series." I understand the need for physical fitness, but I question the legitimacy of born-again generals to define spiritual fitness. There should not be such a program in the military. But there is and it's expensive.

The Military Religious Freedom Foundation reports that a Christian headline group costs between $30,000 and $100,000. Weinstein looked into the Department of Defense contracts for other spiritual fitness events and programs and discovered that one outside consulting firm was paid $3.5 million. A columnist in the dailypress.com commented: "Praise the Lord and pass the military contract."

Why am I so upset about this? Here's my doomsday scenario: As this country is becoming more religiously and culturally diverse the military command is becoming more fundamentally Christian. As America slides into if not third-rate at least second-rate status over the next century there could become a cadre of officers who decide to revitalize us through Christian fundamentalism. I know that I will not live to see this and I pray that my grandchildren will not either. But nightmares sometime come true.

A military that thinks it answers to God and not to the president (whether that president is a Republican or Democrat, white or black, male or female) is a dangerous force in society. I don't want to let the camel's nose into the tent. That's the reason that I'm alarmed over the current situation. That's why Mikey Weinstein and his Military Religious Freedom Foundation is an important organization.

Let's Keep God Out of the Military
11/20/13

If my wife and I are not traveling, almost without exception, I can be found at Friday evening Shabbat services at Congregation B'nai Israel, a Reform synagogue in Boca Raton, not as a rabbi but as a congregant. The service is a combination of traditional Jewish piety combined with 21st century programming and joyful music.

Earlier this month preceding Veterans Day the Kabbalat Shabbat service featured a tribute to those who served in our military. Interspersed with the Hebrew and English Shabbat prayers a trombone quartet played patriotic American music, such as God Bless America and the anthems for the four branches of our military. The rabbi invited all veterans present, who numbered about thirty, to the bima and thanked them for their service to our country and delivered a sensitive blessing.

I found it an inspiring moment. It spoke to my dual identity. I am an unabashed patriot (not a jingoist—I'm not shy in criticizing my government). Tears come to my eyes when I pass the Statue of Liberty, which I did earlier this month on the Staten Island ferry to the starting line of the New York Marathon. That lady with the torch welcomed my grandfather when he arrived in steerage in 1898, and to this day she represents to me the very best instincts of our unique multi-cultured, multi-religious, polyglot experience in nation-building. In short, it's great to be an American.

My second core identity is my Judaism, part of which I express at Friday evening services at Congregation B'nai Israel. Bringing my national identity into the synagogue service was a way for me and for other congregants to express our joy at being able to meld the duality within us and to communally express how fortunate we are to be Jews living in America.

Is this a mixing of church (or synagogue) and state? No. However, the reverse, expressing our religious beliefs through government action, is not just a mixing of church and state, but is dangerous to our personal freedoms that make this country so hospitable to Jews and other minorities. Whenever we foist God upon our national identity we end up with concepts such as Manifest Destiny, the idea that God really ordained our expansion westward to the Pacific Ocean, which, in turn, justified our expulsion and decimation of Native Americans. It also leads to the belief that God is in our foxhole and not the enemy's.

The wall separating church and state is deteriorating with the active help of Congress and the Supreme Court. The faith-based initiative of the Bush era has resulted in proselytizing with the support of the tax dollar, and school vouchers can now be used in parochial schools thanks to a Supreme Court ruling. But these dangers pale in comparison to the infiltration of religion into the military environment.

Some years ago I reported on the situation at the Air Force Academy where cadets were pressured to attend the showing of Mel Gibson's movie, "The Passion of Christ." Christian proselytizing became so blatant that the football coach displayed a banner proclaiming "Team Jesus Christ." I also reported, amongst many other instances, that 80 soldiers at Fort Eustis, Virginia were confined to their barracks and put in "lockdown" because they refused to attend a Christian rock concert.

Although the military promised to rectify these breaches in the wall separating church and state, the problem continues to this day. Blake Page is an ex-cadet at West Point who now is special assistant to Mikey Weinstein, president of the Military Religious Freedom Foundation (MRFF), whose raison d'être is to eliminate Christian proselytizing and influence in the military. He recently reported on his return to West Point for the graduation of a friend and to attend his commissioning ceremony, which took place in the garden of the home of the Superintendant of West Point, Lieutenant General Huntoon.

Major Pickler, the Aide-de-Camp to the Superintendant officiated. Page reports: "It was going wonderfully for a while. Then Major Pickler pontificated: 'Mike is exactly the sort of junior officer I would want in my battalion.' Here he listed a long list of adjectives. Things like strong, intelligent, honorable, etc; all traits that are quite desirable in a good officer. After he appeared to be done with the list, he paused for a second and looked off into the sky before adding with emphasis, 'Christian.'"

Page comments: "As an officer in the army of a pluralistic society, this way of thinking is a problem . . . Imagine if Major Pickler had added Caucasian heterosexual male to his description of preferred junior officers. Would that be tolerable? By saying he prefers Christian subordinates, Major Pickler acknowledged that he would rather not have non-Christian subordinates."

This comment was made in the presence of the Superintendant of West Point, indeed in his own back yard. Although anecdotal, it shows how ubiquitous is overt Christian fundamentalism in the military academies as well as in the field. If you want a more complete picture go to the web site of the Military Religious Freedom Foundation and become depressed.

God's place is not in the military. A military that thinks it answers to God and not to the president (whether that president is a Republican or Democrat, white or black, male or female) is a dangerous force in society. Let's welcome our nationalism into our synagogues and churches, but keep our religions away from the nation-state, especially the military.

Ben Gamla Schools—A Threat to Judaism and the Constitution
2/22/12

Before we begin, a definition is in order. A charter school is a privately run school that receives its funding from the state as an alternative to a public school. It may be in private hands but it must conform to the concept of the separation of church and state as dictated by the First Amendment to the United States Constitution. Charter schools can have many areas of specialty. Some may stress science, others literature, etc. And then there is the expanding movement of Ben Gamla charter schools in South Florida (soon to go nation-wide), the brainchild of ex-Congressman Peter Deutsch.

Ben Gamla schools, named after a High Priest in Israel in the first century of the Common Era who established Jewish religious schools, are charter schools that specialize in teaching the Hebrew language. According to Deutsch there were 900 students enrolled in these schools last year, 1400 this year, and he anticipates 2,000 beginning in the fall of 2012.

At a recent meeting of the Palm Beach Board of Rabbis Deutsch met with rabbis to discuss this movement. I think it is fair to say that the majority of rabbis present expressed great concern over the concept of a Hebrew charter school. The president of the Donna Klein Jewish Academy of Boca Raton, a community day school with over 700 pupils from K to 12, expressed the fears of the rabbis. She succinctly stated the goal of Jewish education: "to instill Jewish life and soul into our Jewish families and the Jewish community"

This goal can be reached by spending your money and sending your kids either to a day school or to a congregational religious school, but either way it is a commitment of resources in the pursuit of instilling a Jewish identity into our children.

Now comes the Ben Gamla charter school, which is free public education, and parents believe that it is a replacement for congregational membership or day school tuition. It is a sort of Day School LIte (as in Bud Lite or Miller Lite). The rabbis and the president of Donna Klein realize that these parents are deluding themselves if they believe that the mere knowledge of the Hebrew language can do that job.

There are over a million Arabs in Israel and scores of Christian academics in the United States who speak fluent Hebrew, but that fact does not attach them to Judaism. The day school president exclaimed: "What is the long-range forecast with parents choosing this option? Yes, perhaps Jews who speak Hebrew, but Jews who speak the language of the Torah without knowing anything about Torah."

Further, they will take their Hebrew language educated son or daughter, hire a rabbi (or facsimile thereof) and have a bar or bat mitzvah without ever belonging to a congregation, thereby undercutting the foundation of Jewish survival in the Diaspora.

My second objection to the Ben Gamla charter schools is not based on Jewish considerations but on protection of the First Amendment and separation of church and state.

If the Ben Gamla schools only taught Hebrew, as presumed in the above quote, there would be no religious education there and no conflict with the Constitution. But that does not seem to be the case. At the Board of Rabbis meeting Deutsch explained that Ben Gamla schools teach Hebrew history, fly the Israeli flag, have Israeli activities, and avoid Halloween since it has Christian derivation. Further, Deutsch effused that the Ben Gamla school "does amazing things—it's not just Hebrew language," and it "changes their (student's) lives."

Deutsch defends all of the Jewish trappings because you can't teach a language without teaching culture, in this case "Hebrew Culture." Baloney. I took Spanish in school without immersing myself in Spanish culture. Anyone who studied a language will tell you that you learn the vocabulary and the grammar, period. Language studies do not do amazing things that change lives; that's what religion does.

I'm not sure the real objective of Ben Gamla schools is the teaching of the Hebrew language, but rather the infusion of this "Hebrew culture," which is really Jewish culture, which is really Judaism in another guise. Here we have mass prevarication (let's use the real word, lying) in the promulgation of religion—that's a fine foundation on which to build a religious experience— and it's unconstitutional.

Deutsch smugly assured the rabbis that he is a Yale Law School graduate and it is perfectly constitutional, whereupon I (smugly I guess) assured the rabbis that I, too, am a Yale Law School graduate and I think that it is not. The decisions of the Supreme Court are very clear (and would take me another column to explain) that you cannot have religion taught in a public school.

And charter schools are public schools, paid for by the taxes of all the people, Christians, Jews, Muslims, etc. If I were a non-Jew I would resent my money going to a Ben Gamla school. The very name of the school, Ben Gamla, is a tip-off. He was a Jewish High Priest and educator who ironically probably spoke Aramaic, the language of the Jews in Israel in the first century of the Common Era. He was not teaching Hebrew; he was teaching Judaism.

These Ben Gamla schools are situated in synagogues, utilizing empty classrooms during the middle of the week. Deutsch indicated that they pay rent in the neighborhood of $100,000 to $150,000 per year (money coming from the state). These congregations are putting money ahead of principle, taking short term gain at the expense of long term Jewish needs and the undercutting of the separation of church and state.

If the Ben Gamla schools are constitutional, what would stop the Catholic Church or the evangelical movement from establishing charter schools based on the study of Western Culture? We know that an integral part of that culture is the rise of Christianity. I do not want to pay for the study of their religion any more than they want to pay for Jewish kids studying Judaism under the guise of Hebrew language study.

Where is the ACLU when we need them? When will some good taxpayer step up and challenge this fraud? These schools are bad for Judaism and bad for America.

Beware of the Nose of the Camel
5/23/12

In late February I wrote a column criticizing the emergence of the government financed Ben Gamla Hebrew language charter school movement. In the guise of teaching Hebrew, which would be perfectly legal, the schools teach Jewish history and culture which are the bedrock of Judaism. Thus they are parochial schools and by receiving tax dollars they violate the prohibition of state support of religion. Eventually a court will have to rule on this.

As I wrote in my previous column, if the Ben Gamla schools are constitutional, what would stop the evangelical movement from establishing charter schools based on the study of Western Culture? We know that an integral part of that culture is the rise of Christianity. If Jews could use sleight of hand to turn a charter school into a parochial school, why not the evangelicals?

A little bit of history is helpful here. There have been periodic waves of fundamental evangelical fervor in this country. The last really big wave began in the Civil War and didn't peter out until the early 1880's. The NRA (not the National Rifle Association, but the National Reform Association), founded in 1864, proposed to rewrite the Preamble of the Constitution as follows:

"We, the people of the United States, humbly acknowledging Almighty God as the source of all authority and power in civil government, the Lord Jesus Christ as the Ruler among the nations . . . do ordain and establish this Constitution for the United States of America."

This was not a fringe movement. Many prominent politicians supported the Christianization of America, including the Democratic vice presidential candidate in the 1872 election. Fortunately, President Grant, who was reelected that year, quashed the movement with his staunch support of the Constitution, declaring that we should "keep the church and state forever separate."

In the face of this evangelical fever in the early 1870's Rabbi Max Lilienthal proclaimed this central tenet of American Judaism: "We are going to lay our cornerstone with the sublime motto, 'Eternal separation of state and church!' For this reason we shall never favor and ask support for our various benevolent institutions by the state; and if offered, we should not only refuse, but reject it with scorn and indignation . . . the public purse and treasury dares not be filled, taxed and emptied for sectarian purposes."

This is no time for American Jewry to stray from this credo. We are now in the midst of a fundamentalist evangelical revival that equals if not surpasses the post Civil War period. You may have noticed that it has changed the character of the Republican Party. It has already dominated many state legislatures and is as close to wielding real power on the federal level as it ever has been.

In fact, this latest iteration is more extreme, if that is possible, than those who proposed the Christian Preamble of the Constitution. The current leaders of the evangelical political movement derive their inspiration from R.J. Rushdoomy, a Christian theologian and primarily from his magnum opus "The Institutes of Biblical Law," published in 1973. Rushdoomy created a movement he named "Christian Reconstructionism" which called for an American theocracy. He advocated stripping citizenship from all non-Christians.

Many of today's political evangelical leaders have studied Christian Reconstructionism and adhere to its beliefs. Most are reluctant to publicly admit this. But not all. I have written about some of these people in a 2005 column, but they warrant a second look. To begin, the Reverend Randall Terry, the leader of Operation Rescue and the man behind the Terri Schiavo fiasco preached: "I want you to just let a wave of intolerance wash over you. I want to let a wave of hatred wash over you. Yes, hate is good. Our goal is a Christian nation. We have a biblical duty. We are called by God to conquer this country. We don't want equal time. We don't want pluralism. Our goal must be simple. We must have a Christian nation built on God's law, on the Ten Commandments. No apologies."

Terry is only one of many willing to spill the beans and let the world know the true aims of the political evangelical right. Gary Bauer, who ran for president in the Republican primary in 2000, served in the Reagan administration and is a prominent Christian Zionist, beloved by AIPAC: "We are engaged in a social, political and cultural war. There's a lot of talk in America about pluralism. But the bottom line is somebody's values will prevail. And the winner gets the right to teach our children what to believe."

Another evangelical leader (Ph.D. in economics and Rushdoomy's son-in-law), Gary North, founder of the Institute for Christian Economics (which he ultimately disbanded), proclaimed: "The long-term goal of Christians in politics should be to gain exclusive control over the franchise. Those who refuse to submit . . . must be denied citizenship . . . Christians are the lawful heirs, not non-Christians."

(Lest you think that this column is somehow anti-Christian, let me state that I am in fear of all fundamentalisms. Ultra-Orthodox Judaism if unchecked will turn Israel into a theocracy and Islam is in the throes of this same problem.)

Here's an alarming statistic—a recent poll indicated that 40 percent of Americans consider themselves evangelical Christians. Of course, not all are as extreme as those I just quoted. But there is fertile ground to plow for the radical leaders among them. Given the chance most evangelicals would lower and even eradicate the wall that currently separates church and state, even if they would not deny citizenship to non-Christians. For sure they would change the pluralistic open acceptance of minorities that we now enjoy.

It is in this climate that we should be aware of any stratagem that a religious school movement uses to secure public money. I believe that you never let the nose of the camel in the tent, for camels have a way of forcing themselves inside to the exclusion of the previous residents.

It is particularly galling to me that Jews, not willing to pay for our own religious and cultural schools, are attempting to nose our way into public funding by the subterfuge of Hebrew language charter schools. If the evangelicals follow our lead, we will have to plead guilty to the moral crime of abetting the undermining of our liberal society.

Beware: Short term monetary gain could lead to long term disaster.

Supporting West Bank Militants With Tax Exempt Contributions
8/4/10

This past month the *New York Times* devoted over two pages to an investigative report on American Jewish charities that funneled $200 million tax-deductible contributions over the past ten years to West Bank, although such settlement activity is in contradiction to American foreign policy.

The legality of this activity depends on legal interpretation, as does all life. Some of this money was used for what appears to be legitimate uses if it were spent in the United States or in Israel proper. The question is whether a community center or a school in a settlement in an area that is not recognized as part of Israel by our government becomes an illegal project. Israel is forbidden to spend direct United States aid in the West Bank, so does this make these privately funded expenditures ineligible for American tax-deductible status?

More clearly, it should be illegal for tax-deductible contributions to be used for guard dogs, bulletproof vests, rifle scopes and other paramilitary devices, as has been spent by these West Bank recipients of American charity dollars. To this point we are talking about settlements that are legal under Israeli law. But American tax-exempt dollars have also flowed to outposts in the West Bank that are illegal under Israeli law. Under any circumstances one would believe that these contributions would not qualify under the tax code as a tax-deductible item.

The crux of the legal question is whether the contribution is used for a religious, educational, humanitarian or political reason. The first three are generally acceptable, but political motivation would negate the tax deduction. This is not an easy question to answer. I was stunned to read in the *Times* that under American law, "Religious groups have no obligation to divulge their finances, meaning settlements may be receiving sums that cannot be traced."

Common sense tells us that these 40 or so relatively unknown charities that quietly work under the radar screen are doing this for political reasons, i.e. they want to populate the West Bank so that the "facts on the ground" will assure that there never will be a Palestinian state in the West Bank or East Jerusalem.

The leaders of these charities are usually circumspect in vocalizing this motivation for obvious reasons, but every so often it slips out. Kimberly Troup, director of the Christian Friends of Israel, commented: "The more that we build, the more that we support and encourage their right to live in the land, (West Bank and East Jerusalem) the harder it's going to be for disengagement, for withdrawal." That's about as clear a political purpose as one can find—which should lead to the conclusion that these charities should lose their tax-exempt status.

Who are the leaders of these charities that funnel money into the West Bank? Some are noted right-wing Jews. The most notorious is Dr. Irving Moskowitz of Miami Beach. Others are less well known, such as the family behind Haagen-Dazs ice cream or operatives in Monsey or Borough Park; and, of course, there are the Christian evangelicals who support a Greater Israel because it is a building block for the return of Jesus, the final rapture and the conversion of all of us Jews. These are our really good friends.

The *Times* noted the disgraced Orthodox Jew and crooked lobbyist Jack Abramoff. A Senate investigation disclosed that through his charitable foundation he donated $140,000 to Kollel Ohel Tiferet, a religious study group in Israel, for "educational and athletic" purposes. The money was used to finance a paramilitary operation on the West Bank. The investigation reported that Abramoff directed the settlers to use the educational and athletic cover because his accountant complained that money for sniper equipment and a jeep "don't look good' in terms of complying with the foundation's tax-exempt status.

How much of this subterfuge is used by these other "charities" that are funneling money to the West Bank, we may never know. We do know that many of the institutions and settlements on the West Bank which are recipients of this money are militant and openly political. The question which we must ask is whether the gun used by a West Bank settler aimed at a Palestinian West Bank village is paid for by tax-exempt American contributions.

One example: Mosques in the West Bank have been desecrated and one was recently torched to the ground. Israeli police arrested the head of the Od Yosef Chai yeshiva in the West Bank, Rabbi Yitzhak Shapira. He was released for lack of evidence. He is the same rabbi who recently published a book declaring that it is morally acceptable to kill Palestinian children because some day they will be Palestinian adults. A plaque inside his yeshiva thanks Dr. Irving Moskowitz of Miami Beach for his contribution. Question: Was the money used only for "educational and athletic" purposes?

J Street has begun a campaign to ask Treasury Secretary Timothy Geithner to launch an investigation into whether these charities which have funneled money into the West Bank have broken the law. It's time that other mainstream Jewish organizations pay attention to this little-recognized problem. If the settlements continue to expand and thrive, an honorable peace agreement will be impossible. Much is at stake, not just the integrity of American tax law.

THE SUPREME COURT

Citizens United—A Shameful Decision
1/27/10

This past week the Supreme Court in a 5-to-4 decision rejected limitations on corporate campaign spending under the McCain-Feingold Act. That law prohibited corporations from spending money from their general funds on national elections 30 days before a primary and 60 days before the general election. The McCain-Feingold restrictions were not overly onerous since corporations were still able to spend from their political actions committees within the blackout periods and outside the specified time windows. The Court ruled those blackout times illegal based on the concept of free speech under the First Amendment.

The majority decision by Justice Anthony Kennedy did indicate that the corporation must disclose its identity on the television or newspaper advertisement and that the money must be spent by an "independent" organization that does not coordinate these expenditures with the candidate's campaign committee. That's a joke. The corporation need only give the money to a trade association or the Chamber of Commerce to hide its identity from the public and to hide its actions from its own stockholders. If one believes that a swift-boating independent political committee cannot coordinate with the candidate without breaking the law, then that person lives on a different planet than I. One needs merely to read a newspaper to decipher the intent of a candidate and to ascertain the message of his or her political campaign.

The majority decision ruled that corporate speech equals human speech and cannot be abridged under the First Amendment. There were five separate opinions written, including Justice John Paul Stevens' 90-page dissent. The dissenters denied the very premise that corporations should have the same rights of real persons. Nowhere in the Constitution is a corporation mentioned. Governments allow corporations to be formed so that people can make money. In a democracy people are not born to make a profit. They are conceived with the expectation that they will live free lives with free speech. This is not the expectation for corporations.

Under the law we treat corporations differently. They are taxed differently than real live people. They are not accountable for crimes in the same way that real people are. I have never seen a corporation serve time in jail (maybe people affiliated with a corporation, but not the incorporeal corporation itself). Justice Stevens stressed that it is a "grave error" in treating corporate speech as that of human speech.

The main objection to this decision is that rather than promoting democracy through unfettered free speech, it will corrupt democracy by further strengthening the corporate forces that already control our government through their lobbyists. Corporations will now have the ability to spend million of dollars in the last week before an election by buying up television time to smear a candidate, leaving no time for him or her to repudiate the charges, even if he or she had the resources to respond.

Further, it strengthens the power of lobbyists, as if they needed more help. As Lawrence Noble, the former general counsel of the Federal Election Commission, responded in the *New York Times*, all the lobbyist has to do now is to say to the legislator, "We have got a million we can spend advertising for you or against you—whichever one you want."

Lest you think that this response is a reflection of knee-jerk liberals, including myself, screaming Chicken Little's refrain that the sky is falling, let me quote Benjamin Ginsberg, a Republican campaign lawyer who worked with the Swift Boat Veterans for Truth, formed to smear John Kerry in 2004. Commenting on the Supreme Court decision, in the *Times*, he said: "It will put on steroids the trend that outside groups are increasingly dominating campaigns. Candidates lose control of their message. Some of these guys lose control of their whole personalities."

Ginsberg continued: "Parties will sort of shrink in the relative importance of things and outside groups will take over more of the functions—advertising support, get out the vote—that parties do now." What Ginsberg doesn't say is that these outside groups are funded by large corporate interests; thus, corporations will increasingly take over the traditional roles of political parties. If we aren't already there, this transforms our government into a corporate oligarchy under the guise of a free democracy of people—real people who actually live and breathe, eat and defecate, love and hate. Rather than maximizing the welfare of these real people the object of government becomes the maximizing of profits.

We saw this coming. In 2006 the Supreme Court in a 5-to-4 decision ruled that a Vermont law limiting the amount of money that a person could spend on a campaign was unconstitutional on the basis that money equals free speech. In 2008 the same conservative majority of five justices ruled that the "millionaire's amendment" of McCain-Feingold was unconstitutional, also based on the proposition that the use of money equals free speech. Justice John Paul Stevens answered these decisions with a simple statement: "Money is property; it is not speech."

That simple concept—money is property; it is not speech—negates the majority decision in last week's case (Citizens United v. Federal Election Commission) in that corporate money spent to manipulate elections is not covered under the First Amendment. Thanks to the appointees of George Bush, that is not the world we live in today.

In its editorial the day after the decision the *Times* summed it up: "The Citizens United ruling is likely to be viewed as a shameful bookend to Bush v. Gore." In 2000 the Conservatives on the Court handed the election to Republicans and now this decision distorts the political system and strengthens Republican candidates.

Supreme Court Diminishes Our Democracy
4/20/11

Unlike revolutions that occur with dramatic frequency, the American legal system changes our society in small incremental steps, with only an occasional case such as *Brown v. Board of Education* that provides a legal tsunami.

This truth is reflected in our conservative Supreme Court's dismantling of election reforms under the 2002 Bipartisan Campaign Reform Act (the McCain-Feingold law), as well as attempts by local and state governments to control political spending. Let's review the steps year by year.

2006—Vermont passed a law limiting the amount of money that a state candidate could spend. On a national level McCain-Feingold limited the amount that an individual can contribute to a candidate. The Vermont law limited the amount that any candidate could spend, no matter the source of the money. The intent was to spur debate and dialogue, rather than having the election turn on who had unlimited money to purchase the most attack ads on television.

The law was immediately attacked by the Republican Party. Before the Supreme Court their argument was that it limited free speech. If you have the money, you have the right to spend it on behalf of your beliefs. In essence, money equals speech.

The counter-argument is that the First Amendment protection of free speech was intended to protect democracy and that unlimited expenditures by the rich undermine democracy. Free speech is a tool toward an end, not an end in itself.

Given the fact that it can cost $5 million for a successful congressional campaign and much more for a senatorial campaign, the office holder is left with due bills and commitments to his funders. Vermont law-makers openly admitted in public hearings that campaign contributions affected what laws won their attention. Show me an office holder who doesn't respond to a call from a major contributor and I'll show you an ex-lawmaker. One can argue that we have the best politicians that money can buy.

The Supreme Court ruled in a 5-4 decision that the Vermont law was unconstitutional. The majority justices (Thomas, Alito, Roberts, Scalia and Kennedy) agreed that money equals speech.

2006—In that same year the identical conservative majority ruled that the provision in McCain-Feingold that prohibited corporations or unions from paying for television ads that attacked individual candidates during the 60 days prior to the general election violated their right of free speech.

2008—The five conservative justices ruled that the "millionaire's amendment" of McCain-Feingold was unconstitutional. That provision stated that when a candidate spent more than $350,000 of his or her own money for a House seat the opponent was allowed to receive triple the usual amount of contributions from a single person, $6,900 rather than $2,300. The rationale of the law was to create a level playing field in the political process. The majority ruled that the millionaire's amendment stifled the free speech of the rich.

Justice John Paul Stevens in his dissent wrote: "The millionaire's amendment quiets no speech at all. On the contrary, it does no more than assist the opponent of a self-funding candidate in his attempts to make his voice heard; this amplification in no way mutes the voice of the millionaire, who remains able to speak as loud and as long as he likes in support of his campaign."

2010—That year will be remembered for the 180-page landmark decision (including a passionate 90-page dissent by Justice Stevens) in the *Citizens United* case. Just in time before the midterm election, the same five conservative justices ruled unconstitutional the provisions in McCain-Feingold that restricted campaign spending by corporations and unions. They decided that for purposes of free speech corporations and unions are like people and deserve First Amendment protection.

I have never seen a corporation go to jail or bleed from bodily attack or even show remorse for a wrongdoing. Corporations are fictional structures that we create to do commerce, but now we are told that they are human, just like you and me. President Obama called the decision "a major victory for big oil, Wall Street banks, health insurance companies and the other powerful interests that marshal their power every day in Washington to drown out the voices of everyday Americans." He was prescient. We saw the results of anonymous corporate funding of front organizations that swamped the airways in the 2010 Republican takeover of the House.

2011—In President Obama's State of the Union address he said that the *Citizens United* decision "will open the floodgates for special interests—including foreign corporations—to spend without limit in our election." Later we learned that the U.S. Chamber of Commerce raised money from foreign corporations and placed it in the same account which funded their political attack ads. The Chamber denies that that portion of the account containing foreign corporate money was used in the campaign. Cmon, all money is fungible. But the issue remained cloudy.

Now two young men working in this country, one a Canadian and the other a dual Israeli-Canadian, have instituted a law suit to overturn the longstanding ban on political contributions from non-U.S. citizens. They are represented by the law firm of Jones Day. In my youth as a labor lawyer I interacted with lawyers from Jones Day who represented one of the Big Three auto companies (I can't remember which one). I can tell you this: it is one of the best law firms in the country. I have nothing but the highest respect for their integrity and expertise.

Jones Day clients include some of the biggest corporate beneficiaries of the *Citizen United* decision, including Koch Industries and the U.S. Chamber of Commerce. They deserve every penny that they charge. My estimate is that the junior lawyers assigned to the case hire out at $500 per hour (senior lawyers probably command $1000 per hour).

Here's the question: Who is paying the bill? Certainly not the two clients, one a young lawyer, the other a medical resident. Obviously, some anonymous corporate giant with foreign interests is attempting to overturn the ban on foreign political contributions. If the Court allows these two young non-Americans to contribute to American political campaigns, it is only another law suit away from opening the floodgates to foreign corporations as well. Remember that the Court in *Citizens United* declared that a corporation is just another person equal before the law to all of us eating and breathing persons.

This Court is the legacy of the appointments of the George W. Bush administration which was bought and paid for by big business. The dividends on that purchase continue to accrue through the work of the Supreme Court. Given enough time, big money will destroy any real democracy in this country. Yes, we will have elections and the outward semblance of freedom, but the outcome will have been preordained, or rather should I say, bought and paid for.

THE UNION MOVEMENT

What's Good for the Unions is Good for America
4/14/09

Senator Ted Kennedy and Representative George Miller have introduced the Employee Free Choice Act (EFCA) and a major battle will be waged with unions on one side and the U.S. Chamber of Commerce on the other. It is this legislation that I want to discuss. I do this from a Jewish perspective. Let us not forget that Jews have been at the forefront of unionization. In the past we have fought for poor Jews working in the sweatshops of the Lower East Side. Today we toil for poor workers regardless of their religious or ethnic identities. It's part of our religious obligation of Tikun Olam (the repair of the world).

My initial premise is that this country needs unions. The US Bureau of Labor statistics show that workers in unions earn 30 percent more than non-union workers. Lest you worry that this overhead hurts union employers, a comparison of Costco (unionized) to Sam's Club (not unionized) shows that Costco has nearly 40 percent more in labor costs than Sam's Club, but has almost double the per-employee profit margin. It is not hindered by an almost 50 percent employee turnover as experienced by Wal-Mart (Sam's Club parent company). Even the bedeviled auto companies have not reached their nadir because of unionization. Only 10 percent of a car's cost is attributable to labor. Poor management decisions and huge health care costs, not unions, got them to the brink of extinction.

Wages aside, unions affect the working conditions. Just this last month I read in the *New York Times* the story of a worker at the deli counter of the Whole Foods store at Union Square in Manhattan. It reported that he was fired for stealing a sandwich and the company challenged his right to receive unemployment benefits. My first reaction was, well, he deserved it. Thieves should be fired. But it turned out that he was throwing away ten sandwiches at the end of the day and he put one aside for himself. His supervisor asked him what he was doing. He explained that since he had to throw away unsold food, he was going to eat the sandwich that he put aside. The government ruled that he had a right to unemployment benefits, but he still lost his job. If there were a union there he would still be working at Whole Foods for $11.50 an hour rather than being currently unemployed.

Under the present law a union must win a secret ballot to be certified as the bargaining agent if the company demands it. The problem with the current system is that the National Labor Relations Board (NLRB) reports that in 30 percent of the elections management has illegally intimidated and fired workers for union activity. The employees are asked to vote in an environment of fear.

After much litigation if the company is found guilty it would have to pay lost wages to the employee (minus what unemployment benefits he or she received). This is a small price to pay for breaking a union organizing drive. And the time line is ludicrous. In one extreme case, Smithfield Foods fired union supporter Keith Ludlum at its North Carolina slaughterhouse in 1994. Under the current NLRB system Ludlum didn't get his job back until 2006.

Even when the plant is unionized many companies "run the clock out." They bargain and bargain for over a year after which they can begin a drive to decertify the union. They never sign a union contract. Bottom line: the current system is stacked in favor of management to the detriment of workers.

The proposed Employee Free Choice Act (EFCA) provides two key changes. First, a union will not have to have a secret ballot. If the majority of workers sign union cards it will automatically be recognized as the bargaining agent. The Chamber of Commerce will claim this is un-American since it denies a secret ballot election. But what good is a secret ballot if you are afraid of losing your job in the process of demanding that ballot? There can be little coercion on a worker to sign a union card. If he refuses a union organizer his job is not at stake.

Second, EFCA requires that if the union and company do not reach agreement within 90 days a mediator must be called. If after 30 days of mediation there is no agreement the contract dispute is sent to arbitration and the arbitration panel can impose a binding two-year contract on both parties. This solves the problem of companies running out the one-year clock so that they can again challenge the union.

The middle class in America is disappearing for many reasons including the greed of top management that redistributes income to the very rich. But a major tool in this process was the destruction of the union movement beginning in the Reagan years. It's time to rebuild the middle class. The Employee Free Choice Act is a good start in that process.

(Postscript: EFCA never saw the light of day in Congress, but hope is eternal and there is always the possibility of seeing it emerge in the future.)

Do We Really Need Unions?
4/28/09

My last column discussed the Employee Free Choice Act (EFCA) pending before Congress. The reaction to that column by a few people was that "unions were important at one time, but we don't need them anymore." This column is dedicated to the premise that we need them now more than ever.

It has always been the position of management that unions were not needed and, indeed, were evil. In 1902 during the great anthracite coal strike George Baer, president of the Reading Railroad which owned the mines, testified before a commission established by President Teddy Roosevelt that the "rights and interests of the laboring man will be protected and cared for—not by the labor agitators, but by the Christian men to whom God in His infinite wisdom has given the control of property interests of the country." Concerning the miners he argued, "These men don't suffer, Why, hell, half of them don't even speak English."

Times have not changed that much; only the language and the presentation have been cleaned up. Before the last presidential election Bernie Marcus, the founder of Home Depot, called the prospect of the enactment of the Employee Free Choice Act "the demise of civilization." Wal-Mart CEO Lee Scott recently said of unions, "We like driving the car and we're not going to give the steering wheel to anybody but us."

We know that it is his obligation to drive that car to the bank with as much money for the stockholders as possible. The question is how many bodies Scott will run over along the road. The aim of a union is not to divert the course of the car, but to make sure that those who service it get a little of the money before management deposits the whole bundle in the bank. This analogy is reminiscent of the old union song: "The banks are made of marble with a guard at every door, and the vaults are stuffed with silver that the miners sweated for."

Are unions needed today? Here are the statistics: The number of workers earning poverty wages approached nearly 25 percent of the workforce at a time when corporate profits doubled from 2001 to the recent economic downturn. Viewing the picture over the last 60 years, inflation-adjusted wages have decreased. This affects white collar as well as blue collar workers. The paychecks of 60 percent of college graduates are inflation-adjusted lower today than they were in 1960. One-sixth of male college graduates earn less today than the least paid high school graduates of the late 1960's.

There is a correlation between these statistics and the fact that in 1955 unionization in the private sector stood at 39 percent of the workforce compared to just over seven percent today. Read that last sentence and underline it. There is a correlation between the decrease of union jobs and the current lower income of the middle class.

I know that there are companies that care for their workers and pay decent wages, but on a macro scale there is no doubt that without unions workers do not receive adequate compensation. As I pointed out in my last column, the US Bureau of Labor statistics show that workers in unions earn 30 percent more than non-union workers. Just one example: In comparable sized cities, where hotels are largely unionized, room maids make $20 an hour; in cities where half the hotels are unionized, they make $12 an hour; in non-union cities, $7 an hour.

Let's get Jewish. The non-unionized workers at the kosher slaughterhouse of the infamous Agriprocessors (where the owners are under indictment for labor crimes) earn $7.25 an hour while unionized Hebrew National (which, it appears, actually does answer to a higher authority) pays $12.65 an hour.

Are unions needed today? Last month the *New York Times* reported that under the Bush administration the Wage and Hour Division of the Labor Department did not protect workers, according to a Government Accountability Office report. It showed that the agency "mishandled 9 of the 10 cases brought by a team of undercover agents posing as aggrieved workers." In one actual case it took 22 months to investigate a complaint that eventually showed that a restaurant owner owed $230,000 in back wages and tips. The government settled the case when he paid the back wages, but he was allowed to steal the tips from his employees.

In another case an employer that owed $200,000 in overtime settled the case with the Labor Department for a paltry $1000. Under the Obama administration, Secretary of Labor Hilda Solis is going to hire an additional 250 investigators, bringing the total to 750. Even assuming that the intention is now to protect workers, the ability of the government is limited. A workforce of over 150 million cannot be protected by 750 government agents. The only real protection is a union at the workplace that can stand up to the George Baers and the Lee Scotts of this world.

Are unions still needed? Yes, now more than ever, especially if we want to get back to the environment of the 1950's when the middle class was not endangered. Unionization is an important tool in our attempt to reach that end and the Employee Free Choice Act (EFCA) will help us get there.

(Postscript: As indicated in the postscript to the preceding column, EFCA was blocked in Congress, but that does not mean that it cannot be revived in a future more union-friendly Congress)

ADDITIONAL TOPICS

HEADING On the Road to Plutocracy
5/22/13

A couple years back my wife and I visited San Francisco, and forgetting how cold that city can be I neglected to bring a light windbreaker. My problem was solved by a street vendor at Fisherman's Wharf who sold me a jacket for eighteen bucks. I still wear it today. It's not expensive but it's a fairly stylish jacket. Skip to last year: On our way to visit our children in Atlanta I realized that I left my windbreaker at home and would need it for the weekend. (They call Atlanta the south, but for this Floridian it's a cold city.)

So while in the Atlanta airport I decided to buy a new jacket. I realized that I would not find one for eighteen bucks, but I'm not poor and I figured that I would have to spend between $75 and $125. I spotted a nice looking windbreaker in the window of Ermenegildo Zegna. I had never heard of this company, but I subsequently learned that it has a fancy outlet on Fifth Avenue in New York and advertises in all of the upscale fashion magazines, of which I was oblivious because I don't read them. I still cannot pronounce its first name.

Anyway, here's the story: I ask the imperious clerk the price. How much would you think it could be? $300? 600? A thousand? He answers, without blinking an eye—you ready for this—$2100. That's not a misprint. $2100. What does this say about our society when the rich spend $2100 on a flimsy windbreaker, which incidentally didn't look much better than my eighteen buck San Francisco special?

At the same time I discovered Ermenegildo Zegna I saw the documentary "The Queen of Versailles" which chronicled Orlando residents David and Jackie Siegel's project of building the largest house in America at 90,000 square feet. During that time they lived in a 26,000 square foot home with a household staff of 19. Speaking of large homes, I live in a condominium on the ocean in Broward County. About a mile down the road someone is building a mansion (it looks like the size of a Jewish Community Center) repudiated to be valued at $65 million.

What is obviously happening in the United States is that the wealthy are prospering while the rest of society is hurting, hurting badly. Enough of the anecdotal evidence. Here are some hard statistics: In 2007 the top one percent earned over 23 percent of all income in this country, more than the bottom 50 percent. The top one percent owns more wealth than the bottom 90 percent. Poverty is increasing and the middle class is disappearing. A two-income family now has less disposable income than a one-income family did thirty years ago. The average median net worth of American households (everything you own) is a mere $67,000. For Caucasians, it's $87,000; for Hispanics, it's $8,000; for African Americans, it's $5,000. Without home ownership, that last figure drops to $1,000.

The disparity between the rich and the poor is growing. The appetite of the rich appears to be insatiable. It always has been. In 1886 Samuel Gompers, a nice Jewish boy who was the founding president of the American Federation of Labor, commented, "The man who has his millions will want everything he can lay his hands on and then raise his voice against the poor devil who wants ten cents more a day."

Except now we are talking about billions, not merely millions. Even though the top tax rate for the wealthy has been increased by three percent, the really rich never pay the top rate because of loopholes. As Warren Buffet has disclosed, he pays a lower rate than his secretary. Hedge fund billionaires pay merely 15 percent, thanks to another loophole. And why should a person who earns money by investing rather than by physical labor pay a lower rate (capital gains limited to 15 percent) while a policeman or teacher could pay 25 percent or higher? The argument that a person or a company would not invest money if he or it had to pay a higher tax rate on profits is fallacious. What is a person or company going to do as an alternative—put the money under a mattress? Capital gains is just another loophole for the rich. It saves me money, but I know it's wrong.

Here are some more statistics: The wealthiest 400 Americans earn an average of $345 million a year and pay an effective tax rate of only 16.6 percent. Thanks to tax loopholes, major corporations pay no taxes at all. This includes companies like Exxon and G.E. The Federal government's General Accounting Office (GAO) reported that two out of three corporations in the United States paid no Federal income taxes between 1998 and 2005. These corporations had a combined $2.5 trillion in sales but paid no income taxes to the IRS.

The outcome of the widening gap between the rich and the poor and the increasing wealth of corporate America at the expense of the average wage earner is that wealth is being concentrated in the hands of the few. This is dangerous to democracy. It leads to something worse than an oligarchic form of government. It leads to a plutocracy. An oligarchy is a government ruled by a few. But those few could be ideologues who care for their people. One can argue whether the communism of the Castro brothers is good or bad for Cuba, but you have to give them credit that the intent of their oligarchy is to increase the welfare of the general public. I would argue that the intent was noble, the outcome a failure.

A plutocracy is government run by a few, but these few are rich, and their intent most often is not to increase the health and welfare of the masses. Rather, it is to increase the wealth of the few. Human nature being what it is, not much has changed since Sam Gompers made his comment in 1886. Our emerging plutocracy is assured through the process of lobbying. In 2009 there were 13,694 registered lobbyists in Washington. They spent $3.47 billion focused on merely 100 senators and 435 members of the House.

Unfortunately, with the recent Supreme Court decisions that corporations are people (I'll believe that when I see one of them put to death in the State of Texas) and as people they have the right to freedom of speech (Citizens United case), i.e. they can spend as much on lobbying and on political campaigns as they like, I do not see an end to the drift toward plutocracy.

Yes, we will have elections and people will think that they really have control over their government, but the very rich will increasingly rule our lives, and it will not be for the better for the average person. Let us hope that a future Supreme Court will change these rulings and reverse this dangerous course of history.

Learning to Live with a Nuclear Iran
2/6/13

Imagine what our world would be today if we followed the advice of the madman General Curtis Le May who was a proponent of a nuclear first strike arguing that we should give the Soviet Union the "Sunday punch" before they did it to us. Absent a nuclear strike, there were those who argued that we should have invaded Russia before it had the capability to go nuclear.

The Cold War was not pretty, but it eventually led to a much saner world where today American capitalists invest heavily in the Russian economy and the superpowers live in peace with one another. This outcome is the result of a policy, primarily attributed to the diplomat George Kennan, called "containment." It reflects careful patience in contrast to using military might to solve problems.

Today containment seems to be a dirty word. President Obama has made it perfectly clear that he will use military force if necessary to stop Iran from acquiring nuclear capacity if economic sanctions fail. He explicitly said that he is not interested in containment, which relies on long term diplomatic negotiations.

It is difficult to know whether this has been political rhetoric during a campaign, whether it was said as a deterrent to Israeli unilateral action before the November election, or whether he really rejects the concept of containment, which has served our country well over the last half-century.

One thing is for sure, the country has taken his words to heart. Even the *New York Times* in an editorial opined, "War, of course, would be disastrous. But so would an Iran with a nuclear weapon." But is that true? Are we involved here in a hysteria reminiscent of the anti-Communist fear of the 1940's and 50's?

Kenneth Waltz, a scholar at the Saltzman Institute and an Adjunct Professor of Political Science at Columbia University, argues in *Foreign Affairs* that a nuclear Iran would restore stability in the Middle East, rather than the reverse. Pakistan and India fought three wars against each other before they acquired the bomb. Now they live in peace, albeit a tense peace. Waltz comments, "There has never been a full-scale war between two nuclear-armed states." Waltz, along with many other Middle East scholars, debunks the idea of "mad mullahs" going wild with the bomb. He writes that they are "perfectly sane ayatollahs who want to survive just like any other leaders," and "they show no propensity for self-destruction."

As a survival technique, it is wise to try to put yourself in the adversary's shoes, to view the world from his/her/its perspective. It is perfectly reasonable from Iran's parochial viewpoint to want a nuclear capacity without having any aggressive motivations. In the not-distant past Iran was invaded by Iraq and fought an eight-year war (six years on its own soil) in which Saddam Hussein was armed and backed by the U.S. government. Its internal democracy was destroyed by the U.S.-backed coup in 1953 that toppled its elected prime minister and ensconced a cruel dictator, the U.S. allied Shah.

Currently, Iran is surrounded by five nuclear powers (Pakistan, India, Israel, Russia and China), not all of whom can be counted on to leave it alone. From a purely defensive viewpoint (not denying that all countries, including Iran, want regional hegemony) it makes sense for Iran to possess nuclear capacity. All human beings and all countries want to be in a situation where one could say, "Don't tread on me."

It's also bad policy for the U.S. to attack Iran's nuclear installations. This would be viewed by the average Iranian as just another American hostile action, consonant with our historical meddling into their country—and it would turn the anti-mullah movement into government supporters. Iran does not have the capacity to wage a conventional war against us, but it could retaliate against Americans world-wide, so that you and I would not want to travel overseas.

An American military action against a Muslim country would increase anti-American hatred and be a boon for Al Qaeda recruitment. Let's not even contemplate the effect on the world economy, with the very real possibility of the disruption of the oil supply, throwing us into another severe recession. Finally, it won't be effective. Iran is a large, proud nation, and there is every reason to believe that a military strike today would only energize it to double its efforts in the future. Ultimately, if it desires, it will obtain nuclear capacity.

The bottom line is that military force is unnecessary and in the long run ineffectual. Containment, long arduous diplomatic maneuvers, is the only sensible response.

President John F. Kennedy, in a speech at American University in 1963, said: "History teaches us that enmities between nations, as between individuals, do not last forever. However fixed our likes and dislikes may seem, the tide of time and events will often bring surprising changes in the relations between nations and neighbors . . . So let us not be blind to our differences, but let us also direct attention to our common interests and the means by which those differences can be resolved."

We learned this lesson vis-à-vis Russia. Now is the time to apply it to Iran.

It's Time to Reconsider the Draft
7/18/12

In 2005 I wrote a column entitled "Bring on the Draft" in which I argued that we need shared sacrifice from all segments of society. We know who joins the military. With the exception of military brats, it is the economically needy, often fighting to get out of the ghetto. A job, any kind of job, and the ability to get training that could someday earn them a decent living are powerful motivators. The middle and upper classes declare our wars while the lower classes fight them.

Certainly the politicians are not sharing the sacrifice. At the time that Congress decided to enter into the Iraqi war only one of 535 members of Congress had a child in the military and that number did not increase during the entire nine years of the war. Compare that to Franklin D. Roosevelt who had sons in World War II and Lyndon B. Johnson whose sons-in-law served in Vietnam. It has been pointed out that in three generations the Bushes went from war hero in World War II, to war evader in Vietnam, to none of the extended family showing up in Iraq.

This was my thesis in the 2005 column: I learn a little bit from history. This country understood the folly of Vietnam only after the children of the middle and upper classes either had to die there or spend great energy to avoid being drafted. As long as poor rural white and urban black kids were dying, it was a convenient war. When we had to share the sacrifice equally, we turned against the war. I believe that as long as we have an all-voluntary Army this country will follow a president (either Obama or Romney, which is a distinct possibility) into another foreign adventure. When the great middle class has to pay with the lives of our children we come to our senses.

This issue has resurfaced this past month. General Stanley McCrystal, the former commander in Afghanistan, called for reinstating the draft: "I think if a nation goes to war, every town, every city needs to be at risk. You make that decision and everybody has skin in the game."

Last week, Thomas Ricks, a fellow at the Center for a New American Security, wrote a lead opinion piece in the *New York Times* entitled "Let's Draft Our Kids." In it he argued for a draft of all 18-year-olds, both male and female, into national service.

But he didn't go all the way. He presented three options. Choose 18 months in the military and receive excellent post-service benefits, including free college tuition. Choose national civilian service for two years (cleaning parks, rebuilding crumbling infrastructure, etc.) and receive good benefits and some form of college tuition assistance, not necessarily totally free. Choose neither of these options and you don't have to serve your country, but neither will you be eligible for government assistance throughout your lifetime, including Medicare, subsidized college loans, government mortgage guarantees, etc.

I believe that this evades the shared sacrifice doctrine in one important way. Two years civilian service is a minor sacrifice in comparison with military service that can put your life at risk. The vast majority of middle and upper class kids will choose civilian service. The whole idea of everyone serving in the military is that if the 535 members of Congress have children and grandchildren in the military they won't be eager to save the world or our presumed national interests at the expense of their own kin.

Also it is very unfair to offer an alternative to opt out to an 18-year-old, a choice that could affect his relationship to his government for the rest of his life. This kind of decision is beyond his maturity level.

If everyone serves in the military it does not mean that there would be no community service. Our current military includes approximately 1,500,000 on active duty with another approximately 850,000 in the Reserves, and a minimum of 250,000 private contractors in Iraq and Afghanistan. We could use a little larger Army so that we would not have recurrent tours of duty.

But a draft of all 18-year-olds would produce four million enlistees per year, meaning an 18-month draft would produce an army of six million—roughly two and one half to three times larger than our present forces, depending on how you factor in the Reserves and the private contractors. Admittedly during peace time we would not need a military of this size.

After basic training the military could assign these soldiers to civilian community service—teachers' aides, social work with the aged, work in national parks, work in day care centers, etc. The key distinction here is that they do this as part of the military, and if we find ourselves in another war they are subject to equal combat duty as the soldier who serves in a more traditional army job. That is the essence of shared responsibility.

Is this a political non-starter? Yes and no. If full college tuition were available to every 18-year-old, the middle class would look at this very seriously. If a single-pay health benefit were also guaranteed after army service (Medicare for veterans and not just for the elderly) this would be a clincher. This model could change our society for the better at the same time providing shared sacrifice on behalf of our country.

Would this raise taxes? Probably, but for the vast middle and lower classes it would be a tax advantage. Who would not agree to a modest tax increase if it meant that you would not have to pay college tuition for your children, or alternatively, your children would not have to mortgage their futures through college loans? Who would not pay a modest tax increase if you knew that your kids would have health insurance guaranteed through an expansion of Medicare as a result of military service?

But I want to get back to my original motivation in my 2005 column. I want to end here with the same conclusion as in that column. The bottom line is that we had a war in Iraq that was being fought by Other People's Children, to use a phrase borrowed from William Broyles (the editor of Texas Monthly). He commented that, "If you support this war, but assume that . . . Other People's Children should fight it, then you are worse than a hypocrite. If it's not worth your family fighting it, then it's not worth it, period."

Only in this way can we keep ourselves from future follies such as Iraq, Vietnam and an over-commitment in Afghanistan, well beyond the earlier task of removing al Qaeda from the country. It would even temper our enthusiasm for a military solution to the Iranian problem.

Dr. Kevorkian and the Right to Die
7/6/11

The recent death of Dr. Jack Kevorkian has brought the whole issue of the right to die back into the public forum after a hiatus of a couple years. Activists on both sides of the issue restated their positions. The conservative columnist Ross Douthat in *The New York Times* was most strident in his denial of the right to die with dignity and his condemnation of Kevorkian, calling him a killer and a murderer.

I disagree. No doubt Kevorkian was an idiosyncratic person, but he shed light on a personal right that is being denied to each of us by our restrictive laws. My position is quite simple: I have the right to die with dignity at the time of my own choosing. Over the past ten years I have written three columns on this issue and I am afraid that what I write today is a rehash of the same arguments, but, since the dialogue has been reignited in the wake of Dr. Kevorkian's demise, I believe that it is a necessity.

I am aware that traditional Judaism, as well as a majority of liberal rabbis, would disagree with my position, but that does not deter me. From my perspective, Torah and Talmud reflect mankind reaching toward God, not God-given dictums imposed upon us. I believe that we are masters over our own bodies and have the right to choose whether we live or die. The Talmud and the traditional commentators assert that this is not true. "The soul is Yours (i.e. God's) and the body Your handiwork" is to be taken literally. We have no right to determine the length of our days without God's permission.

This is in spite of impending Alzheimer's disease or extreme pain and agony or a myriad of disabilities that make life problematic. The question that I ask is, life at what cost? When do we deserve the peace of death? The Talmud could not have envisioned our modern capabilities to prolong breathing well beyond our capabilities to enjoy life. It is painful for me to say that I know some people who are breathing but are really not living.

I cannot conceive that God wants us to suffer pain and indignities beyond our control. I cannot conceive that God wants us to continue existing while not recognizing our spouse or children. Faced with Alzheimer's, why should I not have the right to contact a Dr. Kevorkian? Rabbi Mordecai Kaplan's famous edict applies here: the past has a vote, but not a veto. I read and respect Talmud dictums, but I am not convinced of their wisdom on this issue. I have enough faith in my own moral compass to arrive at a different conclusion.

In his *New York Times* column Douthat opines that it is not "considered merciful to prescribe an overdose to a cancer victim against her will, or to gently smother a sleeping Alzheimer's patient." Of course this is pure fearmongering. We are speaking here of an individual making a decision over his or her own body. We are not talking about mercy killing. But it does bring us to the domino or slippery slope argument, the only non-religious plausible case against free choice.

It goes something like this: If we allow anyone to terminate life, it is a short step toward government deciding that it would be more humane and cost effective to end the lives of old and sick patients and other "drags on society." This certainly has resonance within the Jewish community, thinking of the Nazi atrocities on "defectives" as well as Jews. It evokes the fear of a slippery slope into a moral abyss. It starts with pulling the plug of a respirator; it continues with allowing a person to end his or her own life; it ends with our killing "defective" babies when they are born. It is a powerful argument of fear, but not necessarily logic.

After Auschwitz we know that anything is possible. Yet fear of ultimate consequences down a long, long road can totally immobilize a person or society. No human social laws or curbs on unbridled capitalism would ever be passed because they would be the first steps on the inexorable road to communism. It was precisely this kind of reasoning that kept America 50 years behind Europe in the evolving of social legislation such as Social Security or Medicare. The bottom line is whether we feel comfortable in the stability of our own social system or whether we see a rising Nazi-ism in the future. I feel comfortable enough not to worry about the domino effect.

Legislation in Oregon and Washington have provided for the right to die with dignity for a patient within six months of death from a terminal illness. Unfortunately this does not cover an Alzheimer's victim who could live well beyond this time limit. But their laws are a beginning. The Supreme Court in Montana legalized doctor-assisted euthanasia in that the doctor can provide the terminal pill but the patient must take it himself.

The importance of the Montana decision is that the court decided this case on the Right of Privacy—the right to do to ourselves in our homes what we want without government intrusion (a basic libertarian conservative belief). The Supreme Court of the United States denied this right in 1997 in a complicated split decision (Vacco v. Quill). But that case was argued on the meaning of the Constitution's equal protection clause or its liberty guarantee. It may be time to challenge state laws against the right to die using the Supreme Court's evolving Right of Privacy based on the 4th Amendment, a position explicitly enunciated in a 1967 case (Katz v. U.S.) where Justice Potter Stewart wrote, "The Fourth Amendment protects people, not places."

It's interesting that in Oregon and Washington many people who obtain the right to take a life-ending pill never use it. But it is important to them that they have control over their own lives and how they will die. That is the crux of the matter. Will the government dictate to us how much pain and suffering we will endure or will we be masters of our own fate? I choose self-determination.

Déjà vu—Social Security Under Attack
2/16/11

It may surprise you that Social Security is a Jewish issue. But it really is. Judaism has always stressed communal responsibility. This is reflected in the difference between the words charity and tzedakah. Charity comes from a Greek word meaning compassion. If you feel moved by someone's plight you can contribute.

The mitzvah of tzedakah, translated into English as charity, derives from the Hebrew tzedek, which means justice. It matters not whether you are moved or how much compassion you have, you are obligated to help the less fortunate in our society. This stress upon the communal is taken to such lengths that on Yom Kippur we pray for forgiveness in the plural—forgive us for the sins that we have committed, not forgive me for the sins that I have committed. On our most personal holiday we cannot shake off our responsibility for the entire community.

This brings us to the topic of Social Security, the bedrock of communal responsibility. It is once again under attack. President Bush failed in his attempt to privatize it while he was president, but a campaign toward that end has been reignited. Its first step is to declare that social security is economically unviable.

The *National Review* blared the deceptive headline, "Social Security Now Officially Broke." Even the Associated Press ran a headline that Social Security will be "drained" by 2037. We will discuss what drained really means in a few more paragraphs.

The attackers have even resurrected the ghost of Alf Landon, who was the Republican candidate against FDR in 1936. He called Social Security "a cruel hoax" because "The so-called reserve fund . . . is no reserve fund at all, because the fund will contain nothing but the government's promise to pay."

What's the truth concerning all of this crisis-mongering? Let's start with old Alf Landon's point, which has gained much traction among the Tea Party crowd. By law Social Security must invest its reserve with the government at three percent interest and thus relies merely on the government's promise to pay. But that's true with all U.S. bonds, held by individuals, institutions or other governments. The day our government defaults on payment we can worry about many things even more important than just Social Security.

Social Security has $2.5 trillion in reserve at the present time. It certainly is not "broke." Since income is now lagging behind expenditures this trust fund will be deleted in the year 2037, but Social Security itself will not be "drained." With no change in the law, after that date Social Security will be able to pay out 78 percent of what it does today. We would wish that in the interim there will be tinkering with the law, as there has been in the past, so that Social Security can pay out 100 percent of what it promises. But even at 78 percent, this is not bankruptcy.

There are many reasonable suggestions on the table as to how to tinker. That is a whole different column. I will mention here just the most obvious. Today both the employer and the employee pay Social Security 6.2 percent on earnings only up to $106,800. This means that millionaires and even billionaires pay only $6,622 per year into the trust fund. Over the years the maximum income level has been raised. We can and should increase it again. If we eliminated the cap entirely on both the employer and the employee 70 percent of the shortfall would immediately evaporate.

Tinkering aside, this thrust to either eliminate Social Security entirely or privatize it comes from two different sectors. First there is the Tea Party-Libertarian group that believes that there is no role for government beyond capital punishment and maybe paving roads (although private toll highways are now being used in some states). The other sector is even more ominous. It is Wall Street who will benefit from privatization. This includes traditional country club Republicans and otherwise liberal Democrats who put their lust for money above their social ethics.

The Tea Party politicians who abhor government deficits ignore the fact that if Social Security is privatized it will create an immediate deficit of about $2 trillion (that's trillion with a T). This debt is the result of the "gap."

Let me explain. The way Social Security works is that current retirees are paid from contributions from current workers. If we take a substantial percentage of current workers' payroll tax and divert it into private accounts that the workers own, then that money will not be available to pay the retirement benefits to current retirees. The government will have to step in and pay what it promised them. This figure is referred to as the gap and will probably total $2 trillion or more.

The Wall Street people ignore the fact that private accounts cannot guarantee a set retirement income as does Social Security. If one were to have retired in 2008 when the Dow sank to 6500 he or she would have had to settle for one half or less than was guaranteed under a government plan. It is true that during good times the stock market can outperform Social Security, but this ignores the essence of Social Security. It is an insurance policy, not a pension policy. It is meant to be a bottom line income that will always be there, not a gamble on the market at any given time.

This brings us back to the Jewish issue. During the Bush years most Jewish organizations, including Hadassah and the National Council of Jewish Women, worked against the privatization of Social Security. The notable exception was the UJC (United Jewish Communities, representing the merger of the UJA and the Council of Jewish Federations) which remained "uncharacteristically quiet." JTA (Jewish Telegraphic Agency, the AP of the Jewish world) reported that "Insiders say the pressure to stay out of the debate is coming in part from UJA-Federation of New York, which has many donors and activists tied to the financial sector."

This time around it is imperative that the Jewish community makes it clear that Jewish ethics speak louder than money.

Jonathan Pollard—Twenty Five Years is Enough
2/2/11

This past month marked the 25th year Of Jonathan Pollard's incarceration for the crime of passing classified information to a friendly nation, a crime that usually receives a sentence of three to five years. He was given a life sentence after pleading guilty in a plea bargain gone awry. Secretary of Defense Caspar Weinberger submitted a 46 page secret memorandum to the court that is yet to be declassified.

The general feeling at the time was that Weinberger, a practicing Episcopalian, was exhibiting anti-Semitic animus against his grandparents who were Jewish. A more reasonable explanation was given by John Loftus, a spy expert and author of the "The Secret War Against the Jews." (St. Martin's Press) Loftus reports that immediately after the Pollard incident more than 40 American agents in the Soviet Union were either captured or killed. It was assumed by the Defense Department that Pollard gave their identities to Israel where a Soviet spy in the Mossad transferred them to Russia. This would make Pollard implicit in mass murder.

Loftus debunks this by showing that the agents' names were kept in a locked safe with "blue stripe" security clearance, a level that Pollard never reached. Pollard's Mossad handler, Rafi Eitan (later a Knesset member) stated in 2006 to the Israeli newspaper *Yediot Aharonot* that he never received the identities of American agents in the Soviet Union. Subsequently, the CIA agent Aldrich Ames and the FBI Special Agent Robert Hanssen were convicted of passing these names to the Soviets. Both had "blue stripe" clearance.

The campaign on behalf of Pollard's release was reignited these past few months with a series of dramatic events. Israeli Prime Minister Benjamin Netanyahu wrote a letter to President Obama requesting Pollard's release which he read to the Knesset. Here in America Representative Barney Frank spearheaded a public letter signed by 39 members of the House asking for clemency. Frank purposely waited until after the November elections to avoid any partisan political implications, yet after much effort he could not get one Republican to sign on. (So much for the wooing of the Jewish vote by the political right.)

As of now there are over 500 prominent Jewish individuals and organizations that have requested clemency, ranging from the far right to the humanistic left of the Jewish community—from the ultra-Orthodox establishment to the Religious Action Committee of the Reform Movement. Lawrence Korb, an assistant secretary of defense in 1987, recently wrote a letter to President Obama stating: "Based on my first-hand knowledge, I can say with confidence that the severity of Pollard's sentence is a result of an almost visceral dislike of Israel and the special place it occupies in our foreign policy on the part of my boss at the time, Secretary of Defense Caspar Weinberger."

This advocacy on Pollard's behalf has met with opposition. Joseph DiGenova, the former U.S. Attorney who prosecuted the case, now claims that Pollard tried to entice others to join his operation and received about $500,000 a year plus expenses from Israel. I have been following this case for 25 years and this is the first time such a claim has surfaced. Pollard began his espionage on ideological grounds and was enticed by his Israeli handlers to accept money to tie him in.—money, but nothing like $500,000. DiGenova also claims that Pollard cost the Defense Department between $3 billion and $5 billion to fix what he compromised. He presents no evidence to support his statement. He concludes: "That the country he spied for is seeking clemency is not only unprecedented, it is a joke."

Gil Troy, a professor of history at McGill University, writing in the on-line Jewish *Tablet Magazine* (tabletmag.com), states that Pollard is "the victim of the worst act of official American anti-Semitism in our lifetimes," but then makes a casual remark concerning Pollard's "efforts to shop American secrets to South Africa and possibly Pakistan." Troy presents no footnotes for this assertion in an otherwise fully footnoted essay. We are left with these wild assertions with no way to refute them.

There is one way that all of these issues can be resolved. Our government can declassify Weinberger's 46 page memo to the court. A redacted version was made available to Pollard's lawyers when he appealed to withdraw his guilty plea and stand trial. But it was redacted, and no one is talking about it.

Also, if the Israeli government would provide the U.S. with a full accounting of what it received and what it paid Pollard, it would go a long way to resolve these issues. That's the least that we can expect from a trusted ally that gets $3 billion per year in aid.

All of the above becomes irrelevant when we explore a comment made by Secretary of State Hillary Clinton: "The question for me is around the due process issues concerning the way that he was sentenced." This takes us directly to Pollard's legal fight to change his plea, vacate the sentence and stand trial. It was denied by the trial judge, Aubrey Robinson. (The opinion can be found at 747 F.Supp 797—easily accessible through Google.)

The real arguments in the case are clearly set out by the Decision and the Dissent of the Court of Appeals, District of Columbia Circuit. (959 F.2d 1011—again accessible on Google). By a 2 to 1 decision the court denied Pollard's request. Curiously the two judges in the majority were Jewish (Silberman and Ruth Bader Ginsburg) while the dissenting judge who wrote that "the government's breach of the plea agreement was a fundamental miscarriage of justice" was a Christian, Judge Williams. Judge Williams would not allow a new trial but would have sent it down to the lower court to have a new sentencing hearing, not before Judge Robinson.

There were many legal arguments presented before the court that were discussed in these decisions, but the crux of the case goes to whether the government suckered Pollard into accepting a plea bargain under false pretenses—and then threw the book at him.

The majority opinion acknowledged that "a plea agreement is a form of a contract." The dissenting Judge Williams wrote that the government broke its contract in that it made three promises to Pollard and, "The government complied in spirit with none of its promises; with the third, it complied in neither letter nor spirit."

Here were the promises: First, it would bring to the court's attention the nature, extent and value of Pollard's cooperation with the government. Second, it would not ask for a life sentence. Judge Williams writes that this promise was implicit, but not contested by the government. Third, the government's presentation to the court would be limited to the "facts and circumstances" of Pollard's crimes.

The government then proceeded to bury the review of Pollard's cooperation in a section entitled "Factors Compelling Substantial Sentence." On the second point the government did not explicitly ask for a life sentence but Weinberger's memorandum used such words as "treason," a crime punishable by death, whereas Pollard was indicted for espionage for a friendly country, as I mentioned above, a crime usually punished by a few years in prison. Finally, on the third point, far from limiting its brief to the court to the "facts and circumstances" of the crime, it commented that Pollard's expressions of remorse were "both belated and hollow," that he was "unworthy of trust," that he felt "blind contempt for the U.S. Military," and that he had a "warped" and "skewed" perspective that was "traitorous."

Judge Williams wrote, "As with other contacts, courts ordinarily reject literalism and read plea agreements as a reasonable person would understand them." I urge the reader to read the full 26 pages of the Court of Appeals decision (both the majority opinion and Judge Williams' dissent) and I believe that a reasonable person will come to the conclusion that Pollard was snookered into a plea agreement that the government had no intention of keeping.

So it doesn't really matter whether the Weinberger memorandum is made public, how much Pollard was paid, whether he is remorseful or not, and all of the other arguments. What matters is that our government acted in a duplicitous manner and broke a plea bargain contract. On that issue alone the Pollard sentencing deserves to be rescinded by presidential clemency. Twenty five years is enough.

Should We Forgive Torture?
5/12/09

Having released the Bush administration's torture memorandums President Obama maintains that "nothing will be gained by spending our time and energy laying blame for the past."

Before we begin this discussion we must note that we are talking about much more than waterboarding. The memos define ten techniques, including shackling in a standing position for 180 hours, confinement of people in small dark boxes with insects, banging heads into walls 30 times in a row, repeated slapping, prolonged nudity, dousing people with cold water as low as 41 degrees and sleep deprivation for 11 days. In actual practice, reports indicate that the interrogators went beyond the ten approved torture techniques, including electric shocks to genitals, being suspended in a cage, hooding to electric shocks and being forced to drink urine.

Conservatives may still refer to the above as "enhanced interrogation techniques," but it has become clear that we are talking about torture, plain and simple. The Bush administration knew this reality, otherwise why would they have used "extraordinary rendition" to black holes in Europe or Guantanamo, rather than using these "enhanced interrogation techniques" on American soil?

Conservative commentators and politicians applaud President Obama's forgiving nature. Liberals and those in the middle are sharply divided on this point. The *New York Times* columnist Roger Cohen argues that, "The right balance between retribution and reconciliation is always hard to find in the aftermath of national trauma. Ask the Bosnians or South Africans about the trade-offs between justice and recovery . . . There's work to do. Obama's right: America should look ahead, not back."

The argument goes that we were a traumatized nation immediately after 9/11 and we should forgive our excesses for we were in fear that another attack was imminent. Torture should be viewed in this context. Thus Cohen argues, "There but for the grace of God go I." But this kind of thinking denies the reality that as late as 2006, after the Supreme Court declared that the Geneva Convention applied to Al Qaeda, Steven Bradbury, the head of the Justice Department's Office of Legal Counsel, wrote a new memorandum giving its blessing to almost every technique except waterboarding, which was by then the focus of attention the world over.

Admitting that more than 100 detainees died in U.S. custody in Iraq and Afghanistan, that they were allegedly kicked to death, shot, suffocated or drowned, Thomas Friedman wrote in the *Times* that "Weighing everything, President Obama got it about as right as one could when he decided . . . not to prosecute the lawyers and interrogators who implemented the policy." Friedman argues that it would tear this country apart because an investigation would lead directly to the top, to Rumsfeld, Bush and other top officials.

Paul Krugman, another *Times* columnist, disagrees with his colleagues. Stressing that we are a nation of moral ideals, he writes: "Never before have our leaders so utterly betrayed everything our nation stands for . . . And the only way we can regain our moral compass, not just for the sake of our position in the world, but for the sake of our own national conscience, is to investigate how that happened, and, if necessary, to prosecute those responsible." He continues, "These investigations should, where appropriate, be followed by prosecutions—not out of vindictiveness but because this is a nation of laws. We need to do this for the sake of our future. For this isn't about looking backward, it's about looking forward—because it's about reclaiming America's soul."

I understand Obama's position. For him to call for an investigation of his predecessor's crimes would tumble this country into acrimony and would jeopardize needed legislation covering health care, energy and other vital programs. But this does not say that we need to follow his advice. The clamor should come from Congress, which is an equal branch of government that does not answer to the executive branch. Following President Obama's lead, this past week the Justice Department decided not to prosecute the lawyers who wrote the torture memos. But this is not the end of the matter. Congress can authorize the appointment of a special prosecutor to do what the law requires, i.e. prosecute law-breakers.

I am an American patriot. Whenever I return to this country from abroad, I enter American soil with an adrenalin rush, with an intense appreciation that I am blessed to be an American citizen. If this patriotism is not to morph into unthinking chauvinism, I have to feel that we, as Americans, have something unique to share with this world. Major General Antonio Taguba led an investigation into prisoner abuse at Iraq's Abu Ghraib prison and accused the Bush administration of "war crimes." I cannot abide that my country, which so fills me with pride and devotion, can commit war crimes and not want to purge its communal soul. By consciously deciding not to investigate the miscreants who sullied our flag and our Constitution we betray our heritage.

Krugman is right. Let the chips fall where they may.

It's Time to Reverse Privatization of Government
2/10/10

It's time to reverse privatization of government. I make this statement from the vantage point of my Jewish heritage. Judaism is a religion of communal responsibility.

Throughout the millennia Jews created communal organizations that acted as the agents for money collected through tzedaka. These were in essence governmental instrumentalities. We never feared government. Yes, we feared governments under which we often lived that oppressed us. But we never feared the concept that certain functions could only be provided by governments, and, where we could, we established our own self-regulating "governments."

With the emergence of Reagan conservatives ("Government is the problem, not the answer") and the ferocity of the neocons under George W.Bush, the concept of communal responsibility of government nearly evaporated. Privatization became rampant on both the federal and state levels. Following are some areas of privatization that I believe are either wrong or just plain ludicrous.

Roads—Who would have thought that state governments would sell their turnpikes to private companies? Providing basic infrastructure is a bedrock government function. We toyed with that idea in Florida, but thankfully it went nowhere. However, I recently drove on a privatized freeway in Colorado, paying an inflated premium to private enterprise.

Jails—Most states, including our own, now rely on private jails to incarcerate criminals, with all of the perils that this entails. The profit motive guarantees that basic human needs, even of criminals, would be sacrificed for the bottom line. Witness the many deaths in the privately run detention centers for illegal immigrants. Witness the most egregious crime of a private owner of a juvenile prison bribing two judges to send innocent kids to jail to bolster his profits. This happened in my home town of Wilkes-Barre, Pennsylvania, not in some third world country racked by corruption.

Social Security—Bush Jr. tried to privatize it. Thank God he failed. Can you imagine how many lives would have been destroyed if they had to retire immediately after the near collapse of our banking system when the Dow plummeted to 6,500?

The Military—We have reverted to Colonial times when the British hired 5,000 Hessian soldiers to help them quell our revolutionary spirit. How ancient, even medieval, is the concept of hiring a private army, yet that is exactly what our government is doing today. No longer do the Marines guard our diplomats overseas; it's contracted to Blackwater, who recently changed its name to Xe to hide the stench of its shame. Only a private unregulated military force could kill 17 Iraqis and maim another 20 without paying the price of a military court marshal.

What is even scarier, there are more paid mercenaries in Iraq than American soldiers. Even worse, during the Katrina hurricane the Bush administration hired Blackwater private mercenaries to patrol the streets of New Orleans. Private mercenaries-with-guns having control over civilian populations is the ultimate repudiation of the concept of government responsibility. It is also the beginning of a ghastly nightmare.

Health Care—Obviously we believe that it is the responsibility of government to keep us healthy; otherwise we would not have the Veterans Administration system or Medicare/Medicaid. Well, we believe that it is government's responsibility to keep only some of us healthy, leaving about 45 million without health insurance.

Let's be consistent. If we privatize health care for some, then let's privatize Medicare and the Veterans Administration hospitals. How many of my fellow seniors would buy that? Yet, privatization of health care will continue to expand if for no other reason than in the last six years private health care interests have spent $394 million on contributions to state politicians. Note that this figure does not include payments to national legislators. You wonder why we don't have universal medical coverage?

All of this privatization is the result of two fallacies: First, that government is inherently inefficient, and second, that private enterprise is inherently efficient. The truth is that both are subject to human sloth and error, but government is no more perfect or imperfect than private enterprise.

The bankers have shown that they can destroy the banking system and go broke were it not for government bailouts. General Motors and Chrysler have shown that despite the efficiencies created by the profit motive they can succeed in going belly up, except for government bailouts. On the other hand, our government has shown that it can run an exemplary health system for veterans and an exceedingly efficient postal system that continues to lose money only because it consciously subsidizes us. If it were privatized we would pay 64 cents for a stamp, not 44 cents.

We Americans have this legacy of rugged individualism. It is a virtue in many spheres, but a fatal flaw when it comes to fear of government. There are certain things that only government can do, or at least should do. As Jews we should know this. Communal responsibility is a fundamental concept in Judaism. We don't leave it up to for-profit private enterprise to provide basic services that make life not just bearable but worthwhile. Someone should tell this to our Jewish Republican neocons.

(Postscript: Of course, the Affordable Care Act, otherwise known as Obama Care, is based on privatization, as opposed to Medicare which is based on government management. But it is the best that could be obtained in the present environment.)

Hollywood Moguls, Wall Street and Greed
9/4/13

Next month Harvard University will publish a book by a young historian, Ben Urband, entitled "The Collaboration: Hollywood's Pact With Hitler." In it he reviews newly uncovered evidence of Jewish movie moguls' extensive cooperation (what he terms collaboration) with the Nazis in the 1930s. In order to maintain the ability to distribute their films in the lucrative German market the Jewish Hollywood moguls allowed Hitler's consul in Los Angeles, Georg Gyssling, to censor American movies. Any scenes that were deemed offensive to the Nazis were cut.

MGM, headed by Louis B. Mayer, worked with the Nazis even after 1936 when all Jews associated with the American film industry in Germany were forced to leave the country. In that same year, under pressure from Hitler, Mayer stopped the production of "It Can't Happen Here," a film adaptation of Sinclair Lewis' novel about a fascist takeover of America. Even after Kristallnacht in November of 1938 (one night of Nazi terror that destroyed 267 synagogues, looted approximately 7,500 Jewish owned businesses, desecrated Jewish cemeteries, and killed 91 Jews), the next year ten Nazi newspaper editors, including the editor of the official Nazi Party newspaper, were treated to a "good will tour" of the MGM studio. Further, after the German invasion of Poland, when the inherent evil of the Nazi regime was no longer in doubt, MGM donated 11 of its most popular movies to the cause of German war relief.

In the early 1930s Warner Brothers worked with the Nazis and their appointed censor in Hollywood, obviously with some trepidation because they were shut out of the German market in 1934. (I will have to wait for the publication of the book next month to learn the particulars that led to this.) But still as late as 1937 Jack Warner agreed to Gyssling's demand that the word "Jew" not be spoken in "The Life of Emile Zola," which depicted the Dreyfus case. Warner Brothers assured the German consul that Dreyfus was not a major figure in the movie.

All five of the Hollywood moguls were self identified Jews, some more religious, some more assimilated, but definitely Jewish to the core. Louis B. Mayer was fanatic about morality. He would not allow his daughters to date un-chaperoned. Billy Wilder told the story that when young Mickey Rooney was running wild around the studio, Mayer grabbed him by the lapels and shouted, "You're Andy Hardy! You're the United States! You're the Stars and Stripes. Behave yourself! You're a symbol." Mayer keenly felt his obligation to his nation and what he perceived to be the American way. Yet this did not stop him from cooperating with the Nazis.

Neither did it stop the other moguls. Jack Warner was probably the most Jewish of them all. Neil Gabler, in his informative and entertaining book, "An Empire of Their Own—How the Jews Invented Hollywood," quoted the screenwriter Alvah Bessie concerning Jack Warner's solicitation skills on behalf of the UJA. He described Warner brandishing a rubber truncheon to the assembled employees. He smashed the hose on the table, smiled and then said: "I've been looking at the results of the Jewish Appeal drive, and believe you me, it ain't good. Everybody's gonna double his contribution here and now—or else." Bessie reported that "everyone present reached for their checkbooks." Later, Jack Jr. said, "All he had to say was, 'You won't ever work here again if you don't give to the United Jewish Appeal'" This was in the late 1930s after Warner had finally broken with the Nazis. But for many years he cooperated with Berlin.

Admittedly, these moguls broke no laws. On the whole they were colorful but decent people. But we have to ask ourselves, how could a Jack Warner or a Louis B. Mayer stomach meeting the censorship demands of Hitler's regime? True, their cooperation was before the knowledge of the Final Solution, but there was general consensus, especially among Jews, of the evil nature of

Nazism. The answer is simple: GREED. Money trumps morality, even for many decent people.

People remember Oliver Stone's 1987 movie "Wall Street" and Gordon Gekko's famous creed, "Greed is good." But for me the movie's most important statement was uttered by the young stock trader, played by Charlie Sheen, who commits the crime of insider trading. Ruefully looking back on his mistakes, he laments: "Money makes people do things they don't want to." I'm sure that none of the moguls wanted to work with the Nazis, but somehow they learned to live with themselves as a result of greed.

For the moguls greed triumphed over their personal sense of morality, but nothing was illegal. For Wall Street manipulators greed takes us into the realm of illegality. A recent report of a poll of 250 Wall Street insiders showed that 23 percent said "that they had observed or had first-hand knowledge of wrongdoing in the workplace." Worse, 24 percent said they would "engage in insider trading to make $10 million if they could get away with it." For those under 10 years experience, that number jumps to 38 percent.

I have never been in a position that presented me with the choice of $10 million or a pure conscience. I would like to think that I would make the right choice. But I do understand how decent human beings can rationalize their way through the murkiest waters. Money is a wicked temptress. That's the reason we need strong government regulations to temper human instincts. Capitalism is wonderful and beneficial, but unregulated it becomes a sea of greed into which many people will be tempted to dive.

Alan Greenspan once said, "Rules cannot take the place of character." He was proven wrong by the Wall Street housing bubble which was caused by financial moguls knowingly selling worthless derivatives. Once again, money trumped morality. The recent financial implosion caused by greedy CEOs should teach us that government regulation is crucial for a healthy capitalist system.

Tell that to the Republicans who lobby against effective financial regulations under the Dodd-Frank law and who purposely crippled the EPA, the NLRB and the Consumer Protection Agency by filibustering Obama's nominations for their directors. Yes, a deal was made and the Republicans capitulated. But it was a political compromise, not a philosophical conversion. Someone should tell them that the human instinct of greed requires government vigilance—and that means regulation.

Ambivalence Over the Military Coup in Egypt
8/21/13

On July 3rd, on the eve of our celebration of 237 years of American democracy, the Egyptian military put an end to the first democratically elected government in Egyptian history after merely 369 days of its existence. Most people in the West would have preferred that the Muslim Brotherhood had not emerged victorious. I know that I would not be pleased to live under an Islamic government that is committed to increased religion in the public square, just as I would be discomfited living under an American administration dominated by evangelical leaders.

Putting aside my personal preferences, we must ask the question as to when a coup is justified. Certainly, any party dedicated to the eradication of democracy would be a fair target for a pro-democracy coup. An outstanding example of this would be the rise of the Nazis in Germany. Hitler openly declared that he would abolish democracy after ascending to power. Would had someone assassinated him quickly after the election.

But this is not the case with the Muslim Brotherhood in Egypt. As early as the 1980's, the Brotherhood ceased revolutionary violence in favor of political legitimacy and the democratic process. Yes, once elected, they would use their majority to Islamize (to coin a word) society, much as conservative Christians are attempting to Christianize America, as in making abortion illegal or denying the right to marriage for gays. But this cannot be defined as destroying democracy and justifying a coup in either country.

What then were the sins of the Morsi government that could justify a coup? First, he was intransigent. He could have reached out to the secular parties and not pushed his own agenda with hubris, simply because he had the majority in the People's Assembly, Egypt's parliament. But this same sin has been committed by Republicans in our House of Representatives—my way or no way—yet few would maintain that we should do away with them through a coup.

Secondly, the Morsi administration was incompetent. They were trained in protest, not governance. As a result the economy was in shambles. The International Monetary Fund reported that a year ago 40 percent of Egyptians lived in poverty. That figure increased to 50 percent during the Morsi administration. Immediately before the coup there was an acute shortage of food, fuel and other basic needs. But incompetence should never justify a coup; if it did we would have had the military intervene in our democracy many times, certainly during the Buchanan and Hoover administrations. But we lived through them and democracy endured.

It appears that we are confronted with a standard military repressive regime. Earlier this month, under General Sisi we witnessed the slaughter of almost 300 Morsi protestors. Caught on video in two separate incidents, the military, without provocation, wantonly fired into crowds killing over 70 people each time. As of this writing, August 15, there were at least an additional 500 deaths yesterday in the brutal clearing of Morsi supporters. By the time you read this the number will probably be much higher.

General Sisi has arrested over 200 Brotherhood leaders and placed them in maximum security prisons. He has also trumped up charges against Morsi that human rights organizations have branded ludicrous. Now the General is contemplating the death penalty for the incarcerated democratically elected ex-president, although American pressure has stayed any action. The bedrock of a repressive military regime was established this past week when the generals issued a formal state of emergency which bars unauthorized assembly, restricts freedom of speech and allows police to jail people indefinitely.

A Muslim Brotherhood spokesman commented, "The Mubarak state is back." And well it might be. Khalad M. Abou El Fadl, a law professor at UCLA, wrote in the *New York Times*: "This time, the military agreed with the protestors. But next time, when protestors call for something that isn't in the army's interest, they will meet a very different fate. Today they are called 'the people'; tomorrow they will be labeled seditious saboteurs. A year from now, the dreamy youth who celebrated and danced when Mr. Morsi was overthrown may well find themselves in the cell next door to the Brotherhood."

Do not think that the coup is good for America. It will further radicalize the Islamic Middle East. The *Times* reported an Islamist comment: "What is strange is that we followed the democratic game very well. We joined the elections; we did what they wanted us to. Then we're faced with military force." He then added in English with a pained smile, "Game over." But the game is never over. This coup drives moderate Brotherhood adherents into the camp of the more militant Salafis.

Or worse—The al Qaeda leader Ayman al-Zawahiri has long argued that the West and its proxies will never allow an Islamic government to rule. It's never good for the West to vindicate a Zawahiri prophesy. The Somali al-Qaeda group, Shabab, tweeted: "It's time to remove those rose-tinted spectacles and see the world as accurately as it is. Change comes by the bullet alone, not the ballot."

The Obama administration is struggling with what is happening in Egypt. I understand the fact that if we officially brand the overthrow of Morsi a coup it will require the cut-off of military aid and diminish any leverage that our government possesses. But to hear Secretary of State Kerry declare that General Sisi is "restoring democracy" is a little much. I appreciate the exigencies of *Realpolitik*, but I am aware that in the long run supporting oppressive dictatorships is not in the best interests of American security or our commitment to worldwide democracy.

Israel is also struggling with the coup. Morsi upheld Egypt's commitment to the Israeli-Egyptian peace treaty. Under his authority Egypt acted against Islamic militants in the Sinai who staged cross-border attacks against Israel. The *Times* reported: "Israeli experts said Israeli-Egyptian security coordination over Sinai in the last year had been closer and more intense than during the era of Mr. Morsi's predecessor, Hosni Mubarak." In spite of all of the above, Zvi Mazel, a former Israeli ambassador to Egypt, could say, "If they had stayed in power for another two or three years, they'd have taken control of the military and everything else, and Egypt would have become like Iran." But there is a growing awareness in Israel that its security cannot be based on détente with neighboring dictatorships. In the long run their only real security is signing a peace treaty with the Palestinians.

Sure, I'm ambivalent like most other Americans and Jews concerning what's happening in Egypt. But in the end, I can't support a military coup resulting in a repressive military regime, and my emotional support goes to President Morsi, who languishes in a secret military prison and may well be executed for the sin of participating in democracy.

(Postscript: This is one instance where my instincts were correct. One year later it is clear that General Sisi is a more vicious dictator than Mubarak and has quashed all civil rights in Egypt.)

I Don't Want America to be a Super Power
11/6/13

The debate in Congress as to whether President Obama should militarily strike Syria as a response to its use of poison gas showed that the American people are weary of unilateral foreign intervention. Personally I found it a very difficult decision which transcended the usual political divide. Major figures on both the left and the right joined together in either supporting or rejecting military action.

Ultimately I decided that were I a member of Congress I would have voted against intervention. Bill Keller, in an opinion piece in the *New York Times*, branded this position "Our New Isolationism." Arguing for an "assertive foreign policy" he wrote: "Isolationism is not just an aversion to war, which is an altogether healthy instinct. It is a broader reluctance to engage, to assert responsibility, to commit." He compared opposition to Syrian intervention to the isolationism of Congress (and of the American people) that obstructed President Roosevelt's preparation for the coming world war.

I beg to differ. Isolationism is a process of looking inward and not caring for anything or anyone that is not American. I do not believe that this definition applies to the vast majority of people who opposed bombing Syria. One can want to engage, to assert responsibility and to commit without the use of unilateral military force.

This whole debate over Syria helped me to concretize a thought process with which I have been wrestling for a long time. I hesitate to call it an epiphany, but here is my conclusion: I don't want America to be a super power.

Being a super power led to, as Keller admits, "the blind missionary arrogance of the Bush administration." As the historian and moralist Lord Acton famously said, "Power corrupts and absolute power corrupts absolutely." Our historical abuse of power does not augur well for our prudent future use of it—remembering the rape of the banana republics, the installing of the despicable Pinochet regime in Chile, the overthrowing of the democratically elected president of Iran, etc., etc, etc.(not to mention a useless war in Iraq).

I am not a pacifist, and this is not to say that we should not use military power for our own protection, including violating other countries' sovereignty to ferret out terrorists who are plotting against us. I am sure that Keller would call that an "assertive foreign policy." But there are other ways to engage, to assert responsibility and to commit to world order. Let's start with foreign aid. The United States spends less than one percent of our budget on foreign aid, a figure that is miniscule compared with that of other developed nations.

Military action would be appropriate when there is world consensus, either through the United Nations or other world bodies, that humanity requires action. It's a difficult process to attain this consensus, but it protects one against the arrogance of a super power. And most importantly, the inherent prestige of America allows us to broker peace throughout the world, as in Northern Ireland and President Obama's current efforts with Israel and the Palestinians. All of this does not sound like isolationism to me.

Keller derisively quotes Representative Alan Grayson (a nice Jewish boy from Florida who has the knack to tell it like it is): "We are not the world's policeman or its judge and jury. Our own needs in America are great, and they come first." Grayson is correct. We can't afford being a super power. The fact is that being the sole super power left standing is very expensive.

Although our military budget is held sacrosanct in American politics (God forbid that it should be included in the sequester cuts) it is out of control. We spend $685 billion per year on the military, up from $300 billion in 2001, reflecting our post 9/11 hysteria. We spend 39% of total world military expenditures compared to 5.25% by Russia, 3.5% by the UK and 1.3% by Canada. (Maybe that's why Canada can afford universal health care and essentially free college education for its citizens.)

And what have we gotten for our money? We have no adversaries that we must arm ourselves against. No country is imminently going to attack us. Our vast military complex does not protect us from terrorists; that's the job of our intelligence agencies. We have not attained global peace by the use of our military. To the contrary, our interventions have brought us the enmity of a vast amount of the world community. Let's face it: the Cold War is over, and the military budget is sustained not by need but by lobbying and political contributions of the military-industrial complex.

Would it not be wonderful to go back to 2001 military budget levels when we were just as safe as today? Remember that 9/11 was the result of a breakdown of our intelligence gathering, not of our military capacity. Think what we could do with an extra $385 billion per year domestically.

The real unemployment rate is 13.7%, not 7.3% (including part-time workers and those who have given up looking for employment). Over the past 30 years the cost of a college education has gone up more than 250%. The average college graduate is drowning in debt. One in five children in our country is living in poverty. As a result of the sequester, children are being dropped from the Head Start program, thereby inhibiting their ability to obtain a decent educational experience.

Elders are being dropped from Meals on Wheels, thereby denying them needed nutrition. A personal note: My wife is a Meals on Wheels volunteer, delivering meals each week. The weekly package used to contain meals for the seven days of the week. This was reduced to five. There were 100 seniors receiving meals in her district. This past month it has been reduced to 60.

This is the story of America, where we overspend on the military at the expense of human needs at home. The exact percentage of military expenditures in the overall budget is not an easy figure to ascertain. The problem is that military-related programs are sprinkled throughout the total budget. I have seen responsible sources vary from 20% to 27%, compared to 19% on health care and 15% on responses to poverty.

I don't want America to be a super power.

It's Time to Raise the Minimum Wage
1/8/14

President Obama has called for the minimum wage to be increased from the current $7.25 to $10.10 per hour and to be indexed for inflation. The economist Paul Krugman has estimated that this would affect 30 million workers. Most would benefit because they are currently earning less than $10.10 per hour, but others would indirectly benefit because their salaries are pegged to the minimum. He references fast-food managers who are paid only slightly higher wages than their workers. There is little doubt that there is a ripple effect emanating from the minimum wage.

Surprisingly, 57% of Republicans and 59% of Democrats support the increase, yet it is expected that it will not pass the Republican dominated House of Representatives, if Speaker Boehner will even allow it to come to a vote. Still we will see a major political fight in the next few months, with the slight possibility that it can actually be increased to $10.10.

To understand what's at stake, let's review the situation at the current minimum wage of $7.25 per hour. To begin, there are 3.6 million workers earning minimum wage or *less* and, contrary to what many people believe, they are not primarily teenagers just entering the workforce. Only one in four are teenagers; 38% are in their twenties (43% have some college education); 38% are over 30-years-old, 24% of whom are over 40-years-old. In the fast-food industry the average age is 29, 64% are women, and one in four have children to support.

If one is lucky enough to get a 40-hour-a week job at minimum wage (given the fact that many scummy employers hire multiple part-time workers to avoid paying benefits to full-time employees), the $7.25 translates to $269.70 per week after FICA taxes are subtracted or $14,024 per year— barely enough for one person to survive, let alone enough to support a child.

The 1968 minimum wage was $10.60 adjusted for inflation in today's dollars. Thus the minimum wage has decreased 32% in the last 46 years. The disparity between the rich and the poor and the loss of the middle class are reflected in the statistic that the minimum wage today would be $22.62 if it tracked the percentage increase in incomes of the top one percent of earners.

That's the human story. Now we confront the economists. Arindrajit Dube, a professor at the University of Massachusetts and an acknowledged expert is this field, indicates that a 10% increase in the minimum wage would affect a decrease in employment in the restaurant or retail industries "by much less than 1%; the change is in fact statistically indistinguishable from zero." But we are dealing here with a 40% increase ($7.25 to $10.10). The question is how much would that decrease employment?

To answer that question we must understand where minimum wage work predominates: 44% in food preparation; 15% in sales; 9.7% in personal care and service occupations; 6.5% in building and grounds cleaning and maintenance; 6.8% in transportation and material moving; and 6.4% in office and administrative support. Not much room here for drastic reductions in the workforce. Certainly, very few of these jobs can be shipped offshore or be subject to any form of foreign competition. As Krugman comments, "Americans won't drive to China to pick up their burgers and fries."

There is a possibility of some decrease in employment, but the pain that it would cause would be minuscule compared to the increased quality of life that it would bring to over 30 million people. Dube indicates that a 10% increase in the minimum wage would decrease poverty by 2%. Thus this 40% increase would decrease poverty by something approaching 8%, even taking into account a slight decrease in employment.

And that decrease in employment is not guaranteed. In 1968, when the minimum was higher than $10.10 in comparable dollars, unemployment was at 3.6%, half of the current rate of 7%. Australia has a minimum wage of $15, but an unemployment rate of only 5.7%.

It is true that we are just emerging from the Great Recession and some economists would argue that it would not be advisable to decrease employment even a minuscule amount. My answer to that is that we should work our way out of a recession through government stimulus, not on the backs of our lowest paid workers.

The reason for our slow economic recovery is a lack of consumer demand. An increase in the minimum wage would be a stimulus to the economy. The additional $2.85 per hour would immediately pump $30 billion dollars per year into the hands of minimum wage workers to spend. Given the multiplier effect of wage increases to those above minimum wage, some economists believe that figure can reach $100 billion. And this is not a one-time occurrence. It would be a yearly injection into the economy.

On the whole the majority of economists support this increase to $10.10 per hour. The University of Chicago Booth School of Business asked a panel of leading economists their opinion. A plurality of 47% supported the policy, and only 11% opposed it. The rest were uncertain or had no opinion.

Putting aside economic analyses, let's put this in human terms. No person who gets up in the morning, reports for work, day in and day out, and puts in 40 hours of labor, should have to attempt to support himself or herself or a family on $269.70 per week. It can't be done. That's why children come to school seeking a free breakfast under a federal program because there's no food at home.

An increase of $2.85 per hour would put an extra $106.02 (after FICA taxes are deducted) in a minimum wage worker's pocket per week. It's tough to live on $269.70 per week. It's not great at $375.72 per week, but it's a lot better. That translates to $19,500 per year, not quite up to the poverty level for a family of four in the United States at $23, 550. But if it is not a single parent family, and both adults are lucky enough to get two minimum wage

40-hour-a-week jobs (and not those part-time jobs that so many fast food outlets specialize in), then the family income would rise to $751.44 per week. That translates to $39,000 a year. No one is going to drive a Lexus, but food will be in the refrigerator and children will be clothed. Then those of us who are more fortunate can feel a little better about our country.

Since I am a rabbi, I write this to define the real meaning of Tikun Olam (the repair of the world). To raise the minimum wage is a Jewish imperative.